Inclusion Strategies
That Work
for Adolescent Learners!

Inclusion Strategies
That Work
for Adolescent Learners!

Toby J. Karten

CORWIN
A SAGE Company

For information:

Corwin
A SAGE Company
2455 Teller Road
Thousand Oaks, California 91320
(800) 233-9936
Fax: (800) 417-2466
www.corwinpress.com

SAGE India Pvt. Ltd.
B 1/I 1 Mohan Cooperative
    Industrial Area
Mathura Road, New Delhi 110 044
India

SAGE Ltd.
1 Oliver's Yard
55 City Road
London EC1Y 1SP
United Kingdom

SAGE Asia-Pacific Pte. Ltd.
33 Pekin Street #02-01
Far East Square
Singapore 048763

Printed in the United States of America.

Library of Congress Cataloging-in-Publication Data

Karten, Toby J.
Inclusion strategies that work for adolescent learners! / Toby J. Karten.
    p. cm.
Includes bibliographical references and index.
ISBN 978-1-4129-7045-7 (cloth)
ISBN 978-1-4129-7046-4 (pbk.)
    1. Inclusive education—United States. 2. Teenagers—Education—United States. I. Title.

LC1201.K369 2009
371.9'046—dc22   2008051642

This book is printed on acid-free paper.

09   10   11   12   13   10   9   8   7   6   5   4   3   2   1

Acquisitions Editor:	David Chao
Editorial Assistant:	Brynn Saito
Production Editor:	Libby Larson
Copy Editor:	Teresa Herlinger
Typesetter:	C&M Digitals (P) Ltd.
Proofreader:	Wendy Jo Dymond
Indexer:	Kathy Paparchontis
Cover Designer:	Lisa Riley
Graphic Designer:	Karine Hovsepian

Contents

Preface   ix

Acknowledgments   x

About the Author   xi

Part I: Issues in the Background and Foreground   1

Chapter One: Inclusive Mind-Sets and Best Practices for Adolescents   2

    Adolescent Dynamics   3

       Philosophy of the School District   10

       Administrative Roles   11

       Scheduling Issues and Other Challenges   16

    Teacher Planning, Preparation, Organization, and Reflection   16

    Collaborative Roles of Students, Educators,

       Related Staff, and Families   24

       Coteaching and Collaborative Curriculum

          Applications for Shared Classrooms   31

       Coteaching and Collaboration With Interdisciplinary

          Lessons Involving Chemistry, Social Studies, and English   33

       Family–School Collaboration   33

    Student Responsibility   34

    What About the Students Without Disabilities?   36

Chapter Two: Inclusive Settings   38

    Inclusive Classroom Lessons and Environments   38

    Art and Literature Mimicking Life   39

    Expectations, Concerns, and Reflections: What the Stakeholders Say   43

       Adolescent Statements   44

Part II: Adolescent Cultures: Ways to Teach and Reach   49

Chapter Three: Relating Cognitive and

    Psychological Theories to Adolescents   50

    Entering the Adolescent World   50

    What the Experts Say   51

    Adolescent Scenarios With Emotional and Instructional Implications   57

       What Are Some Possible Factors Involved?   58

Including and Understanding the Adolescent Brain   61
    Why Do We Need to Learn This Stuff
       and When Are We Ever Going to Use It?   64
Prior Knowledge: Is It a Cub or a Cat?   64
Emotional Stimuli   66
Sensory Elements and Kinesthetic Opportunities   70
Applying Creativity, Analysis, and Practicalities
    to Inclusive Adolescent Curriculums   75

Chapter Four: Beyond the Labels and Into
    the Abilities of Adolescent Learners   **78**
Good-bye Childhood Syndrome   78
Societal Pressures: Their Inherited World   79
The Adolescent Department Store   80
Confusions Versus Consistencies   81
Family and Peer Support: Acceptance, Pressure, and Rejection   82
Factors Related to Disabilities, Genders,
    and Diverse Cultures of Adolescents   84

Chapter Five: Applying Inclusive Strategies That
    Correlate With Adolescents' Lives   **89**
Campaigning for Adolescents   89
Connecting With the Daydreamers and Doodlers   90
Behaving Like an Adolescent Angel   97
Empowering Adolescents in Democratic Inclusive Classrooms   101
IEPs and AYP: Adolescents, Families, and School Supports   103
    NCLB = No Child Left Behind (or for This Book's
       Purposes, NALB = No Adolescent Left Behind)   109
    AYP = Adequate Yearly Progress   109

Part III: Focusing Upon Results   **111**

Chapter Six: Meshing Research to Achieve and
    Surpass Standards in Adolescent Classrooms   **112**
Implementing the Trios of Initials   112
    RtI and EBP: Effective Three-Tier Models   112
    UDL: Preplanning for Inclusive Successes
       With Universally Designed Lessons   115
    UbD: Understanding by Design   117
Constructivist Strategies for Inclusive
    Middle School and Secondary Classrooms   121
Instruction That Differentiates But Does Not Segregate   121
Why Cooperative Learning Works   124
Accommodations and Modifications to Create Enthusiastic Learners   128
Appropriate Adolescent Assessments   135
Inclusion Mentoring for Peers, Educators, and Families   144

Chapter Seven: Classroom Dynamics
    That Enhance Learning and Retention   **148**
Kill the "Skill and Drill": Developing Higher-Order Thinking
    Skills Across the Curriculum With Problem-Based Learning   151

Rulers, Rubber Bands, and Sponges   154

Literacy, Numeration, and Much More   154

Poetry, Music, and Art for Adolescent Eyes, Ears, Minds, and Souls   158

    Melting With Music   166

    Artful Connections   168

Ideas for Multiple Curriculum Representations   170

Engagement: Bring Back the Manipulatives!   172

Sample Anchor Activities and Ongoing Stations   175

    Classroom Scenario   175

    Station/Center Directions   177

Curriculum Graphic Organizers (CGOs)   181

    Conceptual Organization   188

Interdisciplinary Lessons and Thematic Units   189

The Role of Technology for Adolescents in Inclusive Classrooms   196

Adolescent WebQuest for Inclusive Teachers   199

**Chapter Eight: Examining Exit Strategies That
Prepare Adolescents to Enter the World**   **200**

Sprinkles and Cherries: More Than the Basics   201

Measure the Learning, Not the Disabilities! Formative,
    Summative, and *Kind* Tests and Evaluations   202

High and Realistic Expectations for Adolescents as Productive Adults   205

Community Integrations   207

Global Connections   209

Professional Development and Enhancement   210

Passing the Torch   211

Bibliography and Resources   **215**

Index   **224**

Part I: Issues in the Background and Foreground

Chapter One:	Chapter Two:
Inclusive Mind-Sets and Best Practices for Adolescents	Inclusive Settings

Part II: Adolescent Cultures: Ways to Teach and Reach

Chapter Three:	Chapter Four:
Relating Cognitive and Psychological Theories to Adolescents	Beyond the Labels and Into the Abilities of Adolescent Learners

Chapter Five:

Applying Inclusive Strategies That Correlate With Adolescents' Lives

Part III: Focusing Upon Results

Chapter Six:	Chapter Seven:
Meshing Research to Achieve and Surpass Standards in Adolescent Classrooms	Classroom Dynamics That Enhance Learning and Retention

Chapter Eight:

Examining Exit Strategies That Prepare Adolescents to Enter the World

Preface

Inclusion Strategies That Work for Adolescent Learners! assists middle school and high school staff in preparing adolescents with the academic, emotional, and social skills for successful postsecondary options. This preparation begins in inclusive environments with secondary educators who administer effective strategies that capitalize upon and maximize their students' abilities and potentials. *Inclusion Strategies That Work for Adolescent Learners!* reviews scheduling, preparation, reflection, student and educator responsibilities, family and community supports, appropriate accommodations, literacy and numeration strategies, interdisciplinary approaches, study skills preparation, development of self-regulated learners, and more. It investigates how to include students with varying ability levels, with both whole-class dynamics and individual needs given merit. The text includes innumerable online resources for educators, students, administrators, and families that outline effective research-based educational programs, strategies, services, and organizations.

This book describes characteristics of adolescent populations with and without disabilities, investigating psychosocial, behavioral, and academic issues that adolescents encounter in schools, home environments, and communities. These characteristics are then addressed within educational scenarios that acknowledge the level at which students are functioning and the skills that must be developed. Assessments and performance indicators that value the best inclusive strategies to effectively deliver the curriculum standards are outlined through constructivist practices with trios of initials such as LREs, IEPs, RtI, UbD, and UDL.

Keeping in sight the goal of ultimate success for the adolescent student, the objectives, materials, and procedures that this book offers aims to achieve those winning results for all adolescents. Peers, educators, administrators, families, and the students themselves are the ones who collaboratively need to believe that with guidance, practice, and perseverance, inclusive players win! Postsecondary options are realized when prepared students are nurtured with competencies to move forward, believing in themselves through realistic, rewarding, inclusive experiences. *Inclusion Strategies That Work for Adolescent Learners* has that desired outcome in mind.

Acknowledgments

This book is dedicated to my first class of students, who are now in their forties. I would like to take this time to issue a formal, collective written apology to all of you. Although my enthusiasm for teaching was enormous, my experience and knowledge base were not equal to my current level. The world was also a different one then, but together, we did thrive. Consequently, I also dedicate this book to the teachers who will lead our next generation of learners out into the world, better prepared to meet the many challenges presented. Be kind to yourselves as you implement the inclusive practices with the adolescents entrusted to your care, as your competencies grow with your students and inclusive experiences.

I would also like to acknowledge the dedicated professionals at Corwin Press as being forerunners who listen to the pulse, heartbeat, and soul of special education. Corwin communicates this knowledge to professionals in the field through its diverse publications. I am honored to be part of this process. Much appreciation to all of Corwin's staff, from the proofreaders to indexers, typesetters, and graphic and cover designers. Specific thanks to my acquisitions editor, David Chao; his assistant, Brynn Saito; my production editor, Libby Larson; and my copyeditor, Teresa Herlinger. Let's continue to march forward together to ensure that inclusion is a concept better understood and practiced by all.

To my supportive family, friends, and colleagues, as always, I am truly blessed to have you in my corner! Life is about passion; thanks for letting me live mine!

In addition, Corwin Press gratefully acknowledges the contributions of the following individuals:

Sarah Miller
Exceptional Needs Specialist/NBCT
Baldwin County School District
Orange Beach, Alabama

Elena Vo
Middle School Teacher of English Language Learners
Gwinnett County Public Schools
Gwinnett County, Georgia

Dr. Harold M. Tarriff
Director of Special Services
School District of the Chathams
Chatham, New Jersey

About the Author

Toby Karten is an experienced educator who has worked in the field of special education since 1976. Ms. Karten has taught K–12 students in public schools within inclusive environments and other settings. She has instructed courses for adults in graduate equivalency programs, at the preservice level, and in MAT programs. Ms. Karten has an undergraduate degree in special education from Brooklyn College, a Master of Science in Special Education from the College of Staten Island, and a supervisory degree from Georgian Court University. Along with being a mentor and resource center teacher in New Jersey, Ms. Karten designed a graduate course entitled Skills and Strategies for Inclusion and disABILITY Awareness and has trained other instructors to teach her course. She is an adjunct professor at Drew University, College of New Jersey, Gratz College in Pennsylvania, and Washington College in Maryland. Ms. Karten has presented at local, state, national, and international staff development workshops and conferences. She has been recognized by both the Council for Exceptional Children and the New Jersey Department of Education as an exemplary educator, receiving two "Teacher of the Year" awards. Ms. Karten has authored several books for Corwin Press about inclusion practices, which are currently used for instruction on many college and university campuses and schools throughout the world. Ms. Karten believes that once we place the adjective *special* in front of the noun *education*, every classroom student is a winner and should receive the best instructional strategies by a highly trained and prepared staff. She currently resides in New Jersey and Vermont, spending time with her husband, son, and two dogs. She loves her family, teaching, art, and discovering the beauty and the upside to all!

PART I

Issues in the Background and Foreground

1

Inclusive Mind-Sets and Best Practices for Adolescents

OVERVIEW This chapter magnifies the value of collaborative teams of administration, staff, students, and families all being on the same page to assist adolescents to "capitalize" on and maximize their potential within inclusive classrooms. Detailed examination of available organizations and resources; a review of scheduling, preparation, reflection, and student responsibility; and a discussion of how to include students with varying ability levels using whole-class dynamics are offered.

Before inclusion strategies can be applied to adolescent classrooms, everyone involved needs to have an inclusive mind-set that says, *"We can make inclusion work with the right strategies!"* If that successful bottom line is the ultimate goal, then the objectives, materials, and procedures will be aimed toward achieving winning results. Peers, educators, administrators, families, and the students themselves are the ones who collaboratively need to believe that with guidance, practice, and perseverance, inclusive players win! Disabilities vary, but believing in abilities and planning lessons for student progress are essential. Yes, inclusive mind-sets precede the inclusive strategies and in turn yield inclusive winning results. Inclusion strategies for adolescents are complex, but they are also that simple.

Inclusion sequence:

1. Inclusive Mind-Sets	2. Inclusive Strategies	3. Inclusive Winning Results

Now, adolescents are unique individuals who sometimes try to exert control, never admit to losing control, test the people in control, and even create their own controls. Adolescents today are living in a world that at times through their eyes also appears *out of control*. How different their world is from ours! Just ask them!

Here is how some adolescents view life:

Adolescent World	Other/Adult World

Fact to share with adolescents: *We live in the same world!* Sharing this knowledge means teaching adolescents that the people who chronologically preceded them are intelligent, caring, trustworthy people. Establishing global adolescent connections is an ongoing inclusive mission that goes beyond individual classrooms into connective communities, cultures, and countries!

Philosophy to share: Here's where the school system comes into play. We as educators must share the controls with the adolescents in our care. We figuratively and literally need to teach adolescents how to drive their own destinies. First, teach the rules of the road; next, practice with test drives; and then follow through with the actual driving test. Metaphorically speaking, classroom objectives lead to effective instructional strategies, which then yield meaningful assessments with passing grades on those *classroom road tests* or curriculum lessons for students of all abilities!

One Global World with *As* +*As* together (Adolescents + Adults)

ADOLESCENT DYNAMICS

The plot thickens, due to adolescent issues in the foreground and background, for students with and without disabilities: adolescent tug-of-wars occur on a daily, hourly, and sometimes minute-by-minute basis. Students with more learning, emotional, behavioral, social, physical, perceptual, and communication needs often struggle to achieve cognitive acumen and peer acceptance in general education classrooms. Adolescents with disabilities in inclusive classrooms require inclusive practices that are able to focus on both background and foreground issues, with tailored strategies that address the diverse personalities and abilities of each adolescent. The following table gives some facts about student differences that may present themselves in inclusive classrooms, along with sensitive classroom strategies. More delineation of inclusive strategies with additional curriculum connections are offered as the book progresses.

Some additional foreground and background issues include adequate yearly progress (AYP), No Child Left Behind (NCLB), individual educational program (IEP), and response to intervention (RtI) which means that adequate yearly progress is expected for all students, legislatively not leaving any child behind. In the past, many students with disabilities were left in the background; now, yearly progress with more accountability is put into the foreground for all students.

IEPs—individualized education programs—are written with specific goals, outlining supports and appropriate accommodations to help students with disabilities to achieve many inclusive successes, if the general education classroom is determined to be the least restrictive environment. RtI—response to intervention—is also implemented in classrooms to help students receive assistance with direct academic training, smaller groups, or more outside help with classifications given as warranted. The National Association of State Directors of Special Education (NASDE, 2006) indicates that there are two main goals of RtI. The first is to deliver evidence-based interventions, and the second is to use students' responses to those interventions as a basis for determining instructional needs and intensity. RtI involves lower student–teacher

(Text continued on page 8)

Adolescents With	Inclusive Strategies
Above Average Skills Online Resources: www.cectag.org www.nagc.org	★ Match the student's maturity/social level without assuming it is the same as higher cognitive abilities indicate; challenge students to explore all multiple intelligences to stretch their stronger and weaker ones; offer students classroom opportunities for acceleration to circumvent boredom; include activities with higher-level thinking skills across a well-organized curriculum and units of study; include open-ended assignments; allow creativity to be displayed; be cognizant of emotional needs; coach as necessary; allow students to expand their knowledge, rather than completing repetitive assignments on same content or always tutoring their peers.
Some facts about students with above average skills: There are approximately 3 million academically gifted children in grades K–12 in the United States—about 6 percent of the student population (www.nagc.org).	
Deafness and Hearing Impairments Online Resources: www.hearingloss.org http://gri.gallaudet.edu/Literacy	★ Talk in a conversational tone and face the student if the student is reading lips; use appropriate facial expressions and meaningful body language; be certain to talk to the student, not his or her interpreter; ask a student to repeat responses or questions to increase clarity; offer the student a copy of your notes, lesson plan, or teacher's manual to follow along; avoid standing near a window to reduce glare if student is lip reading or if you are signing; understand the emotional frustrations that may manifest behaviorally; cushion chairs; avoid noisier environments; coordinate with the speech and language pathologist and home environment to preteach and review content vocabulary.
Some facts about deafness and hearing impairments: 250 million people in the world have disabling hearing impairment, defined as moderate or worse hearing impairment in the better ear, with two-thirds of these people living in developing countries (www.who.int/pbd/deafness/facts/en).	
Learning Differences Online Resources: www.ldanatl.org www.ldinfo.com www.interdys.org www.dyscalculia.org www.ncld.org www.rfbd.org	★ Establish students' prior knowledge, interests, and strengths to connect the learning to their lives; be aware that some students with information processing difficulties may have poor social skills; know that a student with a learning difference may have the same or higher intelligence than his or her peers; model and monitor steps and expectations with direct instruction and guided practice; verbalize learning steps; review informal, formative, and summative assessments and observations; adjust pacing to students' levels to diminish frustrations; allow students opportunities for visual, auditory, and kinesthetic-tactile expressions; increase metacognition; teach study skills, e.g., note taking, calendar organization, highlighting facts during curriculum lessons; offer realistic praise and feedback, but be sensitive to students' reactions to correction and feedback in front of peers to avoid embarrassment or unwanted spotlighting; keep in mind the needs of individual students; honor accommodations and modifications in IEPs; allow students to celebrate their successes in different ways.
Some facts about learning differences: More than 38.7 percent of children with learning disabilities drop out of high school, compared to 11 percent of the general student population (25th Annual Report to Congress, U.S. Department of Education, accessed at www.ncld.org).	

Adolescents With	Inclusive Strategies
Attention Deficit Hyperactivity Disorder (ADHD) Online Resources: www.chadd.org www.help4adhd.org/en/about/what	★ Try to stick to a schedule to avoid confusions; if changes are warranted, offer advance notice if possible; divide larger tasks into more manageable ones; offer positive reinforcement for attention on task; gradually decrease amount of scaffolding given; be kind, yet structured; offer occasional breaks or acceptable motoric outlets, e.g., school errands, classroom centers and stations; incorporate kinesthetic opportunities in lessons, e.g., hold yarn to show latitude and longitude or act out balancing human algebraic equations, plate tectonics; directly teach study skills; if student is on medication, be aware of the type and possible associated side effects, e.g., headaches, abdominal pain, nervousness, insomnia, dizziness, cardiac arrhythmia, stomachache, mouth dryness.

Some facts about ADHD: As of 2003, there are 4.4 million youth ages 4 to 17 diagnosed with ADHD by a health care professional. There are three subtypes of ADHD—inattentive, hyperactive-impulsive, and combined (www.cdc.gov/ncbddd/adhd).

| Emotional Disorders

Online Resources:

www.nmha.org
www.ocfoundation.org
www.mentalhealth.com
www.nimh.nih.gov
www.nami.org/
www.massgeneral.org/schoolpsychiatry/interventions_begin.asp | ★ Educate yourself and your students; understand that students may over- or underreact to stimuli; know that this may be a hidden disability, so be aware of soft signs in dress, writings, attendance; know that the range of emotional disorders can fall under either internalizing or externalizing behavior, with issues such as anxiety, depression, obsessive-compulsive behavior, defiance, conduct disorder, mood disorders, or panic disorders; realize that someone may display inappropriate behavior that is strictly situational and not indicative of an emotional disturbance, e.g., reaction to a divorce, death, loss; since issues with emotional disturbance occur over a long period of time, follow the student's BIP (behavioral intervention plan), observe and monitor the student, and try to understand the triggers or causes with an FBA (functional behavioral assessment), e.g., boredom, frustration, attention seeking; collaborate and communicate concerns with other staff, e.g., school psychologists, guidance counselors, and families; establish a structured behavior modification plan with age-appropriate student reinforcers; encourage positive self-talk. |

Some facts about emotional disorders: Mental illnesses—biologically based brain disorders—cannot be overcome through "will power" and are not related to a person's "character" (www.nami.org).

| Intellectual Disabilities

Online Resources:

www.nacdd.org
www.devdelay.org
www.thearc.org
www.ndss.org | ★ Reach students by working through their strengths, using a step-by-step approach that honors maturity levels and interests, use concrete presentations to teach abstract concepts; promote ongoing communication with families to ensure that the IEP goals are reinforced in home environments; utilize age appropriate reading and writing materials such as magazines, CDs, DVDs, instead of juvenile materials, e.g., no SpongeBob for adolescents; have classroom adaptations for physical and sensory areas, e.g., positioning of desks, pencil grips, secure papers, clutter-free worksheets; relate the content to life experiences; use assistive technology, e.g., adaptive keyboards; acknowledge students' social needs along with cognitive development; have high expectations with an abundance of patience; give opportunities for practice and repetition to retain learning, with attention to the level of support needed: intermittent, limited, extensive and pervasive; help teens with ways to escalate personal |

(Continued)

(Continued)

Adolescents With	Inclusive Strategies
	independence with guided modeling of functional skills, e.g., ordering in a restaurant, shopping for clothes, going to a doctor's appointment, navigating a website; realize that every moment of the day is an educational one.
Some facts about developmental disabilities: Developmental delays can be evidenced in cognitive, speech and language, social, emotional, fine motor, or gross motor developments. Causes can be genetic, e.g., Down syndrome, or environmental, e.g., fetal alcohol syndrome or poor prenatal care or nutrition, while some are unknown or multicausal, e.g., autism with intellectual impairments.	
Autism Online Resources: www.autism-society.org http://ani.autistics.org www.autismspeaks.org www.nas.org.uk/autism www.nichcy.org	★ If students with autism have significant cognitive impairments, address ways that they can work toward meeting the standards with alternate proficiency assessments, e.g., portfolio, dated anecdotal records, dissecting and prioritizing curriculum objectives; realize that symptoms occur before age 3 and that this developmental disability has a wide range of characteristics that can be evidenced in language, social interaction, communication, and cognitive development; understand that some students with autism do not have cognitive delays, allowing them to perform at higher-level activities; give classroom opportunities to improve verbal and nonverbal communication, e.g., brief student presentations; help students to organize information in workable categories; give students practice with social interactions, peer modeling, and mentoring in general education settings, e.g., assemblies, inclusive classrooms; coordinate and collaborate with families, speech and language pathologists, coteachers, paraprofessionals, physical education teachers, art, music, and more; use increased visual aids; outline structure for rules, task completion, and sequencing of daily events; be aware of possible sensitivities to lights and unexpected noises, e.g., allow student to use earplugs or headphones; praise students appropriately; guide students to make choices to create more independence; eliminate unnecessary words, giving direct and explicit directions; capitalize upon affinity for repetition with academic and social presentations.
Some facts about autism: People with autism have a normal life span; research indicates that students with autism learn best in a structured environment (www.nhautism.org/facts_about.asp).	
Asperger Syndrome Online Resources: www.asperger.org	★ Students with Asperger syndrome do not have language delays and often have good cognitive skills; model conventional social rules; help students to increase eye contact; display appropriate social reciprocity through individual behavioral plans and metacognition; limit use of sarcasm; explain figurative language; offer concrete life connections that acknowledge students' interests; teach students self-regulation techniques; help students to problem solve through hypothetical and real models; teach appropriate emotions, facial expressions, and body language through functional social stories, videotaping, and self-analysis; offer quieter and calmer classroom areas; announce major points to increase attention, cueing students to learn, e.g., "this is the main point"; use increased outlines and graphic organizers; vary lesson delivery formats, e.g., cooperative learning, one-to-one, small group,

Adolescents With	Inclusive Strategies
	whole group; ask student to paraphrase understandings; offer breaks; modify assignments to challenge rather than enable students; if instructional assistant or coteacher is involved, be certain the shadowing is invisible with circulation to all students; use strong motivators; encourage peer collaboration.
Some facts about Asperger syndrome: Most students with Asperger syndrome have normal to higher intelligences with no display of cognitive impairments.	
Mobility Impairments: Online Resources: www.naric.com www.ucp.org www.ataccess.org www.customsolutions.us/ adaptatray/index.htm	★ Offer assistance with daily activities as required, trying to increase independence without diluting assignments; utilize technology as appropriate, e.g., word prediction programs, paper stabilizers, commercial switch-activated page turners, electronic books; talk at eye level to a student in a wheelchair; provide students with comfortable access, e.g., bolsters, slant boards, universal mounts attached to wheelchairs, communication boards; coordinate with and refer to occupational therapists, physical therapists, and speech-language pathologists; coordinate with families to decide upon appropriate transitional plans for postsecondary opportunities; realize that students have average intelligences that are not impaired by their physical disabilities; keep individual profiles on each student with his or her IEP goals, accommodations, modifications, medical needs, interests, learning strengths, and family input; realize that the student may have less stamina, and offer breaks and adjust presentation rates accordingly; ensure that content lessons include strategies to maximize memory, attention, and perception, e.g., advance graphic organizers, outlines, study guides, vocabulary cards.
Some facts about mobility impairments: Each student with a physical disability is unique and has a range of strengths, from those who are gifted to those students who may also have learning challenges or sensory impairments, e.g., different types of cerebral palsy, spina bifida, or general categories of musculoskeletal impairments, which involve the joints, limbs, and muscles, or neurological ones that include the central nervous system, e.g., brain, spinal cord, or peripheral nerves (http://education.qld.gov.au/studentservices/learning/disability/generalinfo/physical/pi2.html).	
Traumatic Brain Injury (TBI) Online Resources: www.biausa.org www.nbirtt.org	★ Students need assistance with managing reactions to changes in their levels of performance and functioning such as educational and emotional differences, e.g., adjusting to changes in thinking, learning, sensations, behavior, and communication or language; give direct instruction and modeling of problem solving and ways to strengthen memory; relate learning to functional skills; maximize positive peer interactions and collaborations with guided methods and structured interventions to manage stress and possible emotional triggers; educate yourself and your students about ways to help an adolescent with TBI; accompany verbal directions with written and pictorial ones, by giving examples that delineate new concepts; distribute and follow consistent student routines and schedules; allow additional time to complete school and home tasks; offer multiple ways and opportunities for students to practice and master newer knowledge; coordinate with physical education teachers on strategies to help students improve balance; offer ways to sharpen fine motor skills if muscles are weaker; reduce classroom auditory and visual distractions; allow student periods of rest as needed; communicate and coordinate with health care professionals and families, discussing what care may be required,

(Continued)

(Continued)

Adolescents With	Inclusive Strategies
	e.g., help with possible seizures, short-term and long-term memory problems, concentration; enlist help from the guidance counselor or school psychologists if the student exhibits mood changes, anxiety, or depression; offer positive ways for students to productively release and channel emotions, e.g., yoga, dance, art, writing, group discussion, peer collaboration.
Some facts about TBI: The causes of TBI range from falls to motor vehicle crashes, being struck by or against something, and assaults (www.biausa.org).	
Visual Impairments and Blindness Online Resources: www.afb.org www.rfbd.org www.acb.org/accessible-formats.html www.comeunity.com/disability/vision/index.html www.brl.org/	★ Speak directly to the student; do not speak loudly or shout; if someone is blind, it does not mean he person is also deaf; avoid clutter on worksheets, by offering ample white space; hang signs in the room at a comfortable eye level; enlarge worksheets; use low-vision aids, e.g., magnification pages, handheld telescopes; be certain that ample time is given for textbooks, worksheets; literature, novels, periodicals, and all supplemental written materials to be accurately transcribed into Braille; use talking books; announce physical changes of furniture in the room; reduce classroom clutter that would limit mobility and independence; collaborate with mobility trainers; enlist peer mentors and guides; secure talking Web sites offer additional auditory and kinesthetic ways for students to absorb and demonstrate understandings; announce yourself when walking into a room; do not distract guide dogs.
Some facts about visual impairments: Visual impairments do not just affect the eyes, but the whole person as well as friends and family (www.chrishigh.com/visual_imp.htm).	

ratios, shared responsibility by general education (GE) and special education (SE) teachers and departments, data intervention groups with different delivery models, and more that will be outlined in subsequent chapters.

Classroom Environment: Factors such as class size, coteachers working together; a facilitative vs. authoritarian classroom atmosphere; heterogeneous vs. homogeneous groupings, seating arrangements; and cooperative groups, are just some of the environmental factors that positively or negatively impact adolescent achievements in inclusive environments. Proactive teachers monitor these variables and adjust them to best suit individual student needs without sacrificing the curriculum, emotional, social, and behavioral needs of all classroom students.

Student Dynamics: Issues such as gender; culture; socioeconomic status; physical, perceptual, emotional, behavioral, social, and cognitive abilities; motivation to succeed; self-efficacy; family support; and field-dependent versus field-independent learning styles are just a few student dynamics that enter into successful inclusion implementations.

Cognitive Factors: What about student and teacher prior knowledge, memory issues, varying instructional approaches, matching assessments with the curriculum, and targeting students' strengths? Cognitively speaking, the brain is not to be ignored! Students respond to teachers who honor cognitive differences by offering scaffolding of learning within the students' zone of proximal development to avoid adolescent learning frustrations, but also enhance comprehension of the curriculum with often difficult or unfamiliar topics. Graphic organizers, advance planners, teaching how to create study guides, modeling, offering multiple curriculum examples, and presenting learning with multiple intelligences in mind are just a few ways to respect cognitive differences in inclusive classrooms. More strategies with curriculum details and connections will follow.

Student Crises: Peer pressure, physical appearance, depression, eating disorders, suicide, identity issues, postsecondary decisions, sexual choices, wanting to belong, or wanting to be unnoticed are all potential crises that enter inclusive adolescent classrooms. Teachers who acknowledge these issues will accomplish more curriculum advances. It is often said that students remember how you treat them, long after they forget what you taught them. Kind, supportive teachers offer students nonjudgmental ears that accept differences, but do not magnify them.

Other School Activities: Adolescents with disabilities reap many benefits when they are included in extracurricular activities such as the yearbook committee, drama club, school newspaper, band, chorus, technology club, track and field, cheerleading, future teachers' group, Spanish club, and more!

Review the columns in the next inclusive table to decide what actions (see the list below the table) you believe constitute excellent, good, fair, or noninclusive classrooms. Place the letters where you think they belong in reference to instruction and assessments, and then collaborate with colleagues and share thoughts with families and students.

EXCELLENT INCLUSIVE PRACTICES	GOOD INCLUSIVE PRACTICES	FAIR INCLUSIVE PRACTICES	NONINCLUSIVE PRACTICES

A. High expectations for all students.

B. Belief that students with lower skills do not belong in the same classroom as those students with higher skills.

C. Instruction is test oriented.

D. Instruction is student oriented.

E. Illustrations depicted by artists from different cultures are included.

F. Good grades are the bottom line.

G. Classroom occasionally includes cooperative learning.

H. Students do not keep profiles of their progress.

I. Grading sometimes has multiple purposes.

J. Tests are never weighted.

K. Tests are always weighted.

L. Testing is frequent.

M. Same test format is given throughout the year.

N. Portfolios are used for students with highest abilities.

O. Response time is monitored and limited.

P. Teacher will orally read, explain, or paraphrase test directions and questions.

Q. Critical thinking skill questions are only required for students without IEPs.

R. It's all about students achieving higher grades.

S. Team-building is valued.

T. Multiple strategies are offered.

U. Proactivity is given merit.

V. Assessments are formative and summative.

W. Write what you think constitutes excellent inclusive practices.

Source: Karten, T. (2008). *Facilitator's guide for more inclusion strategies that work!* Thousand Oaks, CA: Corwin Press.

Answers will vary, depending upon the populations of students serviced, individual education programs, environments, and curriculum demands, but the key (see page 11) offers some ideas that constitute an inclusive classroom and letter placements for ones that do not exemplify the best inclusive practices.

Philosophy of the School District

School philosophies are evidenced as soon as you enter a building. You sense a climate that permeates the main office, hallways, school cafeteria, teacher's room, and individual classrooms. Students, educators, administrators, and staff who walk around with a bounce in their gait or a smile upon their faces are saying, *"Things are good here, and I'm happy to be part of this building and district!"* Okay, every given day will not be that rewarding or blissful, but overall, the school tone is set by the philosophy of the school district. A school district that supports its teachers and staff with resources, positive feedback, and respect in turn creates a healthier climate for learning to succeed in individual inclusive classrooms. A school philosophy that

EXCELLENT INCLUSIVE PRACTICES	GOOD INCLUSIVE PRACTICES	FAIR INCLUSIVE PRACTICES	NONINCLUSIVE PRACTICES
A	I	G	B
D		H	F
E		K	N
J		M	O
L		C	Q
P			R
S			
T			
U			
V			

supports its students with disabilities is one that is based upon student needs, not the available resources, latest buzz words, or past practices used.

Philosophies in special education need to match the ongoing and ever-growing research in the field that advocates and delineates effective instructional practices to which students respond best. Reaching students in critical middle school grades helps to prevent students from becoming frustrated with school, and later dropping out in high school, ill prepared for postsecondary options. The earlier students' needs are identified, and they are given appropriate strategies, the better. An inclusive environment has an ongoing and growing inclusive philosophy for all of its students and staff that says, "With the proper support, trained staff, and resources, inclusion can and will benefit all students."

Online resources to view on best practices include the following:

http://research.nichcy.org/whatworks.asp

http://ies.ed.gov/ncee/wwc

www.inclusionresearch.org

Administrative Roles

To increase student achievement, it is recommended that administrators advocate, support, and propagate schoolwide programs for improving literacy for adolescents in inclusive classrooms that give merit to the following research-based strategies as delineated by Biancarosa and Snow (2004). Although this report from the Carnegie Corporation focuses on literacy in middle schools and high schools, the applicable suggestions are valid for all subjects and are not manageable without administrative support. They include direct and detailed instruction in literacy that is embedded in content areas and giving teachers the necessary instruction to implement those programs. Strategies are recommended such as motivation, self-directed learning, strategic tutoring, collaborative peer interactions, increased technology, teacher teams, ongoing assessments to ascertain the effectiveness of the programs, and full support for the necessary professional development. Of course, all of these elements require the encouragement and embrace of principals and administration to champion higher academic skills for adolescents in all content areas with the accompaniment of appropriate staff guidance, backing, and professional nourishment. An administrator's ultimate goal is to provide students with the necessary functional skills to succeed and provide teachers with the appropriate tools to turn that goal into a reality.

Students in inclusive middle schools who lack academic skills may become disillusioned by their lack of progress, while their families quite often experience frustrations with the system. This leads to high school students who very well may be at risk of dropping out. In September 2008, a U.S. Department of Education report entitled *Dropout Prevention: A Practice Guide,* published by the Institute of Education Sciences (IES), highlighted six recommendations to reduce the number of high school dropouts. Administrators are the key players who can turn the suggestions from this report into schoolwide realities for students with and without disabilities (Dynarski et al., 2008).

These recommendations include utilization of realistic diagnostic data systems to determine the following:

★ Students at risk of dropping out
★ Number of students who have dropped out
★ Implementation of targeted interventions such as
  ○ Adult advocates
  ○ Academic support and enrichment
  ○ Social skills and behavioral programs

The report's recommendations also include provision of schoolwide interventions:

★ Personalizing the learning environment and instructional process
★ Providing rigorous and relevant instruction with skills to better prepare students for postsecondary options

Dropout prevention interventions cannot begin until the first step of identifying who is at risk of dropping out is achieved (Kronick & Hargis, 1998). Regularly reviewing records such as students' grades and absences and then trying to intervene with programs to increase student engagement can accomplish this. This can include but is not limited to assigning adult advocates for students at risk, finding ways to increase interest and enthusiasm, creating a schoolwide climate with a sense of belonging, and ultimately encouraging an environment that values not only the curriculum but also students' personal interests. This is tricky, since all of these factors must accompany rigorous as well as relevant instruction that allows students to explore realistic postsecondary options. Educators and administrators who foster and strengthen problem-solving skills and partner with community agencies are creating a culture that goes beyond individual subject areas.

The following programs are some of those listed in the *Dropout Prevention Report* (Dynarski et al., 2008). More details and other promising results can be viewed in the full report or by consulting the following Web sites.

Career Academics: This curriculum is based on career themes, relevant course work, and work experiences with community collaboration, for example, local employers encouraging health careers.

First Things First: Schools are reorganized into smaller learning communities. Kansas City, Kansas Public Schools saw many gains with this program's implementation over a 3-year period, which included lower absences, more proficient reading grades, additional school connections, and graduation rates that increased by almost 40 percent. See www.irre.org/ftf/results.asp.

Talent Development High School Model: Issues such as attendance, discipline, achievement scores, and dropout rates are addressed through organizational and management changes to strengthen school climate, curriculum and course offerings, instructional strategies, professional development, and parent and community involvement. This model offers programs such as Transition to Mathematics, which gives ninth graders increased time and exposure to essential algebraic concepts and other areas to better prepare them for high school–level programs, and Geometry Foundations, giving tenth graders increased course time in that subject area. Other programs include Strategic Reading and Reading and Writing in Your Career, which offer additional literacy opportunities. See http://web.jhu.edu/CSOS/tdhs/index.html.

Quantum Opportunities Program: This program offers life skills training, academic help, tutoring, social mentoring, community service, and financial incentives to primarily ninth-grade adolescents from low-income families, which then extend to their 4 years in high school. See www.childtrends.org/Lifecourse/programs/QuantumOpportunitiesProgram.htm.

High School Redirection: This program encourages teachers to assume roles as not only the people who deliver instruction, but mentors as well, by offering students at risk of dropping out the appropriate support through basic academic skill development, extracurricular activities, and additional monitoring. See http://ies.ed.gov/ncee/wwc/reports/dropout/hs_redirect/.

Check & Connect: Students' attendance levels, academic grades, and suspensions are regularly checked by someone referred to as a monitor or mentor who establishes and ensures increased school connections, for example, literacy and student engagement. See http://ici.umn.edu/checkandconnect.

Achievement for Latinos Through Academic Success (ALAS): This program presents a collaborative approach to preventing students from Latino backgrounds with and without disabilities from dropping out of school, and it includes both problem-solving and social skills. ALAS mainly focuses on Mexican American students from high-poverty neighborhoods who have learning and emotional/behavioral disabilities. Intensive feedback and collaboration with community members, families, and the students themselves are offered. See www.ncset.org/publications/essentialtools/dropout/part3.3.01.asp.

Twelve Together: This program offers peer support and mentors through avenues such as weekly afterschool discussion groups, homework assistance, college visits, and a weekend retreat. Trained adult mentors assist students who are considered at risk for academic failure. See http://promisingpractices.net/program.asp?programid=263.

Administrators have tough jobs. Principals and supervisors in particular frequently deal with school situations that they have not created, but must improve upon. Directives from the central office are often just that, not debatable topics, where input is valued. Some school administrators are merely the conduit between

Proactive strategies	Ideas on how administrators can implement these strategies and programs in inclusive adolescent classrooms
Provision of continuous professional development and promotion of teacher leaders	Inservices and workshops are based upon teachers' communicated needs, not just lip service, e.g., if workshop presenters talk about multiple intelligences or UDL strictly through a lecture format, then no specific curriculum connections are established; offer teachers time to collaboratively plan lessons, design graphic organizers for subjects, and just communicate concerns with each other at faculty meetings; respect each other's days; encourage unity of staff with information, strategies, support, and continuous connections as a principal or administrator who communicates vital messages that not only value the benefits of inclusion, but also turn it into a successful classroom reality with appropriate supports.
Literacy and numeration coaching with direct and explicit instruction	Adolescents with disabilities who learn at varying rates benefit from direct instruction in phonemic awareness, comprehension skills, and mathematical applications; however, the staff or trained student mentors presenting these literacy and numeration strategies need setups for the guidance and suitable time frames to accomplish this, e.g., additional homeroom time, compensation for before- or afterschool tutoring with time for such training periods; lower teacher–student ratios with instructional assistants even if a state's code does not demand it sends out a clear message that support is given; often teachers in middle school and high school grades say that they do not have the time to teach phonics, yet gaps need to be decreased, not widened, e.g., syllabification rules taught with content-related vocabulary; schedule intervention and planning times for this direct instruction into the schedule; offer inservices for those teachers who need more training to develop student fluency, increased comprehension, and phonemic awareness; incorporate tactile approaches in mathematics with the buying of more student manipulatives, e.g., decimal blocks, algebra tiles; offer trainings for reading strategies with career connections; for all content areas, set up teacher skill groups to investigate how to implement best practices.
Strategic tutoring	Administrators and supervisors emphasize that yes, the curriculum is important, using standards as the objectives, but at the same time, specific study skills can be delivered, e.g., organization skills with calendars, teaching how to take notes and other strategies to enhance understandings and completion of short- and long-range assignments; help given to students to process information, refocus, gain more metacognition, and become self-regulated learners. Time should be allotted for this study skill instruction and encouragement given to teachers who innovatively propagate and support these programs.
Interdisciplinary teacher teams	Teachers working together to deliver a curriculum topic or unit achieve greater goals as a team than if operating in isolation with fragmented subjects. Administrators need to encourage the meshing of topics across classrooms and subjects so that students are able to explore more topics in depth, yet gain specific course-related goals across the board.
Ongoing combination of formative and summative assessments of skills	Monitor data on student progress, e.g., reading fluency (www.successforall .net/middle/reading.htm), mathematics (http://balancedassessment.concord .org/packetms.html); use assessment calendars to keep track of different tiers; graph and share students' weekly or monthly progress; monitor those students who require intensive remediation more frequently; establish collaborative data review and intervention groups to ease the burden of data collection on one person.

Proactive strategies	Ideas on how administrators can implement these strategies and programs in inclusive adolescent classrooms
Increased technology	Review *Meridian: A Middle School Computer Technologies Journal* at www.ncsu.edu/meridian to gain ongoing insights into newer technology and curriculum connections; also look at sites such as www.crews.org/curriculum/ex/compsci/index.htm; promote usage of SMART Boards, mastery of word processing systems, and other technology that helps students to gather and present information; be certain that students with physical, attention, language, communication, or sensory issues are given maximum and alternate access to the curriculum, e.g., word prediction programs (www.donjohnston.com/products/cowriter/index.html), wheelchair adaptation trays, wheelchair lap tray with a light, sound-field amplification systems (www.hearingresearch.org/Dr.Ross/classroom_sound_field_systems.htm).
Connected and informed administrators	This is the bottom line: The principal is the key leader who facilitates the inclusive learning and positive mind-sets for his or her staff and students!

communication and deliverance of the philosophy. Other school districts that collaboratively have administrators, teachers, families, and other staff work together yield more fruitful results for all.

Examples of administrative scenarios range from what movies are allowed to be shown to which textbook will be adopted; how back-to-school nights will be scheduled; evacuation plans; earthquake drills; student suspensions; familial concerns; which teacher will receive tenure; and which students with special needs will be assigned to certain classes, teachers, and inclusive programs. This eclectic mix during the day requires leadership that supports its staff's and students' wishes and requirements while abiding by the set district, state, and federal rules; special education regulations; and philosophies.

Then there is the adolescent population, which offers its own set of challenges, concerns, and needs. Students in inclusive classrooms often consume an inordinate amount of administrative and staff time. Issues range from which peers students are to be included with or which ones they should be separated from, how much study skill support time is required, and how to improve literacy and numeration skills, to viable parents' concerns, alternate or interim placements required, and ways to promote positive and accepting inclusive mind-sets. Most important is how to improve postsecondary opportunities for students with and without disabilities, beginning with inclusive classroom environments.

When administrators encourage teacher quality and professional development, they are valuing continuing knowledge for their educators as well as for all students. Administrative policies that encourage team-teaching acknowledge achievement of goals through collaboration. Professional district conferences, meetings, and workshops enhance the quality of instruction in inclusive classrooms. This inclusive training and support includes teacher-generated topics such as ways to implement coteaching, time to plan collaborative interdisciplinary units, classroom management/sharing issues, long-range planning, grading, assessment options, technology training, multiple ways to differentiate the curriculum, and more. When representative teachers share planning with administrators in strategic and tactical meetings, the line between educators and administrators is diminished and replaced with an attitude that says, *"We are in this together, and all inclusive input is valued."*

Improving student achievement is a goal of Making Middle Grades Work (MMGW) (www.sreb.org/programs/middlegrades/publications/06V15_MMGW_ Brochure.pdf). On the 2005 National Assessment of Educational Progress (NAEP) eighth-grade assessment, 29 percent of students scored below Basic in reading, and 32 percent scored below basic testing in mathematics, which revealed that these students are not prepared for challenging high school studies (Southern Regional Education Board, n.d.). According to the MMGW, middle schools need to foster an environment that not only offers academics, but also motivates students' efforts through supportive relationships such as extra help from teachers, and a kind ear and voice that foster challenging work directed toward the standards as well as the students' emotional levels and needs. Administrators that promote this type of school improvement send out a clear humanistic message to the staff that the subjects do not exist in isolation of the educators and students' needs. The table on page 17 offers some ways that administrators can support their staff in implementing inclusion.

Scheduling Issues and Other Challenges

It is often quite taxing to try to set up schedules for educators who work with students with disabilities. Since these students spend the majority of their day in inclusive classes, special education teachers must be highly qualified in their subject areas to not only help students gain more understandings, but to also properly assist their supportive staff and coteachers in general education classes. Allotting common planning time for coteachers, related staff, instructional support teams, and paraprofessionals is also a task that needs much focus. Often, having a floating or rotating substitute in the building frees up staff to plan units of study together and to discuss students' needs. Challenges are the norm when school schedules need to coordinate with lunch periods, basic skills reading sessions, speech services, and individual students' electives.

When districts value collaborative planning, the specific time allotted to educators is proactive time well spent. Since it is not always an ideal world, due to many other constraints, educators can keep ongoing collaborative notebooks with specific issues listed. Administrators, coteachers, and other instructional staff can then view these active and viable shared lists at set meetings during the day or week. Planning times could even include school administrators and supervisors covering classes, which frees up teachers and sends them a clear message that their efforts and collaborative inputs are valued. Keeping a concrete list stops concerns from turning into problems, since collaborative planning sessions are aimed at communication to improve existing issues with classroom management, curriculum delivery, accommodations, assessments, family supports, and more.

TEACHER PLANNING, PREPARATION, ORGANIZATION, AND REFLECTION

What if they don't get it? In most jobs, you may have a plan to accomplish certain tasks by desired dates, but if your idea or time frame does not work out on any given day,

Inclusion Implementation on an Administrative Level	
What and Why?	**How?**
(a) Value educators who support students in inclusive classrooms to increase both students' and teachers' productivity.	Offer inclusive teachers additional planning time on district days and through rotating substitutes or administrative coverage; establish a teacher-recognition program, e.g., inclusion certificates of achievement; send personal notes and e-mails, put positive letters in personnel files; use more verbalization; offer administrative support, both emotional and monetary, with personal accolades and allocation of money from the school budget for appropriate materials and requests.
(b) Listen to educators' concerns to proactively address and promote positive inclusive experiences that honor everyone's efforts and to prevent frustrations from escalating.	Schedule avenues for teachers to voice and network their opinions with team members and all inclusive partners. Value individual student concerns and varying classroom situations, e.g., promptly respond to needs with e-mails, offer viable pragmatic solutions such as administrative intervention with parental contact or student meetings, more classroom assistance via instructional aides, staff consultations, additional supplies and resources.
(c) Advocate a school environment with a proactive support system that specifies what standards students must understand, with a setup ready to handle challenges presented.	Study halls, before and after courses, with tutoring centers, writing workshops for and with teachers and students during the school year, and summer sessions. Train peer tutors and community volunteers to offer assistance with algebra skills, reading strategies, curriculum applications, research papers, study skills, communication needs, social avenues, and all curriculum needs.
(d) Hold continuous high expectations for inclusive progress to send out clear messages to staff, students, and families with a mission statement that the purpose of an inclusive education is to prepare students for life beyond school.	Develop schoolwide system with programs for students and educators to set goals, e.g., build in time in homeroom for student reflection and tracking of progress. Require students to fill out planners that list prior, current, and future courses. Assign teacher leaders to monitor strides toward achieving both academic and social goals. Support professional development that helps students with functional skills to choose career paths. Continually review the curriculum delivery with supervisors and GE and SE teachers to monitor progress in courses before summative, formal, standardized assessments take place.
(e) Connect with communities to maximize everyone's potentials.	Job shadowing, guest speakers, volunteers, and field trips ensure that students within inclusive classes do not view their lives within a microcosm, but instead see that the academics have career connections. Service learning projects are additional ways to develop character education while sharpening academics, e.g., purposeful writing to soldiers overseas or seniors in nursing homes, preparing a personal budget, communicating with peers and adults in appropriate social and school environments.

there isn't always an audience of 25 or more watching you. Teachers in inclusive classrooms not only have lessons that they are preparing, but also have a population of students to whom they are delivering those very lessons at any given moment of every day. The dilemma arises when a teacher thinks that he or she can just wake up in the morning, roll out of bed, stumble into the school, and then just *wing it!* Students with special needs who are matched with teachers who are highly proficient in their subject areas shine in their academics, since the teachers are able to break down the concepts into manageable student doses.

All adolescent learners benefit from highly qualified teachers. Students know when the one in charge doesn't know the topic. They respond to teachers who are prepared with the knowledge, skills, and delivery techniques needed. For example, when introducing a new topic, having a unit planned out with specific lesson goals, and then sharing those goals ahead of time with students in a graphic organizer, will eliminate student frustrations with lack of prior knowledge or surprises about where the unit of study is headed. Sharing the lesson game plan with the students clearly says, "*I am not just teaching a subject; I am teaching it to my class of students.*" This tactic allows students the chance to preview concepts and vocabulary on upcoming text pages. Even sharing calendars with such things as dates of upcoming quizzes, assignments, assemblies, and extracurricular activities can help organize students with self-regulatory study skills. It also organizes collaborative teachers who then have adequate time to prepare essential study guides; maybe brush up on the topic themselves; or conduct mini lessons to gauge students' understandings and further remediate, refocus, or redirect as required. The Chemistry Course Planner on page 19 is designed to concretely assist educators, students, and families to be better prepared and organized with the objectives, instructional approaches, and conceptual skills of upcoming lessons. Sometimes just increased communication can be the correct formula to help adolescent learners achieve further advances. *Classroom chemistry* certainly has literal and figurative connotations here!

Without planning, you may as well just surrender to chaos. Consequently, educators who think that they could go into a classroom and just *wing it* deserve to be permanently grounded! Students know when their teachers do not know the curriculum and cannot properly respond to their questions. Teachers and staff need to be able to assist their coteachers in the deliverance of lessons. There's nothing more harmful than a teacher who introduces a topic and then 20 minutes later says, "Oh, wait a minute, what I just told you was wrong!" or "Oops, I left out a step in that math problem!" Yes, educators are human beings, too, but consistently unprepared teachers are not engaging the minds of their students and only confuse them or increase learning gaps with communicated *pedagogical misconceptions.* Adolescent minds are like sponges, eager to soak up knowledge, despite the learning challenges they might have.

Most students respond to and respect fairness. Personalities that exhibit candor are appreciated, as well as organized classrooms that offer outlines of what is to be expected, with shared lesson objectives. This helps students in inclusive classrooms to see the *big picture.* Prepared educators who plan lessons ahead of time are fueling their adolescent students with excellent modeling for life, since organizational skills are crucial ones that can be applied to many different career avenues. Yes, sometimes gears need to be shifted, but an overall plan guides and structures both adolescents and teachers. In addition, the objectives must be consistent with the instructional

Chemistry Course Planner				
Monday	**Tuesday**	**Wednesday**	**Thursday**	**Friday**
		1 Introduction to the Periodic Table to identify patterns in chemistry HW due 10/3	**2** Half day— No class PM Staff Development Day	**3** Text pp. 55–72 *Concepts: Covalent and ionic bonds and you*
6 Text pp. 73–82 *Concepts: Valences and atomic structures and how they influence reactions* HW Q 1–5 p. 82	**7** Text pp. 83–99 *Concepts: Catalysts & enzymes helping us along* HW Q 1–3, 5 p. 99	**8** Cooperative group research assignments: ➢ ionic bonds ➢ covalent bonds ➢ valences ➢ catalysts ➢ enzymes	**9** In-class research time for cooperative group presentations Outline format with practice questions will be distributed to prepare for 10/15 quiz	**10** In-class research time for cooperative group presentations Student note taking on concepts *Chemistry in Life* assignment explained
13 Cooperative group presentations Student note taking	**14** Cooperative group presentations Student note taking	**15** Chemistry Quiz Chapter One Sections 1–2	**16** Introduction to acids, bases, and salts Chapter 1, Section 3 Text pp. 100–125	**17** Lab experiments on acids, bases, and salts
20 Group discussion question & answer session Outline/study guide for 10/24 test	**21** Lab reports due PowerPoint unit review	**22** Pharmacist as class speaker *Chemistry in Life* assignment due HW: Personal reaction, 250 words See teachers for writing frames and rubrics	**23** Group study session *Chemistry Jeopardy* Open-book class cloze exercises pp. 55–125	**24** Unit test, all concepts from Sections 1–3. Matching, T/F, open-ended responses Individual student/teacher conferences scheduled next week

approach one uses and the types of tests one creates. These three points must be part of all lesson plans:

★ Identify the objectives and goals. (What do you want the students to learn?)
★ Define the procedure. (How will you teach it?)
★ State the criteria for assessment. (How will you determine if the lesson works?)

Some curriculum examples follow in the next table.

Curriculum Subjects/ Activities	Planning Elements Objectives/ Assessments	Preparation	Organization
Biology	Students will be shown how to use a microscope. Assessments will require students to label microscope parts and physically demonstrate their *macroscopic* microscope understandings. Word box will be included on written assessment.	I will have enough labeled slides to view in the biology lab. Students will be given microscope worksheets with and without labeled parts to include a self-checking element for home studying and to ensure that correct answers are reviewed.	The students will gather together for a mini lesson with direct skill instruction and then divide into cooperative groups to view the slides.
Geometry	Pairs of students use Geometer's Sketchpad to learn about the relationships among the angles formed when parallel lines are intersected by a transversal. Students cooperatively construct computer and freehand lines, given certain coordinates. Students work together, but each one completes separate written work.	We modeled the computer program for the entire class on the interactive whiteboard. We have an ample supply of rulers, protractors, and graph paper for freehand work. Group discussion will entertain and clarify student questions.	Students work together in pairs and save all work. Pairs will randomly be assigned and be different from the last cooperative pair groups. Positive interactions and expected outcomes will be outlined on a grading rubric that will be distributed to the students.
Spanish	Students will be able to identify the Spanish names of fruits. The *fruity* assessment will be orally given to test for proper pronunciation.	I will use www.inspiration.com to find fruit pictures that will be matched to the Spanish words.	Classroom setup with stations has Spanish dictionaries and pronunciation guides. Peer tutors from Honors Spanish classes will assist students.
World History	Both oral and written directions will be given to students who will then jigsaw text chapters about World War I. If time permits, they will conduct further research online. Students will then regroup and share knowledge. As an assessment for this unit, students will be given two assignment choices.	Sites to view documents and hear speeches from primary sources will be accessed and shared before students begin research. Students will be given a grading rubric that lists criteria for completed assignments in these categories: superior, good, fair, and more effort needed. www.rubrics4teachers.com	After approximately 15 minutes of instruction and dissemination of resources, heterogeneous groups conduct research for the next two class sessions to either create skits or visual time lines to delineate prominent figures and events from 1914–1918.

Curriculum deliverance by teachers alleviates or elevates student concerns, depending upon whether the motivation, procedure, and ongoing support match students' goals and objectives. Adolescents with and without disabilities are often faced with outside societal and community pressures, home demands from parents, family issues, neighborhood conflicts, peer pressures, and—in case that was not sufficient—internal confusions as well. Teachers are concerned with completing units of study to prepare students for standardized tests, graduation requirements, and future postsecondary choices. Often, general education teachers think that students with disabilities have needs that are not being met under their auspices, due to the variability of the students' class levels. Special education teachers are able to sometimes adapt the curriculum to instruct students in inclusive classrooms, but then they often fear that the right adaptive mix eludes them when there is too much curriculum. The conundrum occurs when knowledge is either sacrificed or diluted. Overall, the needs of all students, both general education and those with special needs, must be met, without emotionally, socially, physically, or behaviorally sacrificing any students. Proactive, collaborative GE and SE teachers who communicate to each other and their students can even use simple techniques such as a Venn diagram or a three-columned chart to figure out how inclusive environments can address adolescent strides. Another representation of concentric circles shows that the SE population under the inclusion model belongs inside the GE domain, with GTP—good teaching practices—acting as the core for both GE and SE, since all students benefit from solid, research-based instructional practices.

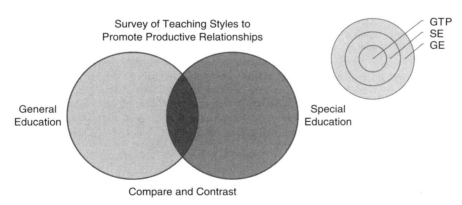

Students with and without disabilities have similar, but not always identical, needs. Comparing and contrasting the two areas concretely reveals that accommodations or modifications need to be offered to both groups of students, with many overlapping interventions. Variables such as complexities of units of study, prior student knowledge, motivation, and interests will influence educators' lesson plans and decisions. Keeping a chart with specific students listed helps teachers to sharpen inclusive reflections with lesson planning. Many general and special educators would agree that the core to student success consists of GTP and the reflection upon those processes. Sample curriculum connections and accommodations for students of all abilities follow.

Students With . . .	Curriculum Concerns	Accommodations
above-average skills	Finishes work ahead of others in science lab	Set up available centers with ongoing science projects and Web sites offering extensive applications; assign positions such as classroom supervisor, equipment manager, safety supervisor.
Asperger syndrome	Needs reminders to refocus in Spanish class	Establish private signals with the student; have structured rules posted with pictorial reminders; privately share photos with examples of positive role models.
Autism	Less prior knowledge about abstract ideas in American History	Offer DVDs and videos pointing out events with multimedia options, e.g., www.brainpop.com, songs, and art without overstimulation; preteach the vocabulary without excessive verbiage but link to student's prior knowledge when possible.
behavioral concerns	Cannot attend for full period during algebra class	Incorporate classroom energizers linking exercise with learning; allow acceptable channels, e.g., getting up to add words to a wall list, writing equations on the chalkboard, computer research, errands; monitor, implement, and enforce individual and classroom behavioral rules with student graphing of strides.
communication/ language needs	Idioms in the novel are confusing.	Have vocabulary pictures that explain the words and idioms; give analogies with student connections; ask students to paraphrase understandings.
hearing impairments	Difficulty hearing the physical education teacher	Utilize a megaphone or sound-field amplification system; speak directly to student with closer proximity; give student a written outline of rules; assign peer to relate instructions.
intellectual disabilities	Less prior knowledge and skills with fractions	Allow usage of more manipulatives and functional associations, e.g., one of your shoes is ½ the total number of shoes on your feet, number of vowels in students' names.
learning disabilities	Different processing speed of directions given during art and music classes	Offer written lesson plan outlines to students with step-by-step written explanations that accompany verbal ones; assign a peer coach/mentor to redirect; allow more wait time for student to process.
visual impairments	Print in mathematics text is too small.	Be certain that magnification pages are available for students to use over text pages; enlarge writings; use line markers.

Reflective teachers revisit their knowledge and teaching practices. It is sometimes from the lessons that do *not* work that teachers learn the most. Changing course is not a sign of defeat, but the application of the knowledge gained. Excellent teaching is an evolutionary and ongoing process.

Directions: Reflectively answer the following statements as true or false.

1. _____ Soliciting comments about the effectiveness of one's teaching methods from students and colleagues and reflecting on these comments is an excellent way to become a better teacher.

2. _____ Students of all abilities need opportunities for exploration, experimentation, and expression.

3. _____When teachers keep a journal, they focus on what they do, why they do it, and how effective they are in inclusive classrooms.

4. _____Educators must continually prepare, observe, and reflect on their lessons, themselves, and their students.

Answer key: All of the above statements are definitely true!

Reflective educators review what was taught and then fine-tune lessons to best meet individual student needs. Students who take the time to candidly reflect upon their learning also determine if the outcomes achieved match their efforts and understandings. Reflections lead to changes, which then result in ultimate inclusive growth for all. It's comparable to an artist who needs to do many sketches before framing a picture, or a writer who revises the first, second, or even third drafts. Perfection, or close to it, is basically an unattainable goal without continual reflections, since there is no template or script to follow for inclusion.

Adolescent learners in inclusive classrooms are not automatically aware of just how crucial these reflections are in order for improvements to occur. Here's where educators can give mini *reflective lessons.* Directly teaching meta-cognitive reflective skills across all disciplines is time well spent. Students need to know how to learn and learn how to know. When students admit that they are responsible for their learning strides, more achievements are attained and retained. The following concise, lower reading-level vocabulary table is intended to increase adolescent inclusive reflections.

My Reflections				
	Yes	Maybe	No	Additional comments/ inclusion support needed
1. I am pleased with my grade.				
2. I could have done better.				
3. Next time I will do things differently.				
4. I thought that I was totally prepared, but I am not sure what happened.				
5. This subject is way too tough for me!				
6. This subject is way too easy!				
7. I need to prepare differently at home and in school.				
8. The test was way too hard and unfair!				
9. I will ask for help if I don't understand something.				
10. Learning more in school will help me in life.				

COLLABORATIVE ROLES OF STUDENTS, EDUCATORS, RELATED STAFF, AND FAMILIES

In order for a team to function successfully, the team members should hold the belief that team teaching provides a more effective teaching environment, which in turn benefits all students, not only those with special needs. (Hammeken, 2007, p. 33)

The acronym below, CHOICES, outlines some key coteaching points:

C urious learners actively seek out more knowledge about best student practices.

H onest communication is essential.

O bservant educators gather and gain valuable student information.

I nnovative ideas are well accepted by attentive students.

C ollaborative attitudes take time to develop.

E xpandable minds happen with proactive inclusive planning.

S tudent- and subject-oriented deliveries yield effective results.

Honest communication between coteachers allows innovative ideas to blossom in professional relationships. If educators are curious learners, eager to expand their content knowledge, then inclusive student-oriented classrooms become realistic ones. On any given day, the coteaching process involves consultation, negotiation, articulation, instruction, assessment, and often resolution. Students who are classified as needing special education services now have additional exposure to the general education curriculum with supports in place. Bauwens and Hourcade (2003) have specified that coteachers trying to achieve collaboration believe in achieving results and also have high confidence levels in their abilities. In addition, coteachers respect each other's imperfections. Most important, coteachers hold high expectations for their students as well as each other.

Research supports that changes need to happen for all parties to achieve maximum benefits in cotaught classrooms. Studies about coteaching practices at the secondary level reveal that teachers need more relevant knowledge about content and strategies, and they also require more awareness and training about disabilities and best practices, aside from keeping their eye exclusively on high-stakes testing (Keefe, Moore, & Duff, 2004; Lindberg, Kelley, Walker-Wied, & Beckwith, 2007; Magiera, Smith, Zigmond, & Gebauer, 2005; Mastropieri & Scruggs, 2006). Negative attitudes regarding coteaching certainly influence outcomes for adolescents, coteachers, and peers. Many students and educators reap benefits when positive attitudes prevail. When asked about cotaught classes, secondary students with and without disabilities interviewed reported benefits; however, one student with emotional issues resented the fact that students could not get away with anything (Dieker, 2001). Overall, students enjoy having multiple educators since it breaks up the monotony with more responsiveness to individual learners (Thousand, Villa, & Nevin, 2007).

Collaboration is a wonderful concept, but its implementation is not always easy. One study reported the lack of differentiation in cotaught world history high school classes (Mastropieri et al., 2005). In 10 cotaught high school mathematics classes, the majority of educators observed used whole-class lecture with independent seat work (Magiera et al., 2005). Options such as parallel teaching, stations, team teaching, and the implementation of differentiated instruction need to be practiced on broader scales at the secondary level. Coteaching models need to include more peer supports, manipulatives, and direct teaching of study skills, with both the expectation and preparation for adolescent differences, without relying solely on lecture-style formats. More class collaboration for educators and students means that more eyes and ears see and hear responses and then match instruction to align with varying levels. Cooperative learning and peer mentoring are valuable instructional delivery tools for adolescents who enjoy learning from each other under teachers' auspices. Somehow, there also needs to be a combination of better curriculum deliverance and the best coteaching practices and staff collaboration that individualizes instruction within inclusive environments to best utilize all resources, both human and physical.

School personnel such as paraeducators, instructional teaching assistants, and one-to-one aides are valuable school employees who work under the guidance of classroom educators, instructional support teams, supervisors, and administrators. These individuals collaborate with qualified school staff to help adolescents practice and review skills, and to assist them in staying on task. Paraeducators can work with students individually and in groups. When they provide assistance in classrooms, the student–staff ratio is lowered, with support given to collect data and offer related services to improve student academics, life skills, and behavior. Most important is that collaboration consistently occur among paraeducators, classroom teachers, students, and families to schedule, monitor, and manage progress and decisions within inclusive environments. Regularly scheduled meetings in pedagogical atmospheres that give merit to ongoing communication and reflections yield benefits for all. Objectives need to be shared, with integral inclusive players holding a team philosophy that respects all staff with constructive modeling, feedback, monitoring, evaluation, and supervision. Different types of coteaching and shared responsibilities include the following:

★ One person leading with support given by another staff member
★ Station teaching with centers set up around the classroom, while staff circulates and assists learners
★ Parallel teaching with the same content simultaneously taught to smaller groups
★ Alternative teaching where different areas of subjects are studied or reviewed with some students practicing subskills, while others move ahead or enhance concepts
★ Team teaching with a complete coordination of all inclusive factors, for example, planning, instruction, assessment

These variations of classroom instruction must be practiced on a wider classroom scale at the middle school and secondary levels for adolescents in inclusive environments to achieve increased successes.

The following sites offer information to help educators assist students, paraeducators, and other professionals within inclusive collaborative settings:

www.paracenter.org

www.specialconnections.ku.edu

Overall, team teachers need a knowledge of the curriculum and individual students' abilities, along with good interpersonal skills, flexibility, and creativity (Klinger & Vaughn, 2002). Even though pedagogical interrelationships are sometimes difficult, with diversification, preparation, coordination, and the right attitudes, benefits are not only possible, but also imperative!

Coteaching itself is often compared to a marriage. Sometimes, coteachers would love to *stay married*, while other teachers would like an *inclusive divorce*. No spouse, no matter how happy he or she claims the marriage to be, will say that every day is a blissful one. Just as no couple skips through a marriage holding hands at every given moment, classroom teachers do not always skip through each and every lesson. Agreements happen about as often as disagreements. The best inclusion case scenarios are wonderful ones, while others represent nightmarish situations for coteachers, students, families, and administrators. Not every inclusion classroom has two teachers working together. Some inclusive classroom configurations have one teacher who may simultaneously feel overwhelmed, underappreciated, frustrated, and delighted by students' progress and support systems. The following table offers perspectives shared by teachers and administrators about inclusive environments. Also check out the following resource: the Center for Effective Collaboration and Practice, at http://cecp.air.org.

The table starting on page 27 offers some positive coteaching approaches to promote collaboration.

Overall, collaborative staff includes team members, coteachers, support staff, and administration who share many roles and responsibilities to ensure inclusive successes. Issues such as scheduling teacher planning time or IEP meetings obviously require administrative support, willing coordination, ongoing flexibility, and the ability to simultaneously and often repeatedly dot your i's and cross your t's. Together, coteachers

★ plan lessons and course units.
★ decide upon appropriate instructional delivery, interventions, and strategies, for example, whole-class, cooperative, multiple intelligences.
★ figure out best formative and summative assessments—oral, written, performance-based, or take-home—that appeal to and maximize students' strengths and abilities.
★ approach grading decisions collaboratively, for example, balancing efforts, progress, achievements.
★ maintain proactive family communications.
★ value continual respect and reflection.

In ideal coteaching situations, educators generally collaborate on all classroom decisions. Whether one coteacher—either general or special education—supports, leads, or accompanies his or her colleagues with instruction that involves parallel or separate classroom groups, collaborative decisions are based upon students' needs. Even though it is not always an easy task, coteachers often exhibit both structure and

Questions and Comments About Inclusion From Teachers and Administrators With Inclusive Solutions & Ideas *(IS&I):*
How do you change the belief system that inclusion is not good for kids?   *IS&I:* Maintain a positive outlook, despite the negative comments; focus upon your convictions. Continually communicate a *can-do* attitude; document and share students' progress with colleagues. Stay on track with your beliefs; realize that inclusion is an evolutionary process for all.
I'm currently implementing "push-in" much more in classes. I'm looking for ideas/tools to make inclusion work more effectively and ideas to help the reluctant teacher who is unsure about others *pushing in.*   *IS&I:* Review and share characteristics of differences by investigating sites like www.nichcy.org, www.cec.sped.org, www.whatworks.ed.gov, www.behavioradvisor.com, www.asperger.org, www.ldinfo.com, and www.thearc.org to determine appropriate strategies. Observe and document students' progress toward goals with reflective and collaborative learning logs. Remember that you are not *pushing in,* but that everyone is *branching out!*
I need more ideas to effectively work with special needs students so that they can progress in the general education setting.   *IS&I:* The first step is to review the curriculum standards and if necessary dissect those standards into their components, taking a step-by-step approach with lesson objectives. Equally important is to determine students' prior knowledge and baseline levels through informal assessments, e.g., class discussions, ungraded assessments, K-W-L charts. Try to relate the learning to students' lives in order to establish personal connections and increase intrinsic motivation. Reward student efforts as well as achievements. Stay connected to professional journals and organizations, such as the National Association of Special Education Teachers (www.naset.org) and Council for Exceptional Children (www.cec.sped.org). Remember to use people-first language: it's not a special needs student, but a student with special needs.
We are a full inclusion high school. I want to be able to help the teachers, SE and GE, be collaborative in a more positive way. (By the way, I am a Special Services Coordinator.)   *IS&I:* Value a team approach with your educators, establishing a committee of both GE and SE teachers, supervisors, and other staff members who collaboratively communicate and plan for students throughout the year. Honor teachers' needs by building weekly or biweekly coplanning time into the schedule and setting up resources for extra materials and help as warranted. Create a library of supplementary instructional and reference materials for all staff. Investigate the *full inclusion* policy, since some students may need a combination of services, given both in the general education class and in a separate smaller setting such as a resource room, study hall, or tutoring, e.g., intensive reading and writing programs, math instruction.
The attitudes of families, teachers, and administrators will determine the success of students with disabilities!   *IS&I:* Absolutely true. Try to share that *bottom line* philosophy that inclusion does and will work!
As a special education teacher, I worked at building relationships with the regular education teachers. I trained them in behavior management strategies to make them more comfortable around my students. Those that opened their arms and hearts to me opened up to the children.   *IS&I:* Yes, and then those teachers train others with a *domino inclusionary effect!* In addition, a welcoming attitude is an essential ingredient for inclusion successes and to increase comfort levels with increased social and academic successes.
I don't always get the help I need from my cooperating teacher.   *IS&I:* Not everyone is attuned or trained to work together. Perhaps the cooperating teacher is unaware of how to help, which means that the door for communication must be opened to voice concerns about how together you can better address students' needs. Listen and learn from each other, valuing different perspectives, background knowledge, and experience.

(Continued)

(Continued)

Questions and Comments About inclusion From Teachers and Administrators With Inclusive Solutions & Ideas *(IS&I):*
I'm worried about short-changing the other students. *IS&I:* Inclusion does not mean that the students without IEPs are on their own. The learning experiences of the students with the most and least needs are equally valuable. Proactively set up the classroom with centers that expand upon concepts, e.g., writing stations, WebQuests, curriculum-related art activities, ongoing research projects, and more. Expect that students will finish assignments in various amounts of time, and work with students to expand their knowledge, assisting all learners. Proactively set up cooperative groups and centers to allow you to circulate about as needed while valuing independent study and differently paced learning times.
As a former teacher, I know that too many general education teachers do not want to take the time, effort, and energy to give accommodations and modifications to students with special needs. How do we change these attitudes and encourage general education teachers to take ownership and responsibility? *IS&I:* That's tough to do if attitudes say, *"Why bother?"* General education teachers' initial discomfort may be attributable to their lack of experiences or apprehensions. Gather instructional support from team members and administration to allow the GE teachers to attend appropriate professional workshops and be mentored by other GE teachers currently practicing inclusion, SE teachers, and other willing staff members.
We need more planning time! *IS&I:* How true! Situations will occur that require collaborative time to plan. Administrators and team members need to honor educators by building time into the schedule or offering district workshop planning days or set times into teachers' programs.
Time is needed to work on functional skills while still trying to help students pass the test. *IS&I:* When study skill strategies are built into curriculum lessons, e.g., modeling how to take notes, then students will be able to not only pass tests, but become better learners. In addition, students with more cognitive needs are required to meet alternate proficiency assessments, even though teaching functional skills may seem like a wiser lesson choice. Dissect the standards and document how students are meeting goals, e.g., an eighth grader with autism learning about negative numbers can take steps toward meeting this math standard with the functional topic of weather and temperature, or if sports oriented, the student can study how a football player gains or loses yards instead of writing abstract equations.
Often teachers are put into an inclusion setting, but not educated on how to work in this setting. *IS&I:* Unfortunately, in some districts' haste to implement inclusion, teachers are not given preparatory training or knowledge about the characteristics of students who will be included. This leads to frustrations for all and many sour attitudes about inclusion. Most important is to allow everyone access to students' IEPs, so all will know the necessary accommodations and modifications needed ahead of time and ensure that the inclusive environment matches specific levels and IEP programs, e.g., increasing physical proximity, reading test questions aloud, not penalizing student for spelling errors, helping with note taking, teaching the students and not just the curriculum.
I am in a very small district that I feel is resistant to inclusion. At my former district, I was an inclusion specialist in an inclusive setting. I would like to know how to get the backing of the powers that be to make that change! *IS&I:* First off, start small, getting the administration's support to share information with the staff, e.g., effective strategies, characteristics of disabilities, study skill resources. Then offer your help to administration to present or arrange workshops and ongoing support for the staff.

Questions and Comments About inclusion From Teachers and Administrators With Inclusive Solutions & Ideas *(IS&I)*:
Families tend to use students' disabilities as a crutch or excuse and sometimes have a lack of concern for student success. *IS&I:* Much more is accomplished when everyone is on the same page with effective and realistic home–school communication supports. Invite family members to attend informal planning sessions to listen to and share their perspectives and concerns. Enlist family support through regular communication, e.g., e-mail, face-to-face conferences, telephone, video conferencing, progress reports.
Some students just don't put forth the effort! *IS&I:* No matter how wonderful a lesson is, nothing is accomplished if students within the inclusive environment do not *buy into* the lesson. Survey students to connect the curriculum with their interests, multiple intelligences, and learning styles. Involve students in more peer interactions within cooperative learning groups to increase focus. Reward efforts and progress toward mastery by giving increased realistic verbal recognition, and by reminding students how close they are to mastery. Definitely share a team mentality that creates self-regulated learners.
Who will be with me during these inclusion classes? *IS&I:* That depends upon a student's specific IEP, but it may be a coteacher, instructional assistant, or just you within the classroom. Realize that you should never feel that you are alone in this process. Always communicate with team members and administration for additional support, strategies, needed resources, or professional development training that may be required.
Will a 1-day lesson turn into 2 or 3 days? *IS&I:* Yes, that is a definite possibility. Remember, however, that the curriculum spirals and that concepts will be reintroduced. All students will not master the standards in the same way. Use your best judgment about how much time to spend on lessons, offering students different ways to absorb concepts without spending an inordinate amount of time on details if the students get the big picture. Each situation will vary, e.g., algebra instruction may require mastery to move on, while some students will understand more or less about the Industrial Revolution. Proactive study centers with trained mentors, e.g., peers, community members, extra teacher tutoring, and online sites, may be viable options to assist students with more difficult concepts.
Inclusion teachers are the ones who receive the reward when students advance. *IS&I:* Teachers who help students achieve beneficial inclusion experiences have an incredible feeling of assisting an adolescent to increase his or her strides toward leading a productive adult life as an integral member of the community. The rewards achieved by both students and educators are immeasurable ones.
Inclusion is sometimes wonderful when I work with the right people, and sometimes it's not so great. *IS&I:* Yes, it's not a perfect world. The same holds true for all occupations and careers.
My inclusion teacher doesn't always show up on time. *IS&I:* Being a support teacher requires that you assume responsibility as a professional, with each person equally sharing the workload of planning, student engagement, and assessments. Remind the inclusion teacher that the periods of support are IEP generated and therefore legislatively mandated.
Inclusion doesn't mean that the kids with IEPs always get 100s on their tests! *IS&I:* Not every student who is included will receive As and Bs on tests. That possibly lower result does not indicate inadequate instruction or that the student is not learning. Students' prior knowledge levels vary. Thus, a grade of 70 percent indicates that the student has mastered 70 percent of the curriculum, but perhaps the entering level was only 50 percent, and a 20 percent gain has occurred. Try to administer pretests and informal assessments to gauge progress, not strictly mastery.
When do I retire? *IS&I:* Tomorrow?

flexibility at any given classroom moment to ensure that student accountability matches student variability, without sacrificing the curriculum. Personality differences between coteachers are fine, as long as the communication is continually open and honest. Even when disagreements occur, they can be excellent opportunities for learning growth. This collaboration also extends to paraprofessionals and instructional assistants who need to be in the loop and also sometimes directed on specific ways to assist students. The following examples offer some collaborative models.

Positive Coteaching Actions
(a) Respect that you and your colleagues have personality differences and unique teaching styles, but remain firmly planted on *common classroom ground* that has positive students' outcomes as your collaborative goals.
(b) Support coteachers in front of other staff members, students, administration, and families.
(c) Have a sense of humor and flexibility in all situations, even the ones that defy all rules or expectations.
(d) Be prepared to agree or disagree on any given day, remembering that it is vital to have ongoing communication.
(e) Adapt course content together, grade together, laugh together, and know when to walk away from each other, too!
(f) Decide ahead of time on acceptable adaptations and modifications for all students, not just those with IEPs.
(g) Vary your teaching styles, assisting, leading, or following one another's lead with shared lesson delivery during whole-class, small-group, or individualized instruction.
(h) Be *two-faced,* which in this case means exchange roles, which allows students to view both of you as equal partners, both worthy of the name *teacher.*
(i) Share ideas with each other and other grade-level teachers privately or in arranged meetings.
(j) Be aware of the standards and course unit planning, but understand that pacing is not racing.
(k) Focus upon hearing each other, not just talking to each other. Definitely talk to each other in front of the students to stimulate more thinking skills.
(l) Raise your own level of professional development by learning and practicing a new strategy each week, belong to organizations, read journals and magazines, learn more about students with different learning needs, and be open to new ideas.
(m) Accept each other's needs, prior experiences, and future potentials.
(n) Give each other space, literally—classroom areas to work, e.g., desks, filing cabinets, book shelves for resources, and also mental space, e.g., time to digest, cool down, rethink, prioritize, and reflect.
(o) Remember that you are both professionals who chose this job for reasons other than the lucrative financial gains!
(p) Be aware of desirability vs. feasibility.
(q) Like what you do; find positive qualities in each other, your students, and life!

Coteaching and Collaborative Curriculum Applications for Shared Classrooms

Literacy Lesson: The lesson begins with introducing the whole class to the literature, implementing direct instruction and modeling of reading strategies with passages in a variety of genres. An informal assessment of prior knowledge about specific literature to be read circumvents misconceptions and establishes personal connections. For example, if the class is introduced to a commentary, speech, short story, or newspaper article in the genre of historical fiction, set in the 1940s in Europe, do the students know some of the political and social conditions that existed at that time? In addition, when students are connected with a motivating hook, focus is increased. At this time, even before the literature is read, students are asked to write down their character traits and then to compare their list to those displayed by the protagonist or antagonist as they read. Even though students have differing word recognition abilities, reading comprehension grade levels, and interests, everyone is learning the principles behind the same basic literacy skills. This lesson includes skills such as the following:

Finding the main idea

Locating supportive details

Sequencing events

Establishing the elements of a story, for example, characters, setting, plot, climax, resolution

Identifying cause–effect relationships

Distinguishing fact from opinion

Understanding propaganda

Applying inferential skills

Next, after the brief direct instruction, teachers or instructional assistants simultaneously instruct separate groups on refining and practicing these literacy skills with differently leveled fiction or nonfiction reading passages, poems, informational articles, short stories, and interest-generated topics or novels from assorted genres. A variation of this coteaching scenario includes offering the same reading materials to all students, with the availability of supplemental materials with options such as prerecorded versions of stories or passages to listen to on headphones, worksheets with guided questions and more explanations, or even flashcards with phonetic pronunciations or visual definitions of more difficult vocabulary. If students are working independently or in smaller groups, this is an ideal time for coteachers, paraprofessionals, and instructional assistants to circulate about the classroom, to give additional guidance to students as needed so as to gauge or clarify understandings. Even when the students do not ask for help, circulating about offers students positive feedback and the chance to check if they are headed in the right direction, as well as an opportunity to circumvent students from heading down learning paths that will detour them from achieving literacy objectives.

Coteaching and Collaboration in Mathematics: Perhaps some students in the inclusive class do not understand how to solve equations and inequalities with variables, while other students do. When more than one adult is in a classroom, students are afforded the opportunity for more guided instruction, either in smaller groups or one on one. In this case, one teacher instructs more advanced students in solving word problems involving one or two variables, while other students receive guided instruction on variables, understanding terminology such as *coefficient* or *inequality*, along with more detailed step-by-step practice on how variables represent numbers or how to solve and balance linear equations. More accelerated students conduct independent practice on approved Web sites. If advanced students desire, under teachers' auspices, they could act as peer tutors and guide other students along their learning path, thereby strengthening and reinforcing their own knowledge while helping their peers achieve mastery. In this case, the initial academic lesson on variables itself varies, to become one that includes behavioral, emotional, and social gains. Knowledge of concepts is reinforced when you communicate those concepts to someone else.

Coteaching and Collaboration in Social Studies: Quite often, students may be excellent at the regurgitation of facts but do not make connections between prior learning and new concepts, especially in areas such as world history, when they often do not see the relevance of the subject matter to their lives. Inclusive classrooms are heterogeneous ones, with students who possess different motivation, attention, study skill levels, cognitive abilities, and social acumen, along with varying physical, communicative, and sensory needs. Yet, despite these differences, there are standards in the social studies curriculum that all students need to acquire. Teachers can ensure that students actually gain the knowledge and make the connections from history to their present lives, while at the same time advance in study skills such as organization, by working in collaborative peer groups. Rather than dictating lessons straight from the textbook, for example on a unit such as Ancient Rome, students collaboratively jigsaw sections of the textbook with different groups learning about subtopics such as the following:

Geography of the Italian peninsula

Formation of the Roman Republic

Expansion of the Roman Empire

Lasting Roman achievements

Reasons for Rome's decline

After the students have a command of the knowledge assigned in the textbook and other references, they then collaboratively figure out ways to present this knowledge to their peers through skits, songs, posters, debates, PowerPoint presentations, WebQuests, newspaper articles, poems, and more. Coteachers or paraprofessionals circulate to assist and guide as needed. A written assessment is collaboratively created and required for each cooperative group, who then grades and records each other's assessments. Valuing both written and verbal acumen, coteachers evaluate students based upon their presentations and their mean performance on student-formulated tests. Coteachers and paraprofessionals encourage and guide cooperative student groups to create written test formats that include essays, multiple choice, and open-ended questions. The advantage of this type of lesson on ancient Rome is that students are still gaining information from the textbook, but now they are becoming self-directed and more regulated learners who figure out the big ideas from minor details and how to communicate this information to their peers. In addition, they are gaining literacy, mathematical, and social skills with deliveries that value their strengths and multiple intelligences. Lessons such as these improve motivation and attention, since students are learning with and from each other, under coteachers' guidance.

Coteaching and Collaboration With Interdisciplinary Lessons Involving Chemistry, Social Studies, and English

I love when effective teaching leaps outside of one classroom and connects with other disciplines. When different subject area teachers collaboratively preplan lessons, they are then teaching students that a unit of study exists beyond one set of classroom walls. In this learning instance, when students enter their next classroom, the vocabulary, basic concepts, and the language are the same. Students do not completely shift learning gears, since there is a common thread that unites disciplines.

While completing an assignment in a graduate class about the adolescent learner, a cooperative group of students ingeniously connected the 19th- to early 20th-century Industrial Revolution with literacy skills, scientific principles, and social studies. Topics in English included the discussion of the conditions described by the writings and books of Dickens, Wordsworth, Gaskell, Melville, Twain, Hawthorne, Thomas Carlyle, John Ruskin, and Matthew Arnold. Themes, metaphors, and symbolism of working conditions presented in factories and the world during this time were explored. Social studies class included lessons that investigated how railroads united the country; explored more about cultural groups who contributed to the growth of the Industrial Revolution; and investigated the development of agriculture, manufacturing, factories, transportation, and communication in the United States and abroad. Students even kinesthetically demonstrated the principles of an assembly line with the division and specialization of labor to create a prototype of a Model T, which yielded a collaboratively created Lego car. Chemistry class discussed the principles behind what made that 1908 car run. Coteachers explored combustion by comparing it to a candle burning. Chemical equations, such as $C_{25}H_{52}(s) + O_2(g) \Longrightarrow CO_2(g) + H_2O(l)$ were then balanced. Comparisons were made between unbalanced equations and incomplete sentences to further connect chemistry with English. The law of conservation was then related to each person's interests. During this demonstration lesson, teachers established prior knowledge, planned together, and displayed incredible enthusiasm. In this scenario, adolescents realize that once their 40-minute chemistry period ends and they walk into another classroom, for example, English or Social Studies, they still explore a given topic, such as the Industrial Revolution, with increased depth. Collaboratively, teachers then grade students with cloze exercises, reflective journals, group projects, and more. Coteaching in this case is certainly *industriously revolutionized!*

Family–School Collaboration

Students often weaken family bonds to bond elsewhere (Sylwester, 2005). When schools embrace families in the mix, with active communication, then accountability extends beyond school walls into homes. Districts that have active Web sites listing items such as school events, teacher e-mails, and family involvement strategies are valuing home connections. Teacher Web sites also send out strong messages to students and families about how everyone needs to collaborate for maximum inclusive results. Web sites can list exam schedules, long-range assignments, conference times, dates for report card distribution, ways to improve literacy or mathematics skills, specifics about the History Day project, track events, college visitation night, and more! This type of setup prevents student miscommunication or lack of communication with parents and also enlists family support. In addition, it helps students who may misplace papers or forget just when the report may be due. If families do not have computers in their homes, they can access one at the local library, or through a neighbor or relative. If possible and desirable, educators can also regularly send communications with progress reports to parents' homes or businesses via postal mail. The ultimate goal to succeed is a shared one for homes and schools. Communication with families leads to increased positive involvement and proactive support, which yields more student advancements when the learning is shared and valued in all environments. When families and students are on board, offering ongoing input and communication into planning and enforcing individualized education programs, then the stakeholders extend beyond the school walls. More positive results are then exhibited across all settings to create inclusive strides that value collaborative attitudes.

STUDENT RESPONSIBILITY

A presentation I heard given by Harry Wong, a renowned educator and author, described how at the end of the day, students are leaping out of their classrooms with a bounce in their gaits and a gleam in their eyes, waiting to tackle whatever afterschool plans are on their plates. Then, several hours later, teachers are dragging themselves out of the school building exhausted, ready to hit the hay before it even turns dark. Now what is possibly wrong with that scenario?

Hmmm, perhaps we could analyze this pedagogical-student description together. First off, learning is a two-way street. Teachers in inclusive environments who deliver incredible lessons cannot succeed unless students are equal partners in the process. Nobody needs exhaustion, just invigoration and responsibility to succeed. Educators want to deliver successful lessons, but the students also require the successes. For some curriculum analogies, integers do not exist without both positive and negative numbers, while rotations and revolutions are both parts of the year, creating day and night and the seasons. The point is that students and teachers have positive or good days, and negative or less desirable ones, too, but we all need to physically and conceptually include each other in our daily rotations and yearly revolutions. Teachers need to plan units of study, but students are ultimately the ones responsible for assuming major roles as learning protagonists who want to achieve higher cognitive, social, emotional, behavioral, communicative, physical, and sensory levels.

When teachers encourage adolescents to assume responsibility for their progress, regardless of the cards they are sometimes dealt or the way the coin is tossed, self-regulated learners are created. Adolescents with disabilities need to realize that although they do not choose their disabilities or learning weaknesses, they can choose their attitudes and ways to approach achieving improvements. As an activity, share these few statements with students and then ask them to fill in their own *heads and tails* versions of a *student coin* on the lines provided.

Decide which side of the coin you would like to be!	
Negative Statements—*Tails down*	**Positive Replacements—*Heads up***
I might pass this course.	I will pass this course.
I'll never get it!	If I review it more, I'll get it!
This stuff is stupid!	Even though I don't like what we are learning, I will concentrate on the lesson. Sometimes there are things we have to do, even though we many not want to do them.
School gets in the way of my life!	School can improve my life!
Explore other comparisons on the lines below.	

Here are some ways for educators to assist students in gaining more responsibility:

★ Provide guided learning experiences.
★ Help students to set realistic goals.
★ Encourage adolescents to ask questions in welcoming classroom environments.
★ Consistently schedule open classroom discussions.
★ Count student participation as part of grading systems.
★ Outline problem-solving steps.
★ Encourage more positive self-talk.
★ Actively provide meta-cognitive strategies and guidance.
★ Observe and assist students as appropriate to help develop self-directed learners.

Just as a family member may provide support to a child learning to ride a two-wheeler, teachers also provide the right amount of support, without exceeding or dismissing the pivotal part where the student rides off on his or her own into that sunset called independence!

The following pledge reaffirms learning commitments and self-responsibilities.

Student Pledge (to be recited with enthusiasm!)
I know it's the *morning* (afternoon)
And we're *still yawning* (leaving soon)
But this is my promise for *today* (now)
When I will *say* (vow)
That I will do my best

And it's not said in jest
To really care
And be sincere
To listen and learn
And respect each in turn
We all have many a need
But we all can succeed
If we use our mind
And to each other be kind
So here I am in school
Where not only teachers rule
But it's each student
That needs to be prudent
If I have a positive attitude
I could master math, reading, and even latitude
The implications are great
I decide my own fate
So I'll give it my best try
And that's no lie
It's my promise, no fingers crossed
I'll ask questions when I'm lost
I'll care about this stuff
Even when the going gets tough
And I think I'll even smile
May as well, I'll be here awhile

Source: Karten, T. (2007). *More inclusion strategies that work!* Thousand Oaks, CA: Corwin Press.

WHAT ABOUT THE STUDENTS WITHOUT DISABILITIES?

Inclusion is not exclusive to students with disability classifications. Inclusion benefits all students. The following few vignettes expand upon this thought. While I was clothes shopping, a true hobby of mine, an adolescent who was a store employee smiled at me. She then approached me and asked if I was a teacher in a school she attended several years ago. Being the ultimate proud educator, I did not deny my profession, but said, "Yes, I am a teacher there." This lovely young lady, who is now a high school senior, then proceeded to thank me for helping her in a sixth-grade math class. Wow! I was floored that I had had such an impact upon her that she not only remembered my support, but wanted to communicate it to me as well! That made me smile the whole day. I was even content to walk out of the store, without a purchase, since the dividends gained far outshone an extra wardrobe piece. She was not a student I was *supposed* to help, but was someone who had responded to an extra pair of eyes and the additional support I offered. Inclusive classrooms have better teacher–student ratios for assisting students without disabilities, too.

The next vignette concretely defines support. I was in a science classroom, nonchalantly sitting near a desk and assisting students while the general education science teacher was leading the lesson. I was not seated next to any of my five inclusive students, since there were no desks available near them. However, my distance from them still allowed me to monitor their attention to the teacher and see if the students were taking notes without stigmatizing them. Basically, I am a realist, and I capitalized on the fact that an available chair existed that belonged to a student who was at a band lesson. (As an aside, I write notes, share outlines, and communicate class and home assignments for those students who are not physically present and who miss part of the instruction, even though they are not classified students with IEPs.) I was seated next to a general education student who is probably one of the brightest science students in the school, destined to become the next Albert Einstein. An outside observer might say, *wrong place for me to be!* Actually, it was a serendipitous location, since what followed now helps me to define what inclusive support can mean *to the other students,* and for the sake of increasing melodrama, just may have saved this student's life. The teacher was discussing the circulatory system, talking about blood transfusions, when all of the sudden, this science prodigy seated next to me went into convulsions, with a tilted head that would have smashed onto a tiled floor a few feet below, had I not quickly caught his head with my outstretched cupped hands. Now how's that for support? We then quickly enlisted the school nurse who was informed by the child's parent that the student faints at the description of blood. This same parent later sent me a thank-you gift—stationery with the following imprint: *Teachers have class!* Not a bad example of what support can mean!

In summary, when inclusion is properly implemented, all students achieve additional gains. The fact is that students with learning disabilities; additional cognitive needs; and auditory, visual, communicative, attention, and physical concerns do require extra support. However, this extra support in no way has to exclude the other general education students who also have needs to be addressed. They, too, deserve the best educational scenario. When I was in that inclusive science class, I taught the whole class study skill strategies with better ways to remember and understand information using mnemonics, vocabulary, and conceptual flashcards. The students created their own study guides, increased research and literacy skills, and just generally learned how to learn! Sometimes I led the lesson, sometimes we taught parallel mini lessons, and sometimes we circulated about, helping students who were completing station work in cooperative groups. The point here is that properly implemented inclusion includes and supports everyone at all inclusive stages. This begins with *Act I, Scene 1,* during the initial planning stage, which considers appropriate services and support needed; and continues to *Act I, Scene 2,* conducting observations and preevaluations; and to *Act II,* the writing and implementing of IEPs with PLAAFP statements (present level of academic achievements and functional performance); and to *Act III Scene 1,* checking and communicating students' progress. The *finale* then creates successful classroom and postsecondary inclusive realities!

2

Inclusive Settings

 This chapter explores inclusive environments from the perspective of various stakeholders and experts in the field. It examines adolescent needs; ways to increase student metacognition; peer awareness; and more sensitivities about varying classroom learning abilities through accepting lessons, books, movies, peer interactions, and other inclusive reflective activities.

INCLUSIVE CLASSROOM LESSONS AND ENVIRONMENTS

Classroom environments in middle schools and high schools are faced with not only the challenge of delivering high-quality instruction, but also the following quagmire: *What can educators do to address the needs of adolescents in inclusive environments?*

The next acrostic sentence outlines many of the factors involved as adolescents learn in inclusive settings under the auspices of skilled educators.

A ctive movement engages the brain.

D iscussion solidifies concepts.

O bservations with ongoing formative and summative assessments gauge plans.

L essons can be direct, cooperative, whole-class, individual, and mini ones.

E xpressions are best when multiple ways of learning are valued.

S elf-efficacy increases performance.

C ollaboration with peers, colleagues, and families accelerates understandings.

E mphasize higher-level learning in enthusiastic environments.

N urture adolescent identity to replace feelings of confusion.

T echnology tunes teens into thinking skills.

S caffold as appropriate.

N oisy inclusive classrooms resound with productive educational results.

E xplore and solve curriculum problems as a class.

E steem of students is valued.

D iversity is honored with appropriate literature to represent genders and cultures.

S ocial skill instruction may be needed with roles, rules, and behavior outlined.

U nderstand that there will be both advances and regressions.

P ortfolios are reviewed by students, teachers, and families.

P rompt, model, and guide as appropriate and provide opportunities for discovery.

O ngoing mentoring by teachers and peers is routine.

R eflective journals are kept by students and teachers.

T each to student strengths to maximize their abilities.

Compare the inclusive lesson statements in the two-columned chart on page 40.

ART AND LITERATURE MIMICKING LIFE

Adolescent cultures are incredibly complex ones composed of diverse individuals budding and emerging to sprout and grow into their own identities. Students with various learning, sensory, emotional, and physical abilities are often caught in the mix of wanting to be just like every other adolescent, despite inner confusions and sometimes outwardly visible differences. Adolescents have also been known to reconstruct or bend rules to suit their immediate needs. Quite often, beneath their tough or apparently apathetic exterior are caring and sensitive teenagers. Adolescents with and without the diagnosis of a disability have their own diagnostic way of looking at others. Adults in schools, homes, and communities often view adolescents as the Dark Ages and Renaissance rolled into one. Someone once explained adolescence to me as the time when the aliens abduct your child and hold him or her captive until the age of 20, when he or she is finally returned and transformed back into the caring person you raised. Both literature and movies highlight some of the identity issues, confusions, and turbulence that are possible during these adolescent years for students with and without disabilities. As indicated by these books and films, the adolescent culture is certainly a unique one.

Several movies depict adolescents in different light, with educators facing the challenge of teaching the required curriculum to a disinterested audience. In *Mr. Holland's Opus*, the teacher's passion for music woke up disinterested students with incredible encouragement and support given through an excellent creative outlet. Ironically, the school bureaucracy ultimately cut Mr. Holland's music position, despite the student connections and the positive impact of his program.

Inclusive Lesson Reflections	
Not-So-Great Lesson (non-example)	**Great Lesson** (model example)
Objective: Same as last year's and the year before!	**Objective:** I'll use Bloom's verbs to outline what I want students to remember, understand, apply, analyze, evaluate, and create.
Motivating hook: Why bother? The students should care about this stuff without me doing an acrobatic song and dance!	**Motivating hook:** Without motivation, the lesson is a futile one! I'll try to incorporate student interests from that personal inventory I asked them to fill out the first week of class. I'll also show a short video from www.brainpop.com; students just love animated curriculum!
Procedure: I'll just wing it! That annoying coteacher better not get in my way!	**Procedure:** When the coteacher and I planned this lesson together, we created some awesome stations for the students to explore the lesson cooperatively. We'll circulate about to gauge understandings.
Class Dynamics: It doesn't matter who is in the class since it is the subject matter that is the most important!	**Class Dynamics:** We need to respond to the diverse cultures, student abilities, and genders. Yes, the subject is important, but the audience is *more* important! Cooperative groups will be heterogeneous ones, with shared roles and accountability for all.
Student Outcomes: By these test results, it's obvious that the majority of the students in the class just don't care, and half of them just don't belong here!	**Student Outcomes:** We'll review the assessments and decide whether the students have responded to our instruction. The data will reveal whether we need to review concepts with some students. Students will understand that it's not always about the grade, but their understandings, too. We might have to verbally retest a few of the students to determine if the reading level or format of the test interfered with them displaying their knowledge of the curriculum.
Reflections: No time for that!	**Reflections:** I love this part! It helps us decide what we did correctly and what we need to fine-tune!

Although he was a passionate teacher, his own son was a child with deafness, unable to mirror his father's achievements. He also struggled to balance his personal life with the hours he devoted to his profession, a dilemma many teachers face. Students with attention issues and other learning challenges respond to teachers like Mr. Holland. There is even a Mr. Holland's Opus Foundation set up to donate musical instruments to underserved students (see the Web site at www.mhopus.org).

In the book and film *Harry Potter and the Goblet of Fire,* we are shown professors who are less perfect than Mr. Holland and most certainly need to attend additional professional training to improve their instructional style, by replacing strong lecture and humiliation with deliveries that help students deal with issues such as depression, fitting in with peers, and identity crises. Hogwarts is not a real school, yet the situations are comparable ones. For example, a teacher in the story who acknowledges Harry's strength in flying is capitalizing upon what a student does best to hook that student into the lesson. At one point in the story, poor Harry is ostracized by his peers with visually concrete *Potter Stinks* badges. Alastor "Mad Eye" Moody is an exciting and concerned teacher, but unfortunately turns out to be a fraud, which just adds more to the adolescents' turbulent confusions. Students with learning, social, physical, and behavioral issues respond to kind teachers who acknowledge what they do best. Even though Harry Potter enters a fantasy school environment, the situations parallel the emotions experienced by students in real-life, inclusive adolescent classrooms trying to fit in.

Another example of a protagonist interacting with adolescents is the teacher, Mr. Keating, in the film *Dead Poets Society*. Mr. Keating passionately connects with his students when he uses the classroom textbook as a reference instead of viewing it as scripture. The fragility of adolescent emotions is also evidenced when a student, Neil, tries to gain his own identity rather than accept the one his dad imposed upon him. Inclusive classrooms also require unscripted classrooms that connect with the curriculum as well as the fragile emotions students experience.

Many films depict the dilemma of being a teenager dealing with influences of peers as well as family, community, cultural, and school factors. For example, a graduate student of mine who is an inclusion teacher related a story about how she recently visited her family in India. When people there asked her about her job, many of them did not understand exactly what she did. However, when she referenced the Hindi movie *Taare Zameen Par: Every Child Is Special* to describe the students she teaches, suddenly there was no need to verbally explain more. The main character, Ishaan, has many frustrations in school as he tries to decode those *dancing letters*. It is through specialized instruction that the student's dyslexia is addressed. Hence, a movie is sometimes worth a thousand words and can teach many lessons.

Some of the information given in the chapters of this book about individual student differences, teacher and student motivation, as well as psychosocial, behavioral, physical, and cognitive adolescent factors can be seen on the screen. Viewing movies that depict various instructional strategies and rapport with students, colleagues, administration, and the community is a way to reflect on your own teaching style. Compare and contrast some of these movies with your personal school experiences, and think about how they are applicable to inclusive classrooms.

The following literature selections also depict turbulent times for adolescents. Holden Caulfield, the disillusioned protagonist in *A Catcher in the Rye* by J. D. Salinger, cannot emotionally deal with the pressures of adulthood. Even though John Knowles's novel *A Separate Peace* is set during World War II, the characters, Gene and Phineas, portray a timeless adolescent message through their complex interactions. *The Adventures of Huckleberry Finn,* by Mark Twain, lets its readers travel down the Mississippi with Huck and Jim as they deal with their unfair environments. Many adolescents in today's inclusive classrooms have their own

Adolescent Movie Options

To Sir, With Love	Dead Poets Society	Dangerous Minds
Kindergarten Cop	Blackboard Jungle	Stand and Deliver
Mr. Holland's Opus	The Outsiders	I Was a Teenage Werewolf
Napoleon Dynamite	My Bodyguard	Fame
Bye Bye Birdie	Harry Potter and the Goblet of Fire	Can't Buy Me Love
The Karate Kid	The Breakfast Club	Brick
Carrie	Thirteen	Grease
Rebel Without a Cause	Taare Zameen Par: Every Child Is Special	_____

Mississippi River adventures that they must transverse. *Hatchet,* by Gary Paulsen, tells how a 13-year-old protagonist handles the Canadian wilderness and his parents' divorce. *Kissing Doorknobs,* by Terry Spencer Hesser, features Tara, a 14-year-old girl, who has issues due to obsessive-compulsive disorder (OCD). *Lord of the Flies,* the allegorical novel by William Golding, is certainly a classic that basically throws out all of the conventional parameters set upon adolescents as the characters must survive on an unpopulated island, handling forces of nature and those within themselves. *My Thirteenth Winter,* by Samantha Abeel, is an autobiography that candidly speaks about how dyscalculia, a learning disability, affects mathematical thoughts and procedures and feelings of self-worth. *Stuck in Neutral,* by Terry Trueman, depicts Shawn McDaniel, a 14-year-old boy with cerebral palsy, who narrates the story from his wheelchair. To gain additional perspectives on Shawn's disability, *Cruise Control,* by the same author, tells how his sibling, Paul, and the whole family are affected by it. *Parrot in the Oven: Mi Vilda,* by Victor Martinez, depicts a Mexican American teen, Manny Hernandez, who struggles with his identity and the environmental influences of poverty, prejudice, and street gangs. *Al Capone Does My Shirts,* by Gennifer Choldenko, is a story about how a family faces the complex acceptance of a diagnosis of autism. *Singing Hands,* by Delia Ray, offers the perspective of a 12-year-old daughter of parents who are deaf. Jonathan Mooney and David Cole's book *Learning Outside the Lines* teaches students that despite learning challenges, with perseverance, successes are always within students' reach. Fitting in, for an adolescent, is a complex issue as shown by these books.

Art such as literature and movies often mirrors life. Adolescents with and without disabilities do not have an easy time dealing with daily school issues with academics, peers, family, other pressures, and just generally transitioning into adulthood. These books and movies depict many situations that help educators, other school staff, families, and the students themselves vicariously understand that they are not alone in their confusions, disillusionments, and daily dilemmas.

Adolescents in inclusive classrooms can cooperatively jigsaw these novels and movies. For example, they can write a synopsis, create a skit, or even design a graphic novel that highlights the major themes of these works, if the movie choices are approved by local schools. In addition, ask adolescents to tell how one of these movies or books compares to their own daily life. Generally, the best part of an assignment such as this one is that it opens up the classroom for further discussion without stigmatizing anyone. Adolescent settings in middle school and high school cultures are more understandable through these fiction and nonfiction genres. Many of these books and movies invite students and adults to develop an enhanced perspective of the world of adolescence and beyond.

EXPECTATIONS, CONCERNS, AND REFLECTIONS: WHAT THE STAKEHOLDERS SAY

Are adolescents predictable? Yes, you can predict that they will be unpredictable! Expecting the unexpected with a wide range of educational repertoires helps all learners to succeed. Educators who remember themselves as adolescents can then relate those understandings to their students. Teachers of adolescents in inclusive classrooms need to reflect upon the following questions and determine how their answers will coincide with the varying abilities and needs of the adolescents under their auspices:

Have you ever been that adolescent who questioned, *Who am I? Where am I going?* whether you had a learning, physical, or emotional difference?

Do you think it is possible for you as a teacher to have a classroom that incorporates open discussion and multiple perspectives, without sacrificing the curriculum, to better connect to students in inclusive classrooms?

Do you agree that delivery and assessment options need to be applied to inclusive adolescent classrooms to help a spectrum of learners achieve gains?

Do you think that gender biases negatively impact students? If so, what can educators do to correct these biases?

Think about your preferred intelligences and your least favorite intelligences with life examples to support each of your choices. Could you apply your least favorite intelligence to meet the needs of an adolescent who requires that kind of delivery?

Remember your own adolescent classroom experiences. How did you learn best?

Describe a situation in which you achieved meaningful learning by associating it with something that you already knew.

Do you use acrostics or acronyms to better understand or remember information, and how can you teach your students to do the same?

Can learning be shaped with clear goals, logical sequencing, self-pacing, organizing the subject matter, and the Premack principle (e.g., eat your vegetables and you can have dessert)?

Do you remember a teacher who had a positive impact on you as a learner? Do you think that you currently affect your students in that same positive way?

How can educators help adolescents to become self-regulated learners?

Many adolescents with disabilities benefit from personalized contact that strengthens learning and perceptual deficits with appropriate attention to study skills. Continually asking adolescents to reflect upon how they learn best, what efforts they have put forth, and just what their overall views on school are, says loudly and clearly that a teacher is not just teaching a subject, but is teaching a student the necessary skills to learn that subject. The following statements are a snapshot into the depth of many adolescent complexities within inclusive environments.

Adolescent Statements

Here are some candid views given by adolescents when questioned about their school experiences by graduate students, colleagues, and myself. Understanding student perspectives gives teachers valuable insights on how to connect the curriculum to student needs and how to establish emotional connections to maximize student growth.

Questions to a 16-year-old boy with Asperger syndrome:

What do you think about school?

Student response: *It's okay, I don't have a lot of friends, but I'm working on that!*

What do you want to improve on?

Student response: *I probably should concentrate more in class, but sometimes my mind just wanders.*

What do you think you might want to do when you are older?

Student response: *Oh, I have plenty of time to decide that, I'm still young!*

Questions to a high school student with attention issues:

What are your favorite and least favorite subjects?

Student response: *Language Arts is my favorite subject because I like to write, while science is my least favorite because it doesn't make sense.*

What makes a class interesting?

Student response: *Classroom discussions and doing projects and experiments that help me to understand more. That way, we are not just taking notes and reading, but we are actually doing something!*

Questions to an adolescent with more advanced cognitive abilities:

Do you like working on class projects as an individual or in a group?

Student response: *Individual, because as a group sometimes the other kids don't put in a lot of effort. You can never persuade them to do more because they slack off and try to get you to do everything. Individually, I know how much I can work. In groups, people rely on me to do the work, but then it counts for everyone. If I do all of the work it's just not fair!*

Define a good teacher.

Student response: *A good teacher is sometimes strict, but is willing to laugh with the kids. When it comes down to schoolwork, they just don't mess around! Sometimes they even talk about personal things and tell us interesting facts.*

What do you like or dislike about school?

Student responses: *The cafeteria raised pretzel and ice cream prices from 50 to 75 cents without telling us why. I also don't like the fact that the double chocolate cookie is banned because of the new healthy eating rules!*

Class monotony, too many notes, and not enough time to sleep.

History is boring.

Friendly teachers are the best.

We need more life skills, not just academics.

We spend too much time learning things we don't need to know!

Teachers talk too much!

I hate the dress code!

Tests are too stressful!

How does school help you to prepare for life afterwards as an adult?

Student responses: *Career day in eighth grade shows you different jobs that you may like to do.*

We do speeches and debates in English.

I don't know, because I'm just not an adult, yet!

What do you want to improve about yourself?

Student responses: *I like constructing stuff and beginning projects, but sometimes I just don't finish them!*

I really don't know what to improve.

I don't think that I need improvements.

What's tough about school?

Student responses: *Trying to get teachers to like you, because if they don't, they sort of pick on you.*

Trying to be everything to everybody, without losing yourself!

Some questions asked of educators:

What are your biggest challenges?

Educators' responses: *Keeping kids on task, and paying attention. We start before 7:30 a.m., so some kids who work after school, end up falling asleep because they are just plain tired from their night jobs.*

Teaching classes with so many different levels.

Raising test scores with pressure from the administration and parents!

Ridiculously simple things that become complicated, like planning a field trip, extra paperwork, and other bureaucracy.

Living up to high standards of parents that at times do not match students' needs or levels.

Not having enough time to plan or reflect on lessons with coteachers.

What's your favorite part about being a teacher?

Educators' responses: *Growing as a person, since kids keep you on your tip toes, on top of your game plan!*

Staying young because of the kids!

Summers off!

Helping kids to be the best that they can be!

Some student and educator comments about what good teachers do:

Listen, and then listen some more!

Care about students and gain their trust.

Know what students know and don't know, even before you introduce what you ultimately want them to know!

Keep the class interesting and get students to return from zoning out.

Make relevant learning connections to student lives.

Set up a classroom atmosphere that values learning.

Help kids help each other!

Help kids deal with transitions, and the other stuff that kids may be going through, outside of the lesson plans and the curriculum.

Keep learning!

Remember back to when you were adolescents, too!

Clear goals, logical thinking, self-pacing, and organization.

Fair tests and fair grades.

Observing kids!

To improve your role as a successful educator in an inclusive classroom, interview adolescents to find out what they like the best and least about classroom instruction, school activities, policies, and requirements. Ask adolescents what tools they think schools should provide to help prepare them to achieve productive adult lives. Ask them what importance peers have in their lives at this age. Gain insights by interviewing families, other teachers, and administrators. Ask these stakeholders to identify and rank their students', children's, colleagues', staff's, and their own most significant academic, emotional, behavioral, and social needs.

Mobility International USA has success stories and blogs from individuals with disabilities who share personal stories about challenges that they have experienced. The Web site can be accessed at www.miusa.org/ncde/stories.

If you ask all groups what challenges they face in achieving success in school as a parent, teacher, student, or administrator, then the knowledge gained can be transmitted into more successful inclusive practices. The ultimate goal is to *include all!*

PART II

Adolescent Cultures

Ways to Teach and Reach

3

Relating Cognitive and Psychological Theories to Adolescents

This chapter magnifies adolescent scenarios as they relate to cognitive and psychological theories. Further examination of sensory elements, emotional stimuli, peer influences, societal pressures, family support systems, gender factors, prior knowledge levels, and instructional implications are included.

ENTERING THE ADOLESCENT WORLD

As shown by the preceding chapter's comments from educators and students, as well as the movie and literature examples, adolescent cultures are complex ones. Schools need to be aware of the problems that adolescents experience as they try to develop a sense of who they are and need to help them positively resolve many difficult issues. Adolescent learners with disabilities in inclusive classrooms are faced with many of the same social, emotional, cognitive, physical, and moral issues as their peers, in addition to specific characteristics that their disabilities may present.

The following outline specifies some of the age-level characteristics of adolescents (Snowman, McCown, & Biehler, 2008):

I. Emotional

    A. Influenced by

        1. family

        2. peers

    B. May have psychiatric disorders

        1. eating disorders, substance abuse, learned helplessness, sense of loss, suicide, illogical thoughts

II. Social

    A. Influenced by parents

        1. long-range plans

        2. values

    B. Role confusion

        1. gender roles

        2. concern about identity

        3. occupational choices

    C. Influenced by peers

        1. immediate status

III. Cognitive

    A. Formal operational thought begins/continues

        1. understand abstractions

        2. engage in mental manipulations

    B. Political thinking (ages 12–16)

    C. Test hypotheses

IV. Physical

    A. At puberty, most are concerned with their physical appearance

    B. Many are sexually active (STD concerns)

Inspiration Software accessible at www.inspiration.com offers educators and students opportunities to create visual representations and organization of academic information with concept webs that are transformed into outlines such as the one above with the click of a button.

WHAT THE EXPERTS SAY

John Dewey, a philosophical educator and one of the first to outline many of the principles of progressive education, valued democratic schools with exploration and growth replacing repressive classroom settings. Sylwester (2007) points out that in the middle of the 20th century, the pendulum shifted back from Dewey's concept of democratic schools to authoritarian ones, and later that century it swung back again to Dewey's initial democratic principles. Now, in the 21st century, many decisions are based upon administrators anxiously deleting student choices in favor of improving student data on standardized tests, thus again sacrificing democratic student choices (www.uvm.edu/~dewey/articles/proged.html).

Dewey emphasized that teachers who just spew out knowledge, without considering the audience present, do not reach their students. Student participation gives merit to social and democratic principles. The unique characteristics of adolescents explain many of the principles behind differentiation of instruction such as teaching in multiple ways with modeling, written examples, more visuals, analogies, vignettes, collaborative work, independent studies, and more. Consistently building upon students' levels, interests, and needs happens when educators acknowledge students' differences and adolescent age-level charac-teristics with valuable lessons that match students' multiple intelligences.

These intelligences, as initially outlined by Howard Gardner (2006; Moran, Kornhaber, & Gardner, 2006), include visual-spatial, verbal-linguistic, bodily-kinesthetic, existentialist, naturalist, logical-mathematical, musical-rhythmic, interpersonal, and intrapersonal ones. Educators who allow students to draw, speak, write, listen, move, question, classify, deduce, compute, tap, interact, and reflect are saying it's okay to be different, and my lessons and assessments will honor your different ways of knowing, whether you are considered to be a gifted student or one who is receiving special services. Democratic classrooms that make use of Dewey's principles honor adolescent differences within inclusive environments.

Similar to Gardner, Robert Sternberg (2006), a cognitive psychologist, proposes that students need to display their intelligence in creative and experiential ways, applying what they know through school lessons and multiple opportunities. Adolescents are at times on a seesaw, seeking balance or equilibrium as they go through different stages. Schools can be that stabilizing force or influence in their lives, when other factors are beyond what adolescents view as sensible or controllable. Jay McGraw describes in his book, *Life Strategies for Teens* (2000), how the world works as a system and advises adolescents that if they learn that system, they will have an advantage over everybody else. He elaborates further by telling about different lenses and roles adolescents have. My favorite quote that he shares with adolescents is the one from Charlie Brown: *To get nowhere, follow the crowd.* Sometimes, adolescents in inclusive classrooms need reminders that their very differences are not to be viewed as negative, but may very well act as their assets when appropriately and creatively recognized and channeled into practical applications.

In Deshler and Schumaker's book, *Teaching Adolescents With Disabilities: Accessing the General Education Curriculum* (2006), it is emphasized that more research needs to be done to offer educators ways to reach all students in inclusive classrooms. Techniques such as graphic organizers, appropriate scaffolding, and establishing prior knowledge are some research-proven ways to better connect with students. These authors emphasize the importance of course unit planning for educators as well as responsibility or ownership of the learning for students as crucial elements for inclusive successes.

Kryza, Stephens, and Duncan in their publication, *Inspiring Middle and Secondary Learners* (2007), talk about valuing the balance of data in environments that honor and inspire students. The big picture they describe includes building communities with physical and emotional environments to create engaging and meaningful lessons that respond to learners' differences. This includes specific objectives and outcomes that match students' interests, learning styles, and of course their varying levels of readiness.

In Mildred Gore's book, *Successful Inclusion Strategies for Secondary and Middle School Teachers* (2004), she speaks about the fact that even though students may have learning problems, we as educators have the keys. She elaborates further, saying that the dilemma is that even though we possess the keys, we have to find the ones that match the correct doors. Issues such as attention, perception, discrimination, sequencing, organization, memory, reasoning, and confusion interfere with students gaining knowledge in inclusive classrooms, but we as educators can alleviate and remediate these issues and more to unlock those *adolescent doors.*

This next table sums up many of the big ideas researchers present that educators need to be aware of to increase successes in inclusive adolescent environments.

Summary of Some Big Ideas About Adolescents to Better Reach Them				
Emotional, social, physical, and cognitive differences exist.	Peers and family influence adolescents.	Students are developing more formal thought to understand abstractions.	Physical changes influence adolescents' behavioral and academic gains.	Students have different roles and lenses from which they view the world.
Adolescents respond to physically and emotionally safe inclusive learning environments.	Certain keys unlock *student doors,* but finding the right one to reach all students in inclusive classrooms is the *key!*	Outcomes and objectives need to be shared with students so they are an active part of the learning plan.	Considering multiple intelligences in lessons and assessments are critical for all students to maximize their strengths.	Prior knowledge connects with students and anchors new knowledge.
Graphic organizers help adolescents to see the *big picture.*	Appropriate scaffolding enhances learning.	Course unit planners advance students and educators.	Prior knowledge needs to be established.	Students' interests, needs, and levels of readiness vary.
Besides academics, perceptual areas must be addressed: attention, discrimination, sequencing, organization, memory, reasoning.	Some adolescents follow the crowd, some lead, and others prefer to be more independent.	Students respond to modeling, written examples, visuals, analogies, vignettes, collaborative work, independent studies.	Creativity and experience spur cognitive thought across the disciplines for both adolescents and educators.	Democratic classrooms value student differences and allow for increased discussion and exploration of concepts.

An important point to remember when considering theories on adolescent behavior is that the students are not always what their outward behavior indicates. Learning is also not just about what concepts are on the textbook pages, but how students will respond to these concepts. Educators need to realize that adolescents are far more complicated than they appear. Classrooms with teachers that not only teach academics but are also aware of cognitive development and psychosocial theories are ones that help students to acquire many lifelong transferable skills through positive, psychologically comforting classroom settings and accepting school cultures. Just the fact that adolescent learners with disabilities are included in general education classrooms speaks volumes in terms of how they perceive themselves and their place with peers.

Lev Vygotsky (1978), a developmental psychologist, affirmed that how we view ourselves is definitely influenced by how others view us as well. I think that Vygotsky would applaud the social benefits that students gain from learning alongside their peers in inclusive classrooms. Inclusion is an excellent way to increase student competencies when academics are skillfully taught within social environments that value the curriculum as well as how diverse student audiences soaking up that knowledge interact with each other. Adolescents also need to know the difference between the logical world and the real world. Sometimes, they are more interested in possibilities than actualities, but direct contextual instruction with modeling and scaffolding can change that. Vygotsky saw social interactions as assisting in cognitive development, and these opportunities are also offered in inclusive environments with scaffolding. Educators can practice mediation, which occurs when a more knowledgeable adult interprets and transforms a child's behavior. Enlisting scaffolding techniques supports student learning when that instruction is embedded within a student's ZPD, or zone of proximal development. How students interact with each other certainly affects their feelings of self-worth and competency. How educators assist students in the learning process—being aware of how information is absorbed, applied, and synthesized—is the most critical factor in helping students to develop more cognitive skills and increased self-efficacy. Positive inclusive results are thus contingent upon the solid factors that exist below the visible student icebergs.

According to Erik Erikson's (1963) theory on psychosocial development, students from ages 12 to 18 experience a stage labeled as *identity vs. role confusion.* That's when middle school and high school students begin to know who they are and start to develop a stable connection with their self-image and their place in the world. Ideas of appropriate behavior are explored. The stage before this is *industry versus inferiority* and the one after it is *intimacy versus isolation.* Most students are not even conscious of these emotions or stages, yet through social situations, they develop a sense of themselves, by experiencing positive and negative emotions or thoughts. Families and educators who are privy to these stages as described by Erikson are able to display more guided empathy and appropriate support that says, *"We understand and respect you as you are!"*

James Marcia (1966) expanded Erikson's thoughts with an identity status model that describes four statuses: diffusion, foreclosure, moratorium, and achievement. The theory refers to domains and crises such as job or career choices, intimate relationships, and politics. In *diffusion,* the adolescent gives no commitment with or without a crisis, while in *foreclosure,* there is a commitment but no crisis—for example, just accepting parents' wishes. During the phase labeled as *moratorium,* the commitment made is an unclear or vague one. Identity *achievement* happens when a crisis results in an adolescent commitment. Identity achievement and moratorium are generally associated with positive characteristics (e.g., high levels of self-esteem, autonomy, reasoning in terms of moral values), while foreclosure and identity diffusion are associated with negative characteristics (e.g., low levels of self-esteem, autonomy, reasoning) (Marcia, 1966, cited in Meeus, 1993).

Piaget's (1965) cognitive theory on intellectual development is based on organization and adaptation. Adaptation refers to how we adjust to the environment, while organization is how we systemize and combine processes. What he described as schemes are organized patterns of behavior or thought. New experiences that don't fit into a scheme must be adapted or accommodated to fit into a new scheme. If no accommodation or modification is necessary, then there is assimilation—the behaviors fit into existing schemes or environments. Educators who are aware of Piaget's theories cautiously introduce new material and consistently try to link it with students' prior knowledge. This approach reduces students' student frustrations when they do not immediately excel at a given subject, which are evidenced by many adolescents in inclusive classrooms.

The chart on page 56 offers more detailed information on Piaget's theory of cognitive development and just how it relates to adolescents.

The psychologist Lawrence Kohlberg (Kohlberg & Turiel, 1971) outlined different levels of moral reasoning that relate to adolescents trying to figure out interactions and morality. For example, should I do the right thing because it is the right thing to do, or because my parents want me to, or because otherwise I might get caught? Adolescent learners are sometimes caught up in immoral activities that are deemed by society as unacceptable. Many schools have character education programs, assemblies, and direct lessons to improve students' moral character. However, research supports that moral thinking does not always lead to moral behavior. It's basically not about what the experts say you should do, or even about what you say you will do, but what you actually do!

This principle applies to classrooms when educators not only teach the curriculum, but continually also emphasize positive student interactions with each other, adults, and in all school and community behavior. No matter what choices students make in terms of postsecondary decisions, without strong moral fiber, the loose threads will unravel and negatively impact them and others. Character education improves academic achievement, behavior, and attitudes, and it affects all life decisions if the principles are consistently modeled and applied. Actions of high moral fiber definitely speak louder than words, since it's not just about what adolescents say they will do, but also how they carry through those words in school, at home, and in the community. Students within inclusive environments have learning needs, but also must improve and grow with strong character education models, moral scaffolding, and guided directions.

Project Wisdom, accessible online at www.projectwisdom.com, offers educators many reflective opportunities to expand students' moral fiber through interdisciplinary activities and appropriate school and community actions. Character education programs such as this one raise the abilities of all students to see beyond their personal needs to establish higher moral connections that not only help others, but ultimately develop more emotional, social, and behavioral fibers within the tapestries of their own lives.

Carol Gilligan (1982), a psychologist who worked with both Erikson and Kohlberg, has more thoughts about adolescents in terms of gender. She delineated

Piaget's Cognitive Theory: How Does an Organism Adapt to Its Environment?				
Adaptation involves taking in new experiences, which leads to intelligent behavioral choices.	**Schemes** are organized behavioral patterns, which then become more complex.	**Assimilation** is taking in new experiences, while **accommodation** is adjusting to existing schemes. They can be simultaneous processes.	Piaget's theory has a **biological** basis with physical maturation involved.	**Equilibration** and **disequilibrium** are learning inconsistencies that occur through school and other experiences.
Piaget's sequence of stages	**Sensorimotor**	**Preoperational**	**Concrete operational**	**Formal operational**
Remember that sometimes these stages overlap as students in early adolescence enter adulthood. Some adolescents with more intellectual disabilities need remediation skills with many of these stages.	**Infancy**	**Toddler & Early Childhood**	**Elementary Early Adolescence**	**Adolescence & Adulthood**
	Knowledge is limited; start of object permanence; beginning of some symbolic language, with most intelligence evidenced through physical activity	Symbols; language matures; memory and imagination more egocentric; less logical thought; thinking in a nonreversible way	Manipulation of symbols related to concrete objects; understanding that mental actions are reversible; less egocentric thought	Intelligence is shown through use of symbols to represent abstract concepts; some return to egocentric thought

How does Piaget's theory relate to adolescents in inclusive classrooms?				
Piaget's theory relates in that teachers who provide concrete experiences to solidify concepts are thereby engaging learners who have variant needs. Teachers who help students with psychological scaffolding to increase their cognitive thought are valuing Piaget's described levels. Adolescents require better ways to soak in and retain the knowledge, e.g., study skills, memory tools, debates, more intellectual stimulation, and discussion. Adolescents need help in the formal operational stage with issues such as the following:				
sarcasm	**analogies**	**experiments**	**figurative language**	**symbolism/ languages mathematics**
thinking skills	**moral behavior**	**safe decisions**	**inferences**	**appropriate curriculum connections**

Source: Snowman, McCown, & Biehler (2008). *Psychology applied to teaching* (12th ed.). Boston: Houghton Mifflin.

some gender theories that view differences as part of a moral issue rather than a developmental one. Educators in inclusive classrooms who treat both genders equally are sending out strong messages that both females and males are capable of academic and social achievements, with neither group viewed as the stronger nor the weaker one. Valuing both genders creates equal environments for female and male adolescents who have varying abilities across their genders and may need additional pedagogical encouragement to show what they know or to take chances within inclusive environments. This means calling on both male and female students for responses to questions and viewing both genders as equally capable in the traditionally male-dominated fields of science and mathematics, which some students with special needs may already not view as their proficient area. Gilligan put forth differences between the genders, with males preferring rules and justice, while females were more involved with deeper emotions, such as developing relationships. Overall, open discussion, student–student interactions, building confidence, and more listening and communication are essential for both genders and students of all abilities. When adolescents are in inclusive environments, it is vital that all students are viewed as equally competent and that they are never stereotyped within a category of disability, past performances, or gender. The main point is that ability should be viewed as an individually applicable concept.

ADOLESCENT SCENARIOS WITH EMOTIONAL AND INSTRUCTIONAL IMPLICATIONS

To further digest more about these theories, with a colleague or solo, read the following classroom scenarios and think about how they are related to the psychosocial, cognitive, and moral developmental theories of Dewey, Erikson, Piaget, Vygotsky, Kohlberg, Gilligan, Gardner, Sternberg, Marcia, and more. Come up with applicable ideas about the theories and educational implications and instructional strategies to improve each scenario. I've offered some of my own connections, which follow the scenarios, but my ideas are not the answer key, since putting the theories into practice is an infinite and collaborative process.

SCENARIO 1

Miguel, an eleventh-grade student with learning differences, is uncertain about whether he will complete his high school studies. Miguel struggles with required school subjects and is unable to understand many abstract concepts presented. He currently has an afterschool job in shoe sales at a local department store, which gives him a sense of achievement, in part because he offers part of his salary to his family. Since his family has recently moved to the town, Miguel does not have a large circle of friends. Miguel often seems both socially and cognitively lost at school.

SCENARIO 2

Amanda, an eighth-grade, 13-year-old girl, has gone from being a student who worked diligently to receive Bs in her classes to a student who is in danger of failing

Mathematics, English, Spanish, Physical Education, and Science. The only two subjects she is passing are American History and Music. Her attendance, preparation, and class motivation is inconsistent. Amanda recently abandoned her longtime childhood friends and replaced them with students who are almost 2 years older. Amanda's sexual characteristics have developed more quickly than her classmates, and she feels awkward in her own body. Her mom was recently diagnosed with cancer.

SCENARIO 3

John, a sophomore in high school, is very athletic. He is currently on the school basketball and football teams, and is popular with the *in crowd*. He struggles with his academics, performing more than two grade levels lower in reading and mathematics. Focusing in school has always been an issue for John. He hopes to receive athletic scholarships and follow in his dad's footsteps. His parents applaud his athletic achievements and are not concerned about his lack of school successes.

SCENARIO 4

Ashley, a seventh-grade adolescent, was recently hospitalized after she collapsed during a school performance of the holiday play. She is an excellent student with high academic grades. Ashley participates in many extracurricular activities and is even the class president. She is well liked by both peers and adults. Despite her academic and social acumen, Ashley has very low self-esteem and is often anxious about upcoming tests and scheduled social events. The doctors just informed her parents that she has severe vitamin deficiencies and is malnourished, weighing far below the norm for her height and age.

SCENARIO 5

Thomas, a high school senior, always had school difficulties. If he could just tell the teachers his answers, he would be fine, but when he is asked to put his thoughts into writing, he is at a loss. The only writing he likes to do is *texting* or *instant messaging* his friends. He was recently arrested for shoplifting gum at the mall. Before this, he had minor run-ins with teachers due to his class misbehavior. Home dynamics are complicated, since both parents have active careers with long hours and frequent business trips away from home. Thomas is often either ignored or showered with clothes, video games, and money by his parents. Past school attempts at increased home–school communication and collaboration have failed.

What Are Some Possible Factors Involved?

Scenario 1

a. Theoretical Framework

Miguel is experiencing identity versus role confusion (Erikson). He is in a state of moratorium, since he is uncertain about his future goals (James Marcia). His lack of social/peer interactions and the fact that the learning is not within his ZPD interfere with his cognitive and social successes at school (Vygotsky). He has not adapted to his new environment and is unable to attach or fit the learning concepts into new schemes (Piaget). His practical intelligence is in play with his job choice (Sternberg), yet he has not totally explored or maximized his other intelligences, for example, interpersonal, intrapersonal.

b. Educational/Instructional Implications and Strategies

Miguel needs instruction that matches his level, within his ZPD, with appropriate scaffolding, for example, more hands-on experiences to concretize and generalize abstract concepts, step-by-step explanations, anchoring learning to prior knowledge and interests. More mediation with adults and peers, for example, open discussions, listening/communication, student–student interactions, and cooperative/collaborative learning will also improve his sense of belonging, personal intelligences, and cognitive growth (Dewey). Family involvement with long-range goals should also be solicited. Overall, Miguel needs cognitively and emotionally supportive classrooms that offer him a range of postsecondary options.

Scenario 2

a. Theoretical Framework

Amanda exhibits difficulties with social choices that are interfering with her cognitive learning (Vygotsky). In addition, Amanda matured at an early age and may be suffering from low self-esteem due to her rapid and uneven physical growth. Her poor schoolwork may be due to the influence of environmental, physical, and social factors that she may perceive as beyond her control (Vygotsky). She is experiencing some identity crisis and a state of disequilibrium with situations that interfere with her existing schemes (Piaget). She is in a possible state of moratorium (Marcia), becoming dissatisfied and resentful of former values. Amanda is unable to establish a sense of security in her self-perception and is uncertain about who she is. She is experiencing role confusion, rejecting her former good student status (Erikson).

b. Educational/Instructional Implications and Strategies

Less concentration on grades and achievement with more focus on progress is recommended. Amanda needs more corrective feedback and increased self-efficacy to realize that she is capable in other subjects as well if she becomes a self-regulated learner. Use Amanda's strengths in American History and Music to improve her weaker areas, for example, create songs to remember Spanish words or mathematics concepts, write stories about events in American History to improve writing and language skills. Allow her to express her thoughts through journal writing or poems to deal with her mom's recent illness. Amanda can also open up dialogue with a caring teacher and guidance counselor. Encourage Amanda to seek out good peer mentors her own age as positive role models by establishing more heterogeneous cooperative classroom groups, peer tutors, and involvement with extracurricular activities, for example, band or chorus. Reward her progress as well as her achievements to shape her academics. Amanda needs an intellectually challenging, yet emotionally safe environment that will allow her to organize new schemata. She needs to adapt and accommodate to changes in her physical body and personal crises. If possible, support groups and more discussion with peers in similar familial situations would open up a chance for nonthreatening dialogue.

Scenario 3

a. Theoretical Framework

John has a strong identity as an athlete, not a student. His peers who influence his identity enamor him (Erikson). Since he is part of the *in crowd*, John also feels superior to some of his peers and is outwardly unconcerned by his lack of academic success. Engagement in formal operational thought and mental manipulations at grade level are difficult for John. He performs best on a concrete operational level, needing specific demonstrations of concepts (Piaget). He is experiencing foreclosure and is definitely influenced by and dependent upon the guidance and approval of his parents in terms of his long-range goals (Marcia). He is also egocentric in his cognitive and social development, limiting his interactions and narrowing his interests (Vygotsky, Piaget). Bodily-kinesthetic and interpersonal intelligences are his strengths, while logical-mathematical and verbal-linguistic intelligences are his weaker intelligences (Gardner).

b. Educational/Instructional Implications and Strategies

Capitalize upon John's interests in sports and his stronger bodily-kinesthetic intelligence. Allow him to read and write stories about basketball and football players to improve his literacy skills, for example, biographies, fiction, nonfiction genres. Relate mathematics to sports as well when possible, for example, percentages of basketball shots made, logical football plays and patterns, word problems involving sports. Honor John's age level by offering appropriately leveled, high-interest texts. Also, offer multiple creative ways for him to demonstrate his knowledge, for example, concrete demonstrations, more cooperative projects with heterogeneous groups, and peer mentors (Sternberg). Offer scaffolding, and avoid strict memorization to help John develop increased cognitive thought; avoid direct instruction, and replace it with more physical manipulation of concepts. Try to decrease egocentrism and replace his need to be on stage with collaborative problem-solving opportunities to develop critical thinking skills and to strengthen reading and mathematical skills through creative and practical applications. Involve John with appropriate educational technology with a more knowledgeable peer or adult to scaffold and strengthen cognitive skills, for example, www.telementor.org.

Scenario 4

a. Theoretical Framework

Ashley's sense of industry is negatively impacted by an unhealthy competition for grades. She has difficulty accepting her own body and may have unrealistic goals and self-concepts concerning her present and future identity. Her distorted body image may be indicative of feelings of worthlessness and depression. Ashley's negative self-image may also be related to gender issues, as she feels unable to voice her thoughts. She may be influenced by false/media-driven conceptions about what girls should look like (Gilligan). Although Ashley is successful both socially and academically, she feels inferior, with no sense of pride in her accomplishments. She is more concerned with possibilities, for example, weight change, than realities, for example, health issues (Erikson). Ashley is capable of formal operational thinking and can deal with abstract concepts (Piaget), but she does not use psychological tools effectively for her own self-image (Piaget, Vygotsky). She may be automatically accepting moral rules (Kohlberg). Ashley has good interpersonal skills, but weaker intrapersonal ones (Gardner). She creatively explores other avenues, such as performing in a school play, but then ignores the practicalities (Sternberg) of her decisions about eating a balanced diet since she has a poor self-image. Although her family has the resources to feed her, she denies herself an appropriate diet and suffers from anorexia.

b. Educational/Instructional Implications and Strategies

Ashley needs emotional guidance in a nonthreatening classroom environment that allows her to realistically identify her present physical needs and accept her own body. Positive and realistic recognition and feedback toward reaching this step should be incrementally rewarded at home and in school. Peer mentors and collaborative partners can help with this as well. Look for signs of depression in writings and body language, and replace it with feedback that is more positive, by giving adult and peer support. Involve the school nurse, guidance counselor, and school psychologist to open up a dialogue with Ashley about appropriate health choices and the consequences of not following them.

Scenario 5

a. Theoretical Framework

Thomas is crying out for attention, behaving in a way to please or impress others. He is seeking social approval from his peers and is thinking of rules as flexible (Kohlberg). He is in a state of identity diffusion, with his values influenced by positive reinforcements. He is alienated from his parents, places little value on authority, and has weak identity formation (Erikson, Marcia).

b. Educational/Instructional Implications and Strategies

Discuss real and hypothetical situations in class. Reward Thomas for compliance with school rules and acceptable academic strides, along with appropriate classroom and moral behavior. Involve parents in appropriate operant conditioning by arranging a mandatory meeting using the administration as liaison. Use more computer tools to improve writing, for example, word prediction programs such as Co:Writer, and those that offer other cues. If students are amenable, allow peers to mentor Thomas to help with his writing skills. Involve Thomas in purposeful writing, for example, creating kids' books for students in younger grades. Investigate Thomas's interests, and connect prompts to writing across the disciplines. Involve multidisciplinary school teams for increased support and observation to intervene with appropriate strategies to alleviate his frustrations with writing assignments. Allow Thomas to dictate his thoughts during assessments rather than solely grading his writing on appearance and mechanics; concentrate on content. Understand that the reason for Thomas's misbehavior may be frustrations with miscommunication with parents and his own past academic performances. Replace that with scaffolding that matches Thomas's current level, by rewarding his progress toward meeting self-determined goals.

The next table tells more about what the experts say and how the research can be translated into successful adolescent classroom practices.

INCLUDING AND UNDERSTANDING THE ADOLESCENT BRAIN

Maya Lin, a prominent architect, poignantly stated, "Without resistance we cannot fly." A plane cannot soar without the proper parts, fuel, and maintenance, and

Experts say that adolescents . . .	Secondary Inclusive Classroom Translations
aged 12–18 experience a stage called identity vs. role confusion (Erikson, 1963).	Honor the confusion by offering structured lessons that allow for feelings of self-worth with realistic reflective student monitoring of accomplishments. Encourage students to use ongoing personal and curriculum journals to communicate thoughts and to clarify emotional or cognitive issues.
are greatly influenced by peers (Vygotsky, 1978).	Use peer modeling and more cooperative learning activities in heterogeneous groups. Encourage social interactions with academic assignments, peer mentoring, and outside activities.
are influenced by parents and other adults concerning their long-range plans (Snowman, McCowan, & Biehler, 2008).	Frequently communicate with families to share students' levels, progress, efforts, and achievements. Invite community mentors to share and discuss their occupations with students.
may weaken family bonds to bond elsewhere (Sylwester, 2007).	Incorporate character education with lessons that mimic positive family values across the curriculum with literature. Channel unsafe bonds to appropriate, safer ones, e.g., technology with approved Web sites.
have a great deal of energy and are smart in different ways (Moran, Kornhaber, & Gardner, 2006).	Integrate multiple intelligences in lessons to allow for bodily-kinesthetic connections and energy releases. Offer curriculum chances to display knowledge through music, dance, art, debates, skits, and other intelligences that incorporate and value reading and logical-mathematical skills, but honor other ways of knowing as well.
will sometimes make unpredictable and unsafe personal choices, think that they are invincible, and have difficulties with controlling impulses, decision making, displaying emotions, planning, and organizing (Deshler & Schumaker, 2006).	Emphasize the importance of nutrition, exercise, and healthy choices. Provide secure, nonthreatening learning environments with open lines of communication. Offer nonjudgmental ears, and be that safe haven. Role-play topical appropriate behavior in varying situations. Connect students with guidance counselors. Address all safety issues in a supportive, yet structured learning environment that not only values individual learners, but also models appropriate personal relationships and decisions.
are more aware of other viewpoints outside of their own perspective with different types of moral reasoning (Power, Higgins, & Kohlberg, 1989); sometimes think that they can change the world.	Allow for more discussion in lessons with viewpoints from diverse cultures, races, and countries. Teach and listen to possibilities and opinions, but then ground adolescents with facts and realities. Honor the adolescent voice. Acknowledge this with lessons that have practical community, national, and global connections.
like challenges, are capable of critical thinking, and are transferring from formal to more abstract thinking (Piaget, 1965).	Strengthen academic skills with motivating lessons that introduce and enhance prior knowledge, minus the frustrations Encourage adolescents to think outside the box through curriculum analogies that relate to their interests, thoughts, and goals. Have ongoing stations and centers set up in the room with anchor activities.
have varying emotional, social, behavioral, and cognitive needs (Crawford, 2008).	Differentiate instruction with subject areas, while varying the grouping. Remember to honor the integrity of the learner, e.g., use age-appropriate lessons and topics that acknowledge different levels. Offer supportive, collaborative, equitable, and caring environments that value adolescent voices.

neither can inclusion. In addition some educators, staff, families, and students may be resistant to inclusive environments, and there are many factors involved that need to be explored before placement decisions are made. Inclusion for adolescents is sometimes as complex as the human brain. The following analogies elaborate more to connect and compare the adolescent brain to many inclusive classroom and school factors before adolescents can soar to achievable heights.

The administrative supports can be thought of as the *skull*—not quite part of the classroom, but protecting and shielding teachers, students, and families from outside forces, encasing the everyday classroom agendas. The *classroom cerebellum* is the positive energy or balance created among coteachers; curriculum choices; and the academic, social, and emotional needs of the students. The *classroom medulla,* like heartbeats, digestion, and breathing, is the involuntary actions comparable to the standardized tests and the goals or objectives that educators follow. The *cerebrum,* the largest part, ultimately controls the positive thoughts and voluntary actions that help shape successful inclusive strategies, such as ways to motivate and prepare students with interest- and IEP-generated lessons.

The *classroom spinal cord* is made up of the instructional methods, processes, and procedures that transport the curriculum content. When the *classroom hypothalamus* is properly functioning, the emotional factors and inclusive classroom climate is well regulated and assessed, without increased frustrations or *inclusive sweating!* The *cerebral classroom cortex* senses all of this, seeing, hearing, touching, smelling, and even tasting the sweet (instead of acrid) messages of inclusion and positive environments. Thus, inclusion is not possible without including and factoring in the dynamics of the complex adolescent brain.

The human brain has two parts, the right and the left hemisphere, each of which controls certain skills. Like the right side of the brain, you could think of one side of inclusion as controlling the skills of reading, writing, talking, and math and problem solving. However we cannot forget the left side of the brain, or another component of the inclusion model that includes emotions, music, art, and spatial organization. Inclusion needs totality and coordination of its parts, too! Allowing students to show what they know through multiple intelligences, rather than solely relying on direct instruction, values individual strengths as well as different parts of the brain.

Theorists such as Gardner, Piaget, Erikson, Kohlberg, Dewey, Sternberg, Marcia, and Vygotsky all acknowledge that children encounter academic and social stages and levels of development, with preferences and choices made at each. Issues such as identity, role confusion, inferiority, feelings of accomplishment, and peer interactions influence school performance. Inclusive classrooms need to acknowledge that varying cognitive, social, emotional, physical, perceptual, and sensory differences relate to future accomplishments. Being proactive with inclusive mindsets accompanied by inclusive, universally designed lessons acknowledges this variability.

Robert Sylwester (2005, 2007), a prominent educator and researcher in the area of cognitive development, expresses many fascinating thoughts on the teenage brain. For example, what we might view as rebelliousness is their definition of creativity. In addition, adolescents are sometimes influenced by their equally immature peers. Our sensory lobes recognize and analyze challenges and mature throughout childhood. Frontal lobes determine an appropriate response, leading students toward finding solutions and making decisions. Sylwester calls to our attention that an adolescent with immature frontal lobes may not even realize that his or her actions were inappropriate and immature until many years later. Adolescents are also vulnerable to stress responses due to these immature frontal lobes. At times, their physical growth does not match their cognitive maturation. In a disability such as autism, the mirror neurons that model language skills or behavioral patterns operate differently. Consequently, the mirror neurons of some students with autism impact their communications and social interactions. I had the pleasure of attending a keynote speech given by Robert Sylwester when he compared the human brain to a *point that took a walk and became a line.* This phrase, borrowed from the artist Paul Klee, can certainly be applied to *points* about the adolescent brain still forming and not quite developed into its full potential. I think that we as educators need to *not only know these points, but walk the line, too!*

Another educator and researcher, David Sousa (2005), states that both general and special educators in inclusive classrooms have imperative roles to translate all of this new knowledge coming forth from brain research into practical classroom applications. The slowly maturing adolescent executive system is the reason that adolescents might lean toward high-risk behavior, thinking more about possibilities than realities. Sousa also points out that adolescents with language disorders may be frustrated by demanding curricula that require them to display more sophisticated language skills in areas such as vocabulary and written composition. This would certainly affect grammar usage, as well as understanding oral directions, written instructions, sarcasm, idioms, jokes, and more. If some adolescents with language disorders never received appropriate interventions when they were younger, then frustrations increase as they enter middle school and high school when they experience poor academic success and difficulties with social inter- actions. Educators need to draw them back into school and help reverse this downward trend with high-interest lessons that help students master academic skills and experience social successes, to circumvent language weaknesses. Fun curriculum-related DVDs, computer programs, assignments such as WebQuests, guided cooperative learning, and peer mentoring are all appropriate ways to address these deficits.

Why Do We Need to Learn This Stuff and When Are We Ever Going to Use It?

Many middle school and high school teachers will affirm that they have heard the preceding comment on more than one occasion from more than one student who thinks school is just plain boring! We as educators need to include the *adolescent brain* in our lesson plans, by motivating it to attend, remember, and apply the vast amount of curriculum that students may very well view as irrelevant, transforming boring lessons into well-remembered ones resulting in adolescent comments such as

Glad that I learned this and paid attention! Great lesson!

PRIOR KNOWLEDGE: IS IT A CUB OR A CAT?

I was walking my dog on a mountain path in Vermont, when suddenly I noticed a huge cat in the distance. I thought to myself, *Wow! I've never seen a feline of that size!* Perhaps this reiterates the reason why I wear eyeglasses for my nearsightedness to see things from afar, because as my dog and I drew closer, I realized that the cat I saw was related to Yogi the Bear. Yikes, it was a cub, not a cat! Being that ultimate calm person, who was internally screaming inside, knowing that Mama Bear was probably not too far away, I proceeded to skedaddle in the other direction with a rapid pace that tried not to communicate my incredible fear! *Why hadn't I initially realized that it was a cub?* This can easily be explained by understanding more about prior knowledge and learning.

Meaningful learning occurs when organized material is associated with stored knowledge. The cub did not fit into my prior knowledge, since where I grew up, in Brooklyn, New York, there were no cubs prowling along Flatbush Avenue! Maybe a rare cat prowler, but no cubs! Now that I was in a different setting, a rural part of Vermont, bears were part of that scene. This new experience was not part of my city background, so I was faced with a process called adaptation. Sticking to animal references, adaptation can refer to climate adjustments, such as when my dogs—yes, I now have two (in case there's another cub sighting)—shed more hair in the summer to stay cooler and have thicker coats to keep warmer in the winter. Bears adapt to climate changes as well when they hibernate in the winter and come out in the spring, ravenously searching for food. Hence, if I had not adapted to the unfamiliar cub encounter, I might not have been able to complete this book. I have stored this experience, so that my prior knowledge now influences where and when I choose to take a Vermont stroll.

When adolescent learners in inclusive classrooms do not adapt or adjust to new learning or social experiences, that negatively influences their understandings. Confusions and misunderstandings then spiral during unit lessons that follow, and are evidenced across all disciplines. Simply put and curriculum-related, a student needs to know what an inequality is before they solve for inequalities. How can adolescents understand cultural diffusions if they do not know the definition of culture or understand the scientific concept of gases diffusing? If adolescents do not have prior knowledge about World War I and Germany's economic conditions during the early 20th century, how will the students understand the events that led to WWII? Sometimes, eager educators who are busily trying to cover the curriculum forget about many of the factors that interfere with students' understandings. Meaningful learning occurs when organized material is associated with stored knowledge. This involves the sensory register attending to, recognizing, and instantly associating information before the information is even formally processed.

Some students with disabilities simply have not had the same prior learning experiences due to processing difficulties; varying cognitive levels; ineffective teaching practices; lack of experience with the same curriculum given in general education classes; and other instructional, cognitive, cultural, sensory, perceptual, and environmental factors. Educators never can assume that all of the students in inclusive classrooms have the same prior knowledge. Teachers somehow must ascertain what students know before they march ahead to teaching concepts that are more complex. One way to accomplish this is to dissect the learning objectives with proactive planning that expects the differences in prior knowledge before they are evidenced. Better-prepared teachers expect that all students will not initially meet their expectations. Informal ungraded pretests; K=W=L charts of what students know, want to know, and have learned; or classroom discussions are great ways to establish prior knowledge and adjust lesson deliveries.

Basically, students need to make sense of the learning! Information processing involves an *art:*

A ttention to stimuli

R ecognition of stimuli

T ransformation of the stimuli into some type of mental representation and comparison with other information

To conclude this section, let me tersely say, *sometimes a cat is really a cub!*

EMOTIONAL STIMULI

Adolescents may over- or under-respond to emotional stimuli. Here's where pedagogical *Goldilocks* wisdom comes into play, assisting adolescents in inclusive classrooms to replace impetuous decisions with more rational alternatives in *just the right amounts!* Learners who require additional guidance to improve behavior, social reciprocity, self-efficacy, study skills, and attention, benefit from direct social skill instruction and modeling opportunities to display appropriate emotions when confronted with varying stimuli. With educators' assistance, adolescents self-monitor how they respond to varying adult and peer interactions and classroom situations. Although adolescents sometimes think that they know a lot about themselves and others, when educators intersperse just the right amount of sensitivities to further engage adolescent reflections, then emotionally safe classrooms are promoted.

The table on page 67 depicts a sample social journal that adolescents keep to develop more metacognition of their emotions. Teachers then discreetly invite students to share and discuss disclosures. As a thought, to combine math, economics, reading, and language skills, students can compare their emotions to stock market, temperature, and class attendance changes from day to day or year to year.

Valuing just the cognitive adolescent side exclusively, without placing importance on the effects of emotional connections and stimuli, devalues learning. Although emotional factors may not be part of the American History class or the Spanish curriculum, they influence just how the history and Spanish words, concepts, and cultures are absorbed. If doubt, confusion, perplexity, humility, low self-esteem, and disappointment are present, these emotions need to be quickly replaced with positive learning scenarios that help adolescents experience reassurance, confidence, understanding, and satisfaction.

As adolescents mature, they often have a *trial-and-error* way of handling stimuli. They might try one approach, and if that does not work, they try Plans B, C, or D. The adolescent brain often reaches for autonomy in a world without autonomy. Students with disabilities in inclusive classrooms may have low self-efficacy and will not tell other teachers, family, and certainly not peers that the rate of teaching is too fast for them to process information. Perhaps the adolescent learner thinks that he or she can handle the stimuli overload, or perhaps the adolescent learner simply does not wish to have undue attention placed on him or her. Trial and error may thus result in more error if left uncorrected.

If educators play favorites, set unfair goals, embarrass students, or speed teach, then concepts are never gained. Some concepts that were previously introduced may

Keeping Track of My Moods and Reactions				
I agree to regularly keep track of my emotions by checking off the appropriate columns. This will help me to be more aware of my reactions to different situations. Maybe, I will even see some patterns that I want to continue with or change. All of this will help me be *a better me* in and out of school! I also agree to regularly review this chart and my thoughts with a selected peer or adult, e.g., teacher, counselor, parent, relative, friend. Signature _____				
Time/Day/Week _____ Brief description of what happened	My emotions were perfect ones for the situation.	I probably overreacted, showing too much emotion, way over the top.	I probably did not show enough emotion, considering the events.	Not sure about how I would rate my response.
My emotions can be compared to _____, because _____. Overall, I think _____ _____ _____.				

even be lost. In contrast, high self-efficacy is promoted within lessons that include clear goals, scaffolding, modeling, realistic challenges, and positive feedback for both efforts and accomplishments. When an adolescent experiences a higher confidence level, it is then translated into increased self-motivation and consequently increased inclusive successes. The curriculum is certainly easier to tackle if you believe that you are capable of tackling it. When this higher self-esteem is accompanied by encouraging, inclusive classroom support from collaborative teachers, family encouragements, and positive cooperative peer learning, then many classroom goals and objectives are scored. Just as students need to keep track of their reactions to lessons and situations, educators need the same if not more amounts of reflection, as shown with the next table.

Keeping Track of My Lessons				
I agree to regularly keep track of my lessons by checking off the appropriate columns. This will help me to be more aware of how my lessons are cognizant of my students' emotions. Maybe I will even see some patterns that I want to continue or change. All of this will help me be a better educator. I also agree to regularly review this chart and my thoughts with selected colleagues, coteachers, parents, or students in the class.				
Signature _____				
Lesson Date: _____	Definitely	Possibly	Not today	More reflections
Clear goals and objectives were communicated to the students.				
Pacing was at the right speed, with pauses for informal assessment and feedback.				
I listened to students' emotional signals.				
I encouraged questioning and open discussion.				
The lesson honored students' multiple intelligences and strengths.				
Modeling was given.				
Challenges were offered.				
Frustrations were minimized.				
Confidence levels were raised.				
Other thoughts about how the lesson stimulated positive emotions:				

The *adolescent emotional elevator* travels both up and down a tall apartment building, with self-esteem and confidence levels stopping at many floors. Adolescents of all abilities experience emotional *ups and downs*. Even students with higher cognitive skills may go through emotional turmoil and frustrations that interfere with their learning. In general, labels such as *disabled* or *gifted* often pigeonhole students into thinking that they are identified by their classification and expected to perform or not perform in a predetermined way, stopping at or having access to only certain floors or levels of learning. Even though some of these *labeled students'* intellectual abilities may deviate from the class norm, quite often, their emotional reactions do not.

Adolescent emotions frequently influence their academics. Students with a conduct disorder display difficulties in recognizing emotional stimuli, with a tendency toward more aggressive behavior (Sterzer, Stadler, Krebs, Kleinschmidt, & Poustka, 2005). Additional findings talk about how exaggerated emotional reactivity during adolescence may increase the need for top-down control and put individuals with less control at greater risk for poor outcomes (Hare et al., 2008). It's not always the words educators or peers verbalize that set off inappropriate reactions; sometimes, a glance or even a lack of a glance can trigger undesirable emotional responses. Proactive, structured classrooms promote acceptance of all individuals, regardless of prior cognitive and emotional successes, looking toward personal growth as the ultimate goal. Inclusive educators need to value the student as a capable individual, despite outward behaviors that may camouflage academic frustrations. It's okay to dislike the behavior exhibited, but not the student!

As the elevator begins its ride, the inclusive classroom is the first floor in promoting the strong message that all students belong. However, physical placement alone does not yield cognitive and emotional successes without skillfully designed lessons that acknowledge how students perceive and react to each other, absorb the learning, and handle their emotions. Glasser (cited in Kryza et al., 2007) advocated that students need to have choices to build this power in themselves within a classroom community that honors personal needs and diversity and that establishes trust. Adolescence itself is sometimes thought of as a time of emotional instability, yet that condition is certainly not irreversible! The following starred list highlights some other floors for educators to stop at to promote emotionally safe classrooms:

★ Valuing adolescent voices and opinions in classroom decision making in democratic classrooms

★ Keeping journals, self-check lists, and graphs of emotional growth and academic progress over time

★ Proceeding at appropriate levels in constructivist classrooms that honor students' voices

★ Nonthreatening, judgment-free classrooms

★ Expressing opinions through respectful discussion

★ Communicating thoughts and ideas, for example, using anonymous suggestion boxes

★ Writing and creating reflective assignments across the curriculum

★ Pairing and partnering peers as mentors and colleagues who share responsibilities

★ Accepting students for who they are, keeping track of likes and dislikes

★ Honoring and inspiring students' multiple ways of knowing

★ Reminding students that with perseverance, many successes will follow

★ Assisting students to understand environmental cues and nonverbal language, for example, body language, personal space

★ Advocating that students always believe in themselves

★ Sharing a classroom philosophy that grades do not define students

★ Allowing students to see personal growth, not make comparisons to each other

★ Collaboratively creating personal improvement plans for achievements

★ Valuing positive reinforcers, for example, more recognition with praise, smiles, and individual reward systems

★ Continuing teacher and student reflections

SENSORY ELEMENTS
AND KINESTHETIC OPPORTUNITIES

Statement One: Adolescents with disabilities in inclusive classrooms respond to teachers who readily realize that materials, presentation deliveries, and assessments must vary.

Statement Two: Adolescents without disabilities in inclusive classrooms respond to teachers who readily realize that materials, presentation deliveries, and assessments must vary.

The juxtaposition of statements one and two purposefully denotes the fact that adolescents with and without disabilities in inclusive classrooms benefit from high-quality teaching strategies. That's part of the principle behind universally designed learning, with *designs designed* to not only meet, but also welcomingly greet the needs of a heterogeneous student population, expecting and accepting differences or disabilities, before such needs are even presented. The positive side effect is that all students' strengths and abilities are acknowledged and maximized. Quite often, difficulties students experience aren't related to the complexity of the curriculum or prior student knowledge; at times, it's more about the process used to deliver or assess that curriculum. Helping students to understand, apply, synthesize, and evaluate the curriculum involves incorporating sensory elements and creating kinesthetic opportunities through concrete multimodal experiences that allow students to see, hear, smell, touch, taste, and move to the concepts! Students in inclusive classrooms, whether they are classified under one of the 13 disability categories or not, also respond to varied sensory approaches and kinesthetic learning opportunities. Bodily-kinesthetic learning and increased sensory experiences allow students to *feel the concepts* and movingly connect with the curriculum in ways that concretize instruction and increase retention beyond the exam date.

VSA arts, connected with the John F. Kennedy Center for the Performing Arts (www.vsarts.org), relates art to many standards, with dance movements and expressions as one of the components. They advocate the benefits achieved, ranging from self-discipline to improved collaboration, replacing possible inappropriate choices through the healthy channeling of body energy. Dance is a form of communication and can reveal much about students themselves, the curriculum, and different cultures. Whether students are physically able to mimic or create their own movement skills, they can still appreciate the underlying dance principles, from folk dancing to ballet. It's a great way to improve attention to detail and can even help with literacy sequencing and logical thought. Dance is capable of strengthening memory skills and social interactions. Some students who dislike reading, but love gymnastics or dance, would be fine learning syllabication rules if they incorporated dance routines with vocabulary words pantomimed, for example, plate tectonics, states of matter. Peers can choreograph curriculum concepts in heterogeneous groups that capitalize upon the bodily-kinesthetic intelligence through well-thought-out steps and curriculum movements that portray any skill or concept, from a book's mood to historical periods or connecting points in a mathematical plane that form angles and polygons. Many times, when the body exercises, the mind follows and stretches as well to achieve higher learning capacities.

Sensory issues impact students with hearing and visual disabilities in inclusive classrooms. However, students with hearing issues and increased visual needs are capable of achieving the same successes as their peers without sensory disabilities, when instructional practices value their strengths. A student with blindness needs to hear and be touched by the curriculum concepts in creative ways, whether it is through more descriptive language, Braille, raised drawings, or additional auditory reinforcement. Students with hearing disabilities or deafness benefit from note takers, more visual aids such as handouts and illustrated text, and sound field systems. Do understand, though, that there is variability within groups of disabilities as well. Just as adolescents in inclusive classrooms are heterogeneous, so are students with visual and hearing needs. All students within these groups do not receive the same instruction because cognitive, emotional, and physical levels vary. For example, some students with deafness prefer oral language, while others use sign language, or even total communication—valuing sign language, speaking with the voice, and a combination of all other ways to communicate. Students with visual needs range from those having partial blindness to students with low vision or total blindness. The point is that sensory and kinesthetic approaches reach and teach these students in moving ways! Concrete, sensible, and hands-on ways to accomplish these increased understandings follow in the table on the next page.

The following sites offer ways to add visual elements to the curriculum.

Webs and outlines with related pictures—http://www.inspiration.com

Picture-assisted reading and writing with Slater Software—http://www.slatersoftware.com

Pics4Learning is a copyright-friendly image library for teachers and students with a wide range of content-related pictures—http://www.pics4learning.com

Eyewitness Books—http://us.dk.com Usborne Books—www.usborneonline.com

Flashcards—www.scholastic.com/kids/homework/flashcards.htm

Online videos and teaching resources with district subscription—www.unitedstreaming.com

Mayer-Johnson has Boardmaker software programs, cards, and many other products for symbol-based communication and learning for students with communication and expressive language needs—www.mayer-johnson.com

Madeline Hunter (2004) distinguishes between emerging and static visuals. Emerging visuals are classified as those that appear as the lesson unfolds, for example, creating diagrams together, or new points illustrated on a chalkboard, overhead, or SMART Board. Examples of static visuals include prepared charts, photos, graphics, and transparencies. Some recommendations regarding both of these types of visuals follow:

★ Use spoken words before asking students to write, for example, if you show the words using PowerPoint, then the students will start taking notes rather than listening to the major points you are outlining.
★ Do not have competing visuals, for example, erase the emerging visuals from the chalkboard, but leave static ones.
★ Use simple, clear diagrams that highlight key words to minimize clutter, for example, appropriate presentations with spacing and positioning to emphasize major concepts and vocabulary.

Sensory and Kinesthetic Ideas for Inclusive Adolescent Classrooms				
Actual and virtual field trips, e.g., online talking museum sites, community visits, http://icom.museum/vlmp	Simulations and dance movements, e.g., pretend that you are solids, liquids, and gases	Role-playing, e.g., describe what you encountered as a crusader	*Doing activities* vs. lecturing, e.g., cooperative assignments	Tactile models, e.g., clay, pipe cleaners, LEGOs, wikki stix
Stretching and exercising to break up longer seated sessions	Gesturing, sign language, e.g., thumbs up/thumbs down for agreements or disagreements	Color coding, e.g., antonyms are written in red and synonyms are written in green letters, colored overlays for reading	Demonstrating concepts, e.g., acting out balanced equations	Sports opportunities, e.g., tossing an inflatable globe for map skills
Multimedia presentations, www.brainpop.com http://illuminations.nctm.org	Approved DVDs that accompany curriculum, e.g., *10,000 BC*	Technology programs, e-text, digital tape recorders, books on tape, speech recognition www.rfbd.org/ www.naunce.com	Animations, e.g., to teach social skills for students with autism	Dancing and moving to learning, e.g., acting out lines of latitude and longitude with skeins of different colored yarn
Singing the learning with curriculum-related lyrics	Allowing break periods, e.g., errands, station/centers	Hands-on activities, e.g., lab experiments, math manipulatives	More visuals, e.g., clip art, freehand, computer images	Reinforcing abstract concepts, e.g., algebra tiles
Concrete demonstrations, e.g., moving about to show meaning of *migration*	Varying materials, e.g., using string to measure perimeter	Descriptive, vivid language if students have visual issues	UDL designs that proactively allow and expect differences	More handouts with written text and Braille if needed
Speaking at the proper volume, clearly and directly, facing students on their level, e.g., bending down or seated in a chair if student is in a wheelchair, not shouting to a student who is blind or overemphasizing words if student is lip reading	Good classroom lighting, e.g., avoiding glares from window light, understanding potential negative effects of fluorescent lights	Alternate formats, e.g., enlarged worksheets, uncluttered handouts, orally reading a written test	Visual warnings, e.g., flashing lights for fire drill signals for those with hearing impairments, signals for changing classes	Better seating, e.g., away from distracting noises or nearer to the front of the room, interactive board, or teachers
Soothing background music	Headphones for additional directions	Magnification sheets to enlarge text and handouts	Raised drawings to touch the concepts, e.g., relief maps	Extended processing time if needed

Quite often, students within inclusive environments will benefit from built-in times to release extra energy. *People searches* physically get students moving to the learning and help those adolescents who need this type of presentation to break up longer periods of sitting. They are another way to maximize students' bodily-kinesthetic and interpersonal intelligences. Adolescents of all ability levels often enjoy collaborating and interacting with peers. With people searches, adolescents survey peers to solicit signatures on the given lines to indicate that the students know the answers to the descriptors they signed. This type of presentation offers adolescents acceptable reasons to move about and talk to their peers, gaining academic and social acumen. Afterward, the class collaboratively shares the knowledge. The following descriptors offer curriculum connections.

Find someone who knows

a. how a seismograph operates. _____

b. reasons for the U.S. Iraq invasion. _____

c. how to find the square root of a number. _____

d. the name of a play written by Tennessee Williams. _____

e. the Spanish word for world. _____

f. the theme of *Macbeth.* _____

g. why the Civil Rights Movement began in the United States. _____

h. what courses they need to graduate from high school. _____

Student searches can also be used to help adolescents bond. The student search on the next page is a kinesthetic way to allow students to discover more about their peers, beyond academics, to form friendships by discovering commonalities and connections. This people search also gives teachers insights on ways to connect to students by incorporating their candid responses into lessons whenever possible to increase motivation, attention, and retention.

Student Search

Name: _____

Directions: Have people sign their name by the descriptor that best matches them. Try to find different class signatures for each number.

Find someone who

1. likes to play video games. _____

2. ran in a marathon. _____

3. loves to sing in the shower. _____

4. has many friends. _____

5. likes to go to the mall alone. _____

6. wishes that he or she owned a car. _____

7. has had a recent argument with a parent or family member. _____

8. plays a musical instrument. _____

9. can speak another language. _____

10. wants to be famous one day. _____

11. interacts with others on a team. _____

12. enjoys writing or reading poems. _____

13. has more than one e-mail address. _____

14. can win a timed text messaging contest. _____

15. spends more than 3 hours a day on a computer. _____

16. has over 100 songs on his or her MP3 player. _____

17. lives with two or more pets. _____

18. thinks learning is fun. _____

19. adds numbers in his or her head. _____

20. wants to be a professional actor. _____

21. wishes he or she were someone else. _____

22. loves this people search. _____

23. dislikes this people search. _____

Overall, sensory lessons that value all modalities with visual, auditory, and kinesthetic-tactile presentations actively demonstrate curriculum concepts that range from population density to *Beowulf* to understanding DNA molecules. Creative teachers who know what facts and knowledge they'd like to disseminate, and then figure out ways to connect them to students, imprint the learning in ways that will be remembered by students in years to come through very *sensible* and *touching* lessons.

APPLYING CREATIVITY, ANALYSIS, AND PRACTICALITIES TO INCLUSIVE ADOLESCENT CURRICULUMS

Views on intelligence today are much different from what the widely used Stanford-Binet or Weshler tests measure. High scores on intelligence quotient tests are simply not the best way to determine if a student will achieve future strides when he or she is an adult. An IQ measurement cannot define who an adolescent is, or how that adolescent will eventually deal with adult situations. Additional difficulties determining intelligence present themselves, since adolescents are undergoing developmental changes that interfere with accurate assessments of their abilities. Students with different abilities in inclusive classrooms do not always show their highest intelligence on standardized tests due to anxiety levels and low self-perceptions. When educators use curriculum-based assessments (CBAs), which are criterion-referenced, the learning is then paralleled to lessons so as to reflect whether students understand the content presented. The traditional tests simply do not allow teachers to have accurate information to ascertain the needs of students with exceptional needs and determine whether these students have mastered the curriculum (Thousand, et al., 2007).

Today's educational views on intelligence include deductive and inductive reasoning as part of adolescent thought to acquire, store, and process information in multidimensional ways, along with the research of other prominent educators. Robert Sternberg (2006), who expanded upon Howard Gardner's theory about multiple intelligences, outlined a *triarchic* theory that includes creative, analytical, and practical applications of learning to demonstrate knowledge. Sternberg advocated that students learn best when all three come into play. The next table gives curriculum examples of ways to allow for multiple adolescent expressions that honor creative, analytic, and practical domains.

Think of your own ways to *intelligently cap the learning* within environments that value creativity, analysis, and practicalities, relating the content to adolescent lives.

Capping the Learning in Intelligent Ways* Creative analysis with practical curriculum interpretations *Based on Sternberg's triarchic theory			
CAP =	Creativity: Solving newly presented, difficult, unknown, or unusual problems	Analysis: Dissections of learning with cognitive thought	Practicalities: Applying the knowledge to yourself, everyday environments, and people
Geometry	Use computer drawing tools, e.g., construct a design with only perpendicular lines.	Compare and contrast two theorems and postulates.	Explain why geometry is essential to an architect. When would geometry be relevant to your life?
Algebra	Formulate an algebraic word problem that can be solved with two or more variables.	Dissect a textbook word problem, telling how to algebraically solve it.	How does understanding about football yard gains and losses relate to positive and negative integers?
Calculus	Originate a problem that can be solved with a single variable calculus equation, e.g., motion of an object along a fixed path.	Evaluate how velocity, acceleration, and slope relate to fundamental theorems of calculus.	Describe how engineers or economists use calculus in their daily jobs.
Chemistry	Set up your own experiment and decide which elements you will use.	Explain how covalent bonds differ from ionic bonds.	Why can chemistry be the answer to many unexplained diseases?
Biology	Draw a diagram or create a model that shows the difference between mitosis and meiosis.	Examine an animal cell and a plant cell, noting similarities and differences.	How can we maintain a healthy heart?
Physics	Initiate an experiment that demonstrates the laws of reflection and refraction.	Evaluate how the Doppler effect relates to a passing siren's sound.	Explain how projectile motion relates to a baseball game.
United States Government	Create a model or a graphic organizer that delineates the functions of the three branches of government.	Judge why some people argue that the Supreme Court is not the voice of the people.	What would happen to the freedoms of citizens in the United States if the U.S. Constitution had never been written?
American History	Rewrite a peace treaty that would have helped Native Americans to procure more rights.	Question the decisions made by Franklin Delano Roosevelt during WWII.	How can learning about past events in a country help to shape its future?
World Languages	Generate a picture dictionary or travel brochure for someone from the United States visiting Spain.	Consider the application of Latin words to the English language.	Think about what the world would be like if we all spoke the same language.

Capping the Learning in Intelligent Ways*			
Creative analysis with practical curriculum interpretations ***Based on Sternberg's triarchic theory**			
CAP =	**Creativity:** **Solving newly presented, difficult, unknown, or unusual problems**	**Analysis:** **Dissections of learning with cognitive thought**	**Practicalities:** **Applying the knowledge to yourself, everyday environments, and people**
Ancient Civilizations	Pretend that you are a Greek citizen in Athens during its early democracy, and write a script about your day in the Agora.	Explore the civilizations of the Nile and Mesopotamia; tell how they are products of cultural invention and diffusion.	Compile an annotated list of ways that ancient achievements have influenced modern society.
Global Events	Coin a slogan that would help develop peace between the Palestinians and Israelis.	Evaluate events in the Sudan in the past decade and offer other options that would have had different consequences.	Tell how the economy of the world can be positively and negatively influenced by the amount of oil production.
English composition/ Poetry	Construct a persuasive letter to a book's character, or create a limerick about a fictional character. Write a haiku about your best friend.	Analyze the word choice in a newspaper article, and offer replacement vocabulary that improves the message.	How have texting and instant messaging affected the rules of grammar? What would the world be like without rhyming words?
Home economics	Create a recipe for a dinner party of 10.	Study the ingredients of recipes from different countries.	Adapt a recipe for someone who is diabetic.

Capping the Learning in Intelligent Ways*			
Creative analysis with practical curriculum interpretations ***Based on Sternberg's triarchic theory**			
CAP =	**Creativity:** **Solving newly presented, difficult, unknown, or unusual problems**	**Analysis:** **Dissections of learning with cognitive thought**	**Practicalities:** **Applying the knowledge to yourself, everyday environments, and people**

4

Beyond the Labels and Into the Abilities of Adolescent Learners

This chapter concentrates on the abilities of adolescents as they encounter internal and external influences with peers in classroom interactions and other settings. It includes an examination of their confusions, pressures, acceptances, and rejections as related to the diverse abilities of adolescents in inclusive environments as developing teens. The text encourages the realization that students are not their labels, but individual children, possessing many diverse abilities, strengths, and potentials, and aids in the development of more knowledge about abilities with increased research, reflections, and sensitivities across cultures and genders.

GOOD-BYE CHILDHOOD SYNDROME

Voice changes, shifts in sleeping patterns, more facial and body hair, developing breasts, changing bodies, and the formation of abstract and more formal thought processes are only a few of the alterations evidenced as adolescents leave childhood and enter into the transitional period called *adolescence,* a step away from being an adult. Adolescents with and without disabilities often compare themselves to others, as they seek their own individuality. Body capabilities and curiosities are also often tested. Adolescent actions may be taken before judgments are made using logical thoughts. Some adolescents have varying respect for authorities such as parents and school personnel, for example, teachers, bus drivers, and administrators.

Interpersonal issues can conflict with academics as some adolescents follow their peers. It is often a tumultuous time for students, especially those in inclusive classrooms, seeking to fit in with their peers. Educators who acknowledge these changes are not minimizing adolescent voices, but maximizing their students' potentials to go beyond the noticeable or internal differences into an inclusive classroom that says, *"It's okay to be confused, but let's work this through together."* Nonjudgmental acceptances in collaborative classrooms that reduce competition and foster healthy, cooperative attitudes are a win–win for all.

SOCIETAL PRESSURES: THEIR INHERITED WORLD

A report from the International Child and Youth Care Network (2001) states, "[A]ll over the world, social, parental or familial developmental interference, peer pressure and collective traumatic experiences may lead to 'adolescent turmoil' among youths during the period of adolescence."

The world is not perfect, and when adolescents start thinking about their place in it, it can be viewed as a pressure-filled one. Adolescents inherit many circumstances from family, schools, neighborhoods, and political leaders. The following alarming facts speak for themselves. The Sudanese Civil War and its effects on the 27,000 displaced and orphaned boys there (they had been targeted for slaughter, and fled across the desert) delineates this point about inherited worlds. In the United States, 1 in 4 children (about 15 million) live below the poverty line (see www.hearts andminds.org/articles/childpov.htm). Globally, 1 billion children live in poverty (1 in 2 children in the world). Almost a billion people entered the 21st century without the skills to read a book or sign their names (see www.global issues.org/issue/2/causes-of-poverty). These startling facts scream that unfairness not only exists, but must also be addressed. Some adolescents are able to cope better than others with changing physical, emotional, cognitive, social, socioeconomic, cultural, and global issues. As indicated by these statistics, all environments do not offer adolescents the same educational opportunities or support. Adolescents are basically a heterogeneous group of individuals who may face either optimistic or pessimistic futures.

In a book titled *Reviving Ophelia: Saving the Selves of Adolescent Girls,* by Mary Pipher, many complex issues such as eating disorders, depression, and suicide are outlined. Nutrition is a serious issue for students who are either underweight or overweight. A report from *JAMA: The Journal of the American Medical Association* (Ogden et al., 2006) announced findings that adolescents aged 15 to 17 who live in poverty are more likely to be overweight than those not living in poverty. Both over- and underweight health issues can lead to severe medical conditions ranging from lack of muscle mass to hypertension, high blood pressure, diabetes, and even death.

Inclusive schools guide both students and parents to deal with other mitigating factors that can trickle into adolescent classrooms such as poverty, lack of home support, poor health conditions, and unequal opportunities. When moral issues or those that concern physical intimacy enter inclusive classrooms, it is quite difficult to deliver a lesson that commands adolescent attention. Physical growth and change combined with societal pressures and increasing difficulties with academics are real societal issues in this not-so-simple world. Adolescents who do not like the world they see often choose to create their own more pleasant world. This is seen through varying dress styles, haircuts, music, movies, and other personal decisions. Morality, commitments, and career choices are just a few of the societal pressures that are on students' shoulders. Despite the differences in their choices, respectful inclusive classrooms offer adolescents space to grow into those people that they envision themselves to be, equipped with the academic skills, guidance, and confidence to make successful choices for future emotional and cognitive developments.

THE ADOLESCENT DEPARTMENT STORE

A report from Editorial Projects in Education (Swanson, 2008) called *Special Education in America* delineates statistical facts about students with disabilities in high schools across the United States. It mentions how inclusive policies, which resulted from much litigation over the past few decades, have led to an increase in the number of students with disabilities who are now educated in general education high school settings. The LRE continuum, which says that the general education classroom is the "least restrictive environment," means that efforts must be made to see if students can be placed in this setting with their nondisabled peers to the greatest extent possible before more restrictive environments are considered.

The report outlines how a rapid increase in the total number of students in SE programs is primarily attributable to a rise in two disability classifications: SLD (specific learning disabilities) and OHI (other health impairments, including ADHD). The report emphasizes how knowledge is certainly a powerful tool, with increased monitoring of programs that have meaningful outcomes and expectations that are evaluated. Most important is the need to carefully scrutinize special education practices to determine effectiveness. The report examines diagnostic, instructional, and transitional services, along with looking at settings, school disciplines, and rates of high school completion. When teachers keep accurate records with grade books that reflect observations, performances on informal and formal academic and behavioral assessments, portfolios, anecdotal records, and more, the information revealed is invaluable. Administrators who listen to educators and carefully determine the progress achieved by adolescents in SE programs can then make recommendations to continue, modify, abandon, replace, fine-tune, and emotionally and financially support classroom interventions to raise student achievements.

The next list shows statistics regarding disability categories of high school students (Office of Special Education Programs [OSEP] 2006 data, cited in Swanson, 2008):

Specific learning disabilities—57 percent

Other health impairments—11 percent

Emotional disturbance—11 percent

Mental retardation—10 percent

All other disabilities—11 percent (The other categories under IDEA include autism, visual impairment including blindness, hearing impairments, deafness, multiple disabilities, traumatic brain injury, deaf-blindness, orthopedic impairments, and speech or language impairments.)

Students with disabilities constitute approximately 9 percent of the school-age population, with almost one-third of the students with disabilities aged 14 to 17.

Overall, as this report and many other researchers note, students with disabilities are a diverse rather than homogeneous group. Anyone who shops in a department store is no doubt amazed at the wide array of merchandise choices, ranging from clothing for toddlers to young adult fashions, men's shoes, or women's hats. Choices are good, yet in the case of the adolescent department store, too many different options offer confusions. The figure headings in the cognitive, physical, emotional, social, and moral domains below delineate that adolescents have a vast array of unique items *stored within.*

Welcome to the Adolescent Department Store			
Cognitive Shops	**Physical Items**	**Emotional Accessories**	**Social/Moral Sweets**
A few items for purchase here include shelves filled with formal thought and free mental manipulations to test hypotheses and political thinking. Now if you prefer to buy discount items, that's when schoolwork is cut due to other distractions, poor performances, or restless feelings.	Watch out as you walk through these aisles, since uneven growth spurts and puberty influences are quite apparent. Tread carefully! The items may appear ripe, but the maturation dates vary. What the items look like is sometimes more important than their function, and they may be different from how they appear to be once the items are unpackaged.	These are sometimes the most fragile, sensitive items, and they need to be handled and packaged carefully. They almost shout at you to buy them, since they often crave acceptance due to some negative self-concepts. These emotional accessories are constantly gazing in the mirror, often with anxious thoughts that may depress or sometimes with smiles, communicating high self-direction.	These social and moral sweets are often self-conscious about their popularity, yet at times are uncertain or confused about just what role they fill. Overall, acceptance is crucial, with these sweets looking toward peers for immediate answers and toward family for long-range goals. Once you make your purchase, offer set rules for them to follow with appropriate peer *mannequins* and models.

CONFUSIONS VERSUS CONSISTENCIES

Nobody knows what I am going through!

I just can't seem to get to the heart of the matter!

I kind of think I'm okay, but I'm not sure.

I'll meet you tomorrow, unless things change.

No need to explain, because it just doesn't make sense.

Sometimes I just want to fit in!

(And, my personal favorite, that sums it up rather well) Whatever!

The book *Get Out of My Life, But First Could You Drive Me and Cheryl to the Mall: A Parent's Guide to the New Teenager,* by Anthony Wolf, is specifically written to help adults understand teenagers who desperately require additional love, attention, guidance, and compassionate environments, even though these teens may appear as unruly, disobedient, and defiant. The How I Survived Middle School series, by Nancy Krulik, offer students many insights through the genre of fiction. The protagonist, Jenny McAfee, goes through events ranging from not fitting in with the popular crowd, to discovering about courage and confidence. In her memoirs, *My Thirteenth Winter*, about dyscalculia, Samantha Abeel candidly offers insights about her mathematical learning difficulties. Many teens would respond to reading and hearing about other people who have faced such challenges and thrived. When Michael Phelps won his Olympic gold medals, many students with ADHD felt that they shared the podium with Mr. Phelps, who triumphed over the negativity of the label of ADHD, displaying his ability to productively channel his hyperactivity. Family members and educators can also offer more support. Teachers who acknowledge confusions and replace them with meaningful, constructive classroom experiences validate both academics and positive relationships, increase teen self-efficacies, and establish environments that encourage emotional and academic growth for students with and without disabilities in inclusive classrooms and in their communities.

Students with learning issues, such as those missing prior knowledge or teens who have processing difficulties, are very often confused by discomforting surprises and learning puzzlements when educators do not communicate effectively to outline goals, objectives, and learning steps with the class. The following starred list highlights ways for teachers in inclusive adolescent classrooms to increase student understandings and diminish these confusions. Ongoing proactive lessons acknowledge their adolescent audiences, offering and communicating a variety of learning *accessories* such as

- ★ informal establishment of prior knowledge through informal assessments, for example, K-W-L charts.
- ★ collaboration and communication of goals and objectives to and with administrators, coteachers, students, and families.
- ★ organization of lessons, from simpler to more complex concepts, with course outlines and advance planners consistently available to students.
- ★ dissection of misunderstandings to explain or reteach in mini lessons as needed.
- ★ classrooms that welcome participation and questions.
- ★ informal and formal evaluations and constructive feedback that lead to more insightful reflections.

FAMILY AND PEER SUPPORT: ACCEPTANCE, PRESSURE, AND REJECTION

In adolescent attempts to please peers and families, sometimes, teens' own needs are sacrificed. Acceptance and rejection often affect how adolescent learners view themselves and how they will perform in classrooms. Some adolescents with disabilities compare themselves to peers, thinking that they do not meet the levels of the other students or self-imposed expectations. Motivation is frequently distracted and influenced by other internal and external pressures. In addition, onset of maturation affects acceptance by peer groups and how others view the students, even though interiors do not always match physical appearances. When an adolescent experiences rejection, the results are sometimes detrimental. The following tables ask peers and families to think about their levels of acceptance of a disability.

Dis*ability* Awareness Peer Rubric: Circle one choice in each row.

Lousy Outlook (LO) ↓ 1 point for each circled in the column below	Fair Outlook (FO) ←→ 2 points for each circled in the column below	Mature Outlook (MO) ↑ 3 points for each circled in the column below
If I'm friends with *that kid*, people will think I'm weird!	I guess I could talk to *that kid*, but only in school!	I think I'd like *that kid* to be my friend!
I have no time to help someone like that! No way is she working with me on this project. She'll mess it up!	I understand that she has difficulties, so I'll try to help her sometimes. Just don't make me do it all of the time.	Everyone needs help sometimes, including me! She can definitely work with me on this project and add her thoughts.
How could anyone look or act like that? He's strange!	It's not right to poke fun at someone because of what he or she can or cannot do.	I'm going to stop those mean kids who are teasing that boy or girl just because he or she is different.
I feel sorry for that kid. What a lousy life!	I wonder if I could help that kid!	I admire that kid's courage and perseverance.
I hope that *weirdness* never happens to me!	I'm curious about what happened to that kid and if that could affect me.	It's not about me!

Scores:

5–7   Just what are you thinking?

8–11   Getting better

12–15   You're a true friend!

Source: Karten, T. (2008). *Embracing disabilities in the classroom: Strategies to maximize students' assets.* Thousand Oaks, CA: Corwin Press.

This is a complicated rubric to conceive, since no one can imagine exactly what it's like to be the parent or guardian of an adolescent with a disability. Levels of support and degree of severity of each disability will most often influence parental/guardian attitudes. Again, it's difficult to understand other people's lives when you're on the outside looking in, without experiencing the daily agenda, complications, interruptions, and triumphs presented.

Disability Awareness Parent/Guardian Rubric: Circle one choice in each row.

Lower Level of Acceptance (LA) ↓ 1 point for each circled in column below	Medial Level of Acceptance (MA) ← → 2 points for each circled in the column below	High Level of Acceptance (HA) ↑ 3 points for each circled in the column below
Thinks his or her child is a burden, resenting the interference the adolescent presents to the family dynamics and other social relationships	Realizes extra responsibility his or her adolescent demands; may isolate other family members and social contacts	Acknowledges the unique needs his or her son or daughter presents and embraces their adolescent as an integral, contributing family member
Skewed view of current performance level of teen	Accepts adolescent's current performance level	Accepts adolescent's current performance level and envisions future potentials and strides
Blames self and others for adolescent's lack of successes, with a level of hostility toward school personnel	Complacent about adolescent's performance level and indifferent toward school personnel	Supportive of adolescent's current level and appreciative toward school personnel's efforts Partners with teachers
Ashamed of adolescent and somewhat guilt-ridden	Indifferent about adolescent	Proud of son or daughter
Actively looking for a cure	Hoping for a miraculous change or reversal	Accepts disability and ways to attain future strides
Shattered self-esteem	Fragile self-esteem	Good self-esteem
Disinterest or disengagement in adolescent's life with some avoidance of parental/guardian involvement	Performs necessary parental/guardian tasks to maintain adolescent's health and daily needs	Thinks of innovative and positive ways to perform parental/guardian tasks to joyously be part of adolescent's life

Scores:

7–10   Need more help with adjustments

11–14 You are dealing with situations.

15–21 Total acceptance and an embracing attitude

Source: Adapted from Karten, T. (2008). *Embracing disabilities in the classroom: Strategies to maximize students' assets.* Thousand Oaks, CA: Corwin Press.

FACTORS RELATED TO DISABILITIES, GENDERS, AND DIVERSE CULTURES OF ADOLESCENTS

Disabilities are complex. Within each disability group, such as autism or learning disabilities, so many different characteristics are evidenced. Yes, there are similarities, but it's important to remember that adolescents are not just about their disabilities. Disabilities do not define people; they are just one petal of a flower that changes and develops with nurturing. In school scenarios, this translates to appropriate instruction and inclusive support.

First of all, students should always be spoken about in *people-first language:* It's the student with Asperger syndrome or the student with blindness, not the *blind kid* or the *Asperger boy.* Again, the disability is just one part of a student's makeup. In addition, not all accommodations need to be complex ones. Simply reducing distractions or helping students to increase perception, memory, metacognition, and attention to lessons could be the keys that students need to be successful. Even though students with attention deficit hyperactivity disorder (ADHD) may be impulsive, hyperactive, or inattentive, providing stimulating, interest-generated lessons can increase motivation. The Web sites noted on page 86 can be consulted to gain additional information about instructional methods and appropriate accommodations to assist students with specific disabilities in both school and home environments, and to maximize their abilities to lead productive adult lives. Many of the Web sites also offer support and increased knowledge for peers and adults regarding students with different abilities.

Diversity was always the norm in special education. Now, with inclusion more prevalent, diversity is the norm in general education classes as well. For adolescents, this includes students with varying cognitive, physical, emotional, and behavioral needs, as well as different cultural backgrounds. Labels—which are sometimes used to group individuals with similarities for convenience, organization, or funding reasons—often stigmatize people as a group, rather than recognizing individuality. Another issue that is huge is the overrepresentation of students of color in special education, accompanied by the underrepresentation of the same population in programs for the gifted. Inclusion means that we must not only include but also offer all students the opportunities to shine with the proper academic preparation and social experience that mimic life's natural settings.

Culture is a complex issue for students with and without disabilities. African Americans and Native Americans are more likely to receive special education services, while Asian students are less likely to receive them. African Americans, when compared to other racial and ethnic groups, are about 40 percent more likely to receive services than other students (Swanson, 2008). Differences in levels of cultural participation, access to services, advocacy, and views of special education can influence students' school performances and future successes (Harry, 2002). Some cultures are also more accepting of disabilities, while other cultures view a disability as a familial punishment or something that is associated with shame.

Teenagers themselves are even said to have their own culture, with set rules and ways of thinking. In addition, gender issues are also complicated. Various maturation levels of adolescents present particular challenges. For example, late-maturing boys need opportunities to gain status and self-confidence, while late-maturing girls require extra attention to build their self-esteem. Early-maturing boys may have more social interactions with older peers and may even engage in more risky behavior, while early-maturing girls may have lower self-esteem with a propensity toward eating disorders and depression (Snowman et al., 2008). Gender bias in classrooms refers to treating males and females differently, such as not valuing girls as scientists or mathematicians or conversely, boys as chefs or artists. Educators need to motivate both sexes equally across the board, by allowing each one to shine according to individual interests, not based upon preconceived sexual

Inclusion accommodations and ideas for students with . . . Online Resources	Communication Disorders www.asha.org	Executive Dysfunction www.schoolbehavior .com/conditions_ edf.htm	Specific Learning Disability www.ldanatl.org www.ncld.org www.schwablearning.org www.ldinfo.com
Above Average Skills www.cectag.org www.nagc.org	Conduct Disorders www.nmha.org www.nimh.nih.gov	Intellectual Disabilities www.thearc.org www.aamr.org	Tourette Syndrome www.tsa-usa.org
Asperger Syndrome www.asperger.org	Deafness/ Hearing Loss www.agbell.org www.hearingloss.org www.deafchildren.org	Obsessive Compulsive Disorder www.ocfoundation.org www.adaa.org	Traumatic Brain Disorder www.biausa.org
Attention Deficit Hyperactivity Disorder www.chadd.org	Depression www.nimh.nih.gov	Oppositional Defiant Disorder www.nmha.org www.mentalhealth.com	Twice Exceptional www.uniquelygifted.org
Auditory Processing Needs www.ncapd.org/php	Developmental Disorder www.devdelay.org www.thearc.org www.aamr.org	Physical Impairment www.ucpa.org http://specialed.about .com/od/physicaldisa bilities/a/physical.htm www.kidsource.com/ kidsource/pages/dis .physical.html	Visual Impairments/ Blindness www.afb.org www.rfbd.org
Autism www.autism-society.org www.autismspeaks.org www.autismspeaks.org	Dyscalculia www.dyscalculia.org Dysgraphia www.ldinfo.com www.hwtears.com Dyslexia www.rfbd.org www.interdys.org		

Learning more about different ABILITIES	www.cec.sped.org www.adl.org www.nichcy.org www.whatworks.ed.gov www.behavioradvisor.com www.teach-nology.com/teachers/special_ed/organizations www.disabilitystudiesforteachers.org/index.php www.disabilityresources.org.DIS-AWARE.html

stereotypes or biased film or media portrayals (Gilligan, 1982). In special education, gender disparities are evident in that males are diagnosed with a disability twice as often as female students (Office for Civil Rights, 2006, cited in Snowman et al., 2008). Both genders of adolescents need role models, ways to express their voices, and support to overcome or compensate for existing barriers and obstacles based upon preconceived notions. Everyone benefits from consistent structured mentoring, exploring issues, and learning from one another.

Family situations certainly impact students' successes as well. The British government is addressing the fact that some students miss out on many cultural exposures and experiences due to familial reasons, such as not being able to afford these types of trips. The government is piloting and funding school programs for students to participate in 5 weekly hours of cultural activities, such as visiting art museums, going to concerts, learning to play instruments, and more in an attempt to balance their exposure to the arts. The reasoning is that all students need equal opportunities to make broader future occupational or recreational choices (Ross, 2008).

Family situations vary, as shown with a National Health Interview Survey (NHIS) study, conducted from 1998 to 2002, on how many parents with disabilities are raising teens. The study used a scientific sample of 40,000 families across the United States and revealed a range from a low estimate of 2.6 million parents to a high estimate of 4.7 million parents with disabilities raising teens. The study notes that if the high estimate is used, then of all the parents of adolescents, 15 percent of them have a disability. Education and income levels of these parents were also lower than those of nondisabled parents. Familial situations are thus not always equal ones, with family and environmental issues impacting teens both with and without disabilities.

The obverse side of the familial coin is that teens with disabilities also impact families. Many families who hear negative reports from schools then go through a gamut of emotions such as guilt, denial, anger, and grief, depending upon the severity of the disability and the family member's level of acceptance. Different reactions to a teen's disability may influence a marriage and other social and familial relationships in both positive and negative ways. In my opinion, no one sums up the complexity of emotions of raising a child with a disability better than Emily Kingsley in her inspirational piece, *Welcome to Holland,* when she writes about finding out that her daughter has Down syndrome. She analogously compares this experience to having a flight change from a trip planned to Italy to an emergency landing in Holland, a different destination. She poignantly invites readers to always enjoy the very special things about *Holland* even though the Rembrandts differ from the Michelangelos.

A compilation of parent essays in a book entitled *You Will Dream New Dreams: Inspiring Personal Stories by Parents of Children with Disabilities,* edited by Klein and Schive (2001), offers many familial perspectives to help staff and other parents understand more about the complexities involved in raising a child with a disability, beyond what meets the eye within inclusive environments. Parents who read a resource such as this one are sent a strong message that they are not alone in their emotions and may very well relate to and feel affirmed by the perspectives of other families undergoing similar thoughts and situations. When a staff member recommends a resource like this one to families, or personally reads essays such as these to gain additional perspectives, the gains for all adolescents are immeasurable ones.

Family reactions and acceptance of their children with disabilities certainly impact educators in school settings. If teachers meet parents when they are frustrated or depressed, sometimes the school system can be the recipient of undue anger. Many other times, families know their teens best and will offer workable solutions. Before educators play defense, they should review the family's suggestions and concerns.

Ferguson (2002) recommends that educators always stay positive with families, by communicating students' strides, accompanied by productive comments and strategies and the offering of ways to collaborate with school efforts.

Sometimes, families need to hear kind pedagogical words, or they just require a forum to vent their thoughts and concerns to someone who knows their children. Guidance that involves home learning suggestions to maximize students' abilities is the way to go here. So much more is accomplished when families, students, and the curriculum concepts are on the same side. Trying to connect academic skills with independent living skills is also important for teens with developmental disabilities and their families. Although it is a bit dated, the *Adolescent Autonomy Checklist* from the Youth in Transition Project (1984–1987) at the University of Washington Division of Adolescent Medicine offers excellent community, health, leisure, and home ways to promote and assess independent living skills (see http://depts.washington.edu/ healthtr/Checklists/intro.htm and www.family-networks.org/teens.cfm). Skills such as balancing a checkbook, knowing how to use public transportation, or even figuring out how to read a menu are life-related appropriate ones that schools cannot ignore. Overall, adolescent issues involving gender, family, culture, and abilities are important ones that merit the attention of all educators if we are to connect with our students.

Applying Inclusive Strategies That Correlate With Adolescents' Lives

This chapter examines the emotional and self-regulation factors involved in inclusive classrooms to increase student time and engagement on task. It investigates the development and reinforcement of appropriate behavior to empower and connect to adolescents with study skill strategies. In addition, it explores the IEP and career goals, and the best inclusive teaching strategies that connect to the curriculum and the students themselves. Students need to know their subjects better, but most important, they must know who they are as responsible learners. This chapter encourages a realization of how students learn best and a review of personal goals to maximize individual growth under educators' auspices and guidance.

CAMPAIGNING FOR ADOLESCENTS

Danica McKellar, an actress, author, and mathematician, wrote a book entitled *Math Doesn't Suck: How to Survive Middle-School Math Without Losing Your Mind or Breaking a Nail*. The book's content, geared toward adolescent girls, says, "*Okay, I know that you might think math is uncool, but it's not only doable, you can succeed at it!*" McKellar sends the strong message that mathematical success is not restricted to those of the male gender. She campaigns for middle school girls to view their abilities in a different light as she shares many mathematical strategies.

Based upon this premise, I've written some *campaign slogans* that you might like to tackle or expand upon with your students. Some of these may very well proactively generate increased class discussion and higher student motivation. Adolescents with disabilities should never feel helpless, but instead should feel empowered to increase their present knowledge with proactive learning strategies and increased self-efficacy. Some adolescent campaigns follow, with the last one left blank so that adolescents in your class can creatively campaign for themselves. In cooperative groups, adolescents in inclusive classrooms choose one of these campaign slogans and use it to write an essay, act out a skit, carry out a debate, make a PowerPoint presentation, create a poem, design a graphic novel, or draw a poster. It's an exercise in creative writing that yields more than literacy gains. It's a campaign that any adolescent would join!

Maximize Your Potential: Ignore the Ridiculous!	*Change the Channel: Don't Listen to the Crowd!*	*Figure Out the Abstract: Picasso Was Cool!*	*Explore the Unknown: Take a Journey to Learning!*
Decide Upon Goals: Kicking Your Own Football!	*Who Cares About This Stuff? Apathy Is Overrated!*	*No Speed Limits Cause Road Rage: The Art of Slowing Down*	*Risking it All for Peers: What Fools Do!*
Families Bother Me: Loving them Anyway!	*Music, Dance, and Computers: Creating My Own Learning Files*	*Tough Choices: Getting Through the School Maze!*	_____ _____ _____!

CONNECTING WITH THE DAYDREAMERS AND DOODLERS

Daydreamers and doodlers often see little value to the whole school concept, disconnecting them from gaining behavioral, social, and learning advancements. Studies of Japanese classrooms (Linn, Lewis, Tsuchida, & Songer, 2002) point out that aside from valuing cognitive strides, effective classrooms are humanistic ones that place social and ethical growth on high pedestals. These Japanese classrooms consist of students who have classroom responsibilities that encourage valuing caring student interactions and both individual and group contributions. This approach is said to be the reason for student successes in mathematics and science at younger grades. If students have these earlier successes, then as adolescent learners, their solid background knowledge will contribute to more strides. Connecting to the students as contributing class members means that students are not just sitting in the room, but are a vital part of the room—they are not merely passive recipients of knowledge. I once instructed a classroom with students who loved using the electric pencil sharpener and answering the class phone. Consequently, pencil sharpener and class receptionist were added to job descriptions, along with other classroom responsibilities such as computer manager, windows and chairs director, homework collector, peer mentors, and more. This creates a collaborative classroom environment that allows students to productively bond. Once a caring, comfortable atmosphere is established, students are then more apt to focus on lessons, satisfied to be an integral part of the class and school community.

One of the most important ways to connect with daydreamers and doodlers is to solicit more student comments and reflections. With increased metacognition, adolescents gain insights into how they learn. Metacognition does not happen overnight, but needs to be continually introduced and emphasized in all lessons. By the time students reach middle school and high school grades, it is even more crucial that they learn how to become self-regulated learners, prepared to tackle higher academics or demands in chosen careers. Study skill strategies are lifelong skills that can be applied across the curriculum and with many postsecondary decisions. Ultimately, the daydreamers and doodlers are the ones who need to be the major stakeholders in their learning. The next table lists a variety of strategies for teachers to infuse into their curriculum lessons to help adolescents gain vital study skills to better understand, evaluate, analyze, and synthesize not only the content presented, but themselves as well. The organizer that follows offers specific benefits of these strategies with valuable and more detailed ways to infuse these study skills across the curriculum in inclusive environments.

Study Skill Strategies				
Writing an outline of concepts	Using an index to find information	Knowing a text's format	Creating mnemonics, e.g., acrostic sentence	Chunking information
Identifying the big picture, or main ideas	Finding ways to visualize the information	Taking notes	Learning how to study for tests with more retention	Organizing information
Supporting opinions with facts	Conducting research	Using word processing tools	Keeping a calendar	Understanding vocabulary
Paying attention	Developing active listening skills	Identifying and capitalizing upon strengths	Being involved in study groups	Developing more metacognition

As these study skills indicate, adolescents in inclusive environments need more than a dry delivery of academic concepts. All adolescents and adults vary in their personalities, abilities, perceptions, cognitions, and more. The Myers-Briggs Type Indicator (MBTI) classifies personality types, with an available online inventory to investigate (www.personalitypathways.com/type_inventory.html).

Many different adolescent personalities are evidenced in inclusive classrooms with students, educators, assistants, and all staff. The following two personality scenarios point out the necessity of honoring differences to help students exhibit a

(Text continued on page 96)

Study Skill Strategies	Learning Benefits for Adolescents	Educator & Student Applications
(1) Setting goals	Self-direction, emotional exploration, personal focus, and priorities are strengthened to take the steps to plan for future attainable goals and accomplishments.	Verbal and written surveys, discussions, and recordings of short-term and long-term student aspirations, teacher–student conferences; enlist home communications and support through e-mails, written communications, telephone, face-to-face conferences.
(2) Keeping a calendar/ schedule	Time management, prioritization of assignments, procrastination circumvented, accuracy increased; ability to first record, then visualize and act out the day, week, month, year; increased organization with meshing of school and personal agendas that help students prepare for today, tomorrow, and their futures	Teacher modeling, student practice, and monitoring of independent application of daily to-do lists, weekly schedules, and monthly calendars specifying quizzes, tests, research reports, presentations, assemblies, appointments, holidays, birthdays; teach students to understand the importance of setting specific times for reviewing calendars, schedules, notes, homework; allow students to write or sketch out their day in the morning; remind students that adherence and schedule success takes time and may require revisions
(3) Preparing and maintaining minds and materials	Proactive display of a ready-to-learn attitude with concrete items that match the curriculum to heighten overall achievements	Checklist to review and monitor items to bring from class to class, school to home, and home to school, e.g., pencils, homework assignments, signed forms, calculators, reports; review A.S.P.I.R.E. Study System to develop a better approach to studying (www.studygs.net/aspire.htm)
(4) Developing metacognition	Self-reflection and responsibility that increase the development of self-regulated learners who proofread written work and completed assignments, knowing personal strengths and needs to develop individual profiles to consistently improve upon	Not correcting student's work, but circling or pointing out where corrections need to be made, e.g., offer students comparative lists or answer keys to match their answers instead of always being handed teacher-corrected work; encourage self-reflection by having students graph their grades on quizzes, tests, and reports to notice patterns and improvements over time; encourage students to observe and interview successful peers or adults whom they admire and wish to emulate, asking them for advice
(5) Identifying strengths Web sites: Index of Learning Styles Questionnaire (Felder/Silverman) —www.engr.ncsu.edu/learningstyles/ilsweb.html	Capitalize upon students' learning styles and multiple intelligences to create independent, lifelong learners who know how to learn best no matter what the lesson's contents, to improve personal motivation and concentration with increased student connections that value	Centers or strategy boxes set up in the classroom containing student- or teacher-generated materials with contents such as generic writing frames, lists of transitional words, visual dictionaries, electronic spellers, maps, pencil grips, erasers, protractors, colored overlays to help with reading glare, blockers to handle cluttered worksheets, graph paper to organize math calculations, headphones to listen to music during independent work, computer headphones,

Study Skill Strategies	Learning Benefits for Adolescents	Educator & Student Applications
Success Types Learning Style Type Indicator (Pelley), based on Myers-Briggs Type Indicators (extraversion, introversion, sensing, intuition, thinking, feeling, judging, perceiving)— http://www.human metrics.com/cgi-win/JTypes2.asp Self-Assessment Resources— www.fullcirc.com/ community/assess mentlinks.htm www.rileyguide.com/ assess.html	individual profiles within the inclusive classroom with words, images, motions, songs, dances, logical thinking, independent work, or cooperative group activities	markers, highlighters, Post-It Notes, blank outlines, digitized texts, CDs; offer a wide combination of kinesthetic-tactile, visual, and auditory opportunities during lessons and assessments that match curriculum topics and lesson's objectives
(6) Paying attention	Visual and auditory concentration increased, academic concepts better understood, social interactions improved, receptive and expressive language skills developed	Active listening with classroom teacher—student signals and monitoring, e.g., thumbs up/thumbs down, student tallying time-on-task, private reminders, student conferences, self-monitoring system, functional attention assessment; *do the unexpected* within reason to control classroom boredom and invigorate lesson deliveries
(7) Regulating self-discipline	Responsibility for one's actions, impulse control is heightened, higher self-esteem is established, more respect attained from both peers and adults, self-satisfaction of thinking before doing	Behavior is self-monitored with teacher setup, suggestion of strategies, recognition of positive strides, e.g., writing thoughts down before calling out, counting to self to delay immediate reactions, verbalization with trusting peer or adult, intermittent and appropriate recognition of behavioral strides.
(8) Knowing a textbook's format	Creation of independent learners able to achieve more self-direction with written materials to access and apply knowledge	Direct instruction on how to use a table of contents, glossary, index; knowing why certain words are highlighted; using the section headings as outlines for the main ideas; reading titles and captions, interpreting graphs and other illustrative text materials
(9) Understanding vocabulary	Prior knowledge established to better understand the concepts with increased context clues, preventing reading difficulties from interfering with	Before units are assigned, students receive a list of the vocabulary words, if necessary phonetically spelled next to the correct spelling with visuals, e.g., visual dictionaries, or have collaborative student searches for Google images, clip art programs;

(Continued)

(Continued)

Study Skill Strategies	Learning Benefits for Adolescents	Educator & Student Applications
	comprehensions across curriculum content areas	encourage hand-drawn visuals; direct instruction on using a dictionary, text glossary, computer tools, e.g., thesaurus tool for synonyms, electronic dictionaries; when possible, relate vocabulary to adolescent experiences through appropriate analogies and classroom discussions.
(10) Identifying the big picture	Making sure main idea is understood first before students focus on extraneous details or isolated thoughts allows for anchoring of the curriculum to prior knowledge, concretizes further learning, increases attention	K-W-L charts to establish and check that prior knowledge is solid, highlighting, underlining, marking photocopied text pages with symbols, e.g., * = important, – = minor detail
(11) Organizing information	Alternative ways given to students that spotlight, sort, arrange, classify, rank, sequence, strengthen, and retain class learning objectives without the formal writing of sentences, to better focus on concepts with the removal of extraneous information	Guided note taking, with spaces for students to fill in facts, e.g., cloze exercises, concept maps (David Ausubel, www.fullcirc.com/community/assessmentlinks.htm); graphic and advance organizers are demonstrated; three-columned chart—main idea/details/personal connections (www.inspiration.com)—to first view concepts as a visual with ellipses connected and then use the conversion tool to create an outline with main ideas, ordered items, subtopics, and details
(12) Visualizing concepts	Internalization of concepts, development of intrinsic motivation, personal connections of abstract formal thought	Ask students to place themselves in another historical time period; pretend that they were an apprentice to Benjamin Franklin, aboard the space shuttle, an advisor to the president, an architect designing a new building, visiting Egypt, a farmer tilling the fields, astronomer identifying a newly found constellation, and more.
(13) Chunking information	Skills in summarization, with information and main concepts more easily understood when grouped together	Model chunking and show examples with phone numbers and familiar non-curriculum items; then move to the big pictures in content areas.
(14) Supporting opinions with facts	Creation of critical thinkers, developing research skills	Teach students the Socratic method through questioning and discussion; allow students time to reflect and research answers.
(15) Collaborating with peers	Common goals are shared, with a team approach that values positive interdependence and contributions of peers to focus on issues, mediate together, mentor one	Start with smaller heterogeneous groups, gradually increasing size, purpose, and task qualifications to promote successes; allow students to work together in cooperative, democratic study groups with specific roles assigned that value accountability for all students; give direction to students who may

Study Skill Strategies	Learning Benefits for Adolescents	Educator & Student Applications
	another, and share strengths.	need more social help, e.g., students with conduct disorders, quieter students, students with Asperger syndrome or autism.
(16) Identifying and solving problems	Maximizing available human and material resources in the decision-making process; prioritization skills are strengthened through adaptation, research, collaboration, implementation, and communication to find possible solutions to specific tasks or predicaments.	Model how to first define a problem and then gather information and strategies for step-by-step strategies that lead to documented solutions; give non-examples, e.g., dissecting ill-structured problems; peer groups can collect data, analyze, and brainstorm solutions together; try to connect problems with the curriculum as well as student interests when possible.
(17) Asking for academic, social, emotional, or behavioral help	Communication, intrinsic motivation, social reciprocity, self-regulation, and performance levels are increased with clearer understandings as misconceptions are clarified and stumbling blocks or shutdowns are avoided.	Encourage students to ask for help by being a kind, trustworthy, and nonjudgmental ear when students are *not getting* the concepts; help them to clear their minds of negative self-fulfilling prophecies and replace them with relaxation techniques such as meditation or kinesthetic opportunities, e.g., for adolescent with ADHD; connect students with guidance counselors if emotional support is needed; offer academic peer tutoring with mentors; teach students the benefits of positive self-talk and increased metacognition.
(18) Maximizing usage of technology	Alternate routes of obtaining and communicating information are valued; appropriate social networking is encouraged.	Write schedules on spreadsheets or calendar templates; use electronic spellers, Web sites for math help, peer mentoring, online clip art, approved research sites, WebQuests, telementoring with e-mails and electronic mailing lists (www.thinkers.co.nz/telementoring).
(19) Conducting research	Value of multiple sources for information, exploration of information from reputable cites, learning how to paraphrase, focusing on a main idea	Collaborate with librarians and colleagues on interdisciplinary lessons; model how to create a bibliography; outline copyright rules; allow students to use notes, digitized books, encyclopedias (both hard copy and online); teach how to identify reputable sources; allow for differences with age-appropriate but lower reading-level sites
(20) Retaining learning	Concepts solidified in long-term memory (LTM) for future reference and stronger learning foundations as the curriculum spirals	Give frequent quizzes and informal assessments to value reviewing work, even if you move on to the next unit; scaffold with students within their zone of proximal development (ZPD); teach students information processing techniques, e.g., mnemonics, acrostics, visualization, concept and mind maps.

(Continued)

(Continued)

Study Skill Strategies	Learning Benefits for Adolescents	Educator & Student Applications
(21) Becoming a better test-taker	Stress is alleviated and replaced with preparation that values understanding versus strict memorization and regurgitation.	Teach students how to create study guides using index cards, flashcards, notes, textbooks, templates, mnemonics, e.g., PEMDAS (order of operations), HOMES (for the Great Lakes); review basic study skills and test-taking tips, e.g., narrowing down choices, time management, letting a teacher read a question if it is an IEP-generated accommodation; emphasize good sleep, nutrition, relaxation techniques, and exercise as healthy ways to perform your best.
(22) Valuing feedback	Personal academic and social growth as students transition into adulthood	Create self-regulated learners who grow from reflections to constructively accept personal feedback to improve future work.
(23) Revisiting work	Retention is increased with the development of a mentality that says, *"I am not just studying this for the test; these concepts will have meaning for me again and again."*	Move ahead, but review the learning; since the curriculum spirals, repetition ensures solidification of concepts.

balance of behavior. Maximizing both emotional and academic growth gives students a feeling of belonging, rather than being singled out or excluded because of extremes in personality.

Extraversion: This student may have ADHD and impulsively act out before thinking, exhibit inappropriate social interactions with peers, and always want to be the center of attention. A private behavior modification program offering the student increased metacognition is warranted. Allow this type of student appropriate ways to channel outgoingness through cooperative learning, discussion groups, curriculum presentations, and more kinesthetic lesson activities.

Introversion: This student may be one with an internal emotional disorder, being extremely shy, unwilling to interact with peers, focusing on his or her own interests, unable to switch channels to concentrate on lesson objectives, possibly experiencing signs of depression. Encourage this student to gradually reach out to other peers and adults; for example, partner the student with a study buddy during a Think-Pair-Share activity, connect the student with a guidance counselor or adult advocate. Value this student's desire to reflect more by giving the student extra time to respond to questions, rather than spotlighting his or her more reflective personality and causing stress or embarrassment in front of peers. Be sensitive to the student's writings that may reveal more about his or her inner thoughts as an avenue of communication.

The next questionnaire is a multipurpose one. It allows adolescents to rate themselves in terms of their likes and dislikes. It's also a way for adolescents to communicate their individual needs to educators and for educators to then try to incorporate these likes and dislikes into lessons when appropriate, for example, writing a mathematical word problem about the Jonas Brothers or Miley Cyrus, choosing genres for novels, varying lesson presentations, offering assessment options. Counting this questionnaire as students' first quiz grade sends out a strong message to adolescents that what they think is truly valued by their teachers.

BEHAVING LIKE AN ADOLESCENT ANGEL

Classroom management issues quite often perplex qualified teachers who are skilled in their curriculum areas but can't handle less-than-angelic students who march to different drummers, and quite often lead a whole marching band! That's where reinforcement comes into play, since positive behavior needs to be more than an occasional incident. Educators, students, and families who understand the crucial roles external stimuli and reinforcement play in the lives of adolescents of all abilities are helping these individuals to achieve many more strides.

According to B. F. Skinner, the environment can be *operated on* through a process called operant conditioning (Wagner, 2009). This involves voluntary responses that are *strengthened* or *weakened* by consequences that follow, as shown in the table on page 98.

A reinforcing stimulus can make desired behavior occur more often, and less desired behavior disappear. For example, if a student with Asperger syndrome is rewarded for making more eye contact—for example, given extra computer time or another mutually agreed-upon reward—then the message is clearly sent that eye contact is desirable, and that student is then likely to repeat the desired and reinforced behavior. Conversely, if an adolescent impulsively calls out in class and is not given recognition, while he or she sees students who behave appropriately receiving more positive attention, then through observation, emulation, and lack of reinforcement, that student may stop that impulsive behavior since it is not having desirable effects. Many students, including those with less intellectual abilities and more developmental delays, must receive guided instruction in processes known as generalization and discrimination. *Generalization* refers to responding in similar ways to stimuli, while *discrimination* means responding in different ways to similar stimuli. An example of generalization is knowing that the fire is always hot, whether it is in a kitchen or a flame in a chemistry lab. Discrimination involves discerning skills, from knowing that it is okay to converse in cooperative groups but not okay to converse during fire drills, to understanding that there are different appropriate social ways to interact with a stranger, a family member, and so on.

An inclusive classroom has different types of reinforcement, given at variable or fixed intervals. A classroom example of a fixed interval would be when teachers test regularly, while a variable interval involves random or surprise quizzes. Another classroom example of reinforcement is when educators encourage longer time on tasks and higher test scores to reduce disruptive behavior and increase academic performance, such as by saying, *"We love the way you are collaboratively completing the research assignment; looks like we'll have time for that movie on Friday,"* or *"Those students who received a higher grade may have additional computer time and two homework passes."* Think of another scenario. Suppose a teacher wanted his or her students to come to class, prepared and ready to learn, but many of the students display undesirable behavior—they repeatedly forget their homework, or do not open texts or notebooks to required pages. What if the teacher then gave students who were consistently prepared 5 extra points on their next quiz grade? Wouldn't that send out a strong message that reinforces preparedness and organization? Often students are physically present, but emotionally elsewhere. Even though adolescents are older, they still need frequent pats on their *teen shoulders,* with some students having behavioral goals specifically stated in their BIP (behavior intervention plan) in their IEP.

Student Directions: Honestly answer the following questions. The answers to this questionnaire will count as your first quiz grade, revealing more about you; how you learn; and how you plan to succeed in this course, other school subjects, and life! There are no correct answers on my teacher's answer key, because each answer is the right one for each of you. No judgment is given; every response is valued. Your answers will be used to help match lessons with your strengths, interests, and prior knowledge. Additional comments are welcomed in the far-right column, or on the reverse side of this paper.

NAME _____	Yes	Not sure	No	Other Comments/ Examples
1. School is my ticket to the future.				
2. I know a lot about this subject.				
3. I take learning seriously.				
4. I prefer someone showing me an example of what to do.				
5. I like doing things my own way, rather than listening to others.				
6. I enjoy listening to or playing music.				
7. Spending time on the computer is a huge part of my day.				
8. My favorite lessons are the ones that get me moving about.				
9. I am sometimes shy about sharing my thoughts in front of others.				
10. I enjoy learning new things.				
11. When working with peers, I like to follow their lead.				
12. Paying attention is something I'm great at.				
13. I love to doodle in class.				
14. I sometimes need more help getting organized.				
15. Honesty is highly important.				
16. I like to have extra time to respond.				
17. If I do not know the answer, I'll ask someone or research it more.				
18. I like quieter classrooms.				
19. Home situations are often intense.				
20. Making friends is easy.				
21. Working at a job after school is important.				
22. I prefer accuracy over speed.				
23. Books are awesome.				

NAME _____	Yes	Not	No	Other Comments/ Examples
24. Pictures are worth a thousand words.				
25. I enjoy group work and discussion.				
26. We should care more about nature.				
27. I could get lost in a movie or TV show.				
28. I love to write.				
29. I often set future goals.				

Behavior	Consequences: Reinforcement or Punishment		Reinforced behavior is repeated and will happen more since it is strengthened.	Ignored behavior is extinguished since it is weakened; punishment may have positive or negative effects on behavior.
——————→ Principles of operant conditioning and behavior modification	Positive behavior is reinforced in different schedules.	Negative behavior is ignored (reinforcement is removed).		

The following chart (retrieved from www.pbis.org/schoolwide.htm) illustrates positive behavioral interventions and supports of the Office of Special Education Program (OSEP). Data-based intervention programs with increased decision-making, self-assessments, and schoolwide discipline programs are advocated and illustrated with this model.

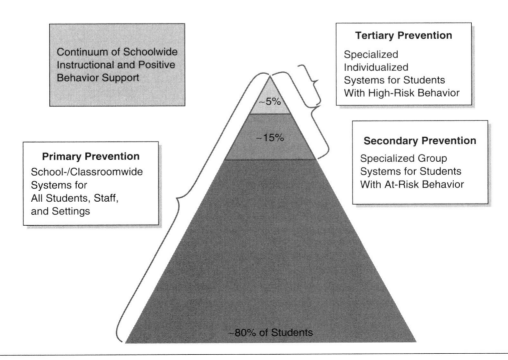

Source: Reprinted with permission from the National Center on Positive Behavioral Interventions and Supports at www.pbis.org.

Valuable behaviorally based programs advocate teaching environments that give merit to learning, responsibility, cooperation, and individual differences for students with and without disabilities. PBS—positive behavior support—has a main goal of decreasing inappropriate behavior and enhancing more positive behavior through proactive, schoolwide interventions. Behavioral supports are given to students with targeted programs and interventions that do not value punishments, but instead offer positive behavioral supports to recognize higher behavioral expectations, rather than noncompliance with the rules. It's a multilevel approach that offers a primary behavioral policy for all students with a setup of positive classroom expectations; secondary ones, for example, homework clubs, study groups, and other remediations; or tertiary ones, for example, assigned adult or peer mentors working on a one-to-one basis with students for more intensive assistance.

In addition, educators need to understand some reasons for *misbehavior* through a functional behavioral analysis, which can include classroom reasons such as boring work, threatening environments, frustrations at not understanding the lesson, or the fear of failure. Inclusive adolescent classrooms equally acknowledge adolescents' motivations and affects, along with their cognitive levels. Creative educators have lesson plans that draw students into them, with excitement and curiosity replacing boredom, anxiety, frustrations, or depression.

Higher-level thinking skills are certainly not exclusive to those students labeled as gifted or well-behaved; rather, they need to be part of every student's repertoire. Students with learning disabilities require learning challenges and are capable of much advancement when quality instruction is accompanied by appropriate reinforcements that increase the likelihood of desired behavioral results. Neither academics nor behavior should be considered as rote applications. The following list outlines applicable research worth investigating further.

★ Without treatment, depressed teens are at increased risk for school failure, social isolation, unsafe sexual behavior, drug and alcohol abuse, and long-term life problems. (Cash, 2003)

★ From age 13 onward, symptoms of clinical depression increase in girls and reach a peak in terms of the greatest gender differences with females higher having higher vulnerability than males in teens aged 15 to 18 (Hankin et al., 1998).

★ Students with emotional behavioral disorders who exhibit externalizing behaviors such as aggression, attention-getting acts, or acting out are more likely to display language deficits than students who experience internalizing behavioral disorders, such as depression or social withdrawal (Nelson, Benner, & Cheney, 2005).

★ When students with emotional behavioral disability (EBD) receive one-on-one training by teachers, peers, or trained adult volunteers, both reading skills and motivation are increased (Coleman & Vaughn, 2000; Elbaum, Vaughn, Hughes, & Moody, 2000).

★ The academic processing speed of students with EBD appears to lag behind those without disabilities and contributes to academic and behavioral functioning (Benner, Allor, & Mooney, 2008).

* The reading scores of students with learning disabilities improve significantly over a 5-year period, while the reading achievement scores of students with EBD tend to plateau or decline over 5 years (Anderson, Kutash, & Duchnowski, 2001).
* Symptoms of depression are higher in girls with associative lower self-concepts and lower academic performances (Harter, 1999; Marsh, 1989).
* Students with learning disabilities (LD) had higher scores of depression and lower self-concept than students without disabilities (Maag & Reid, 2006).
* When adolescents experience depression, it is more likely that there will be additional episodes when they enter adulthood (Rao, Hammen, & Daley, 1999).

Inclusive classrooms shape students' behaviors into positive ones by setting high goals that recognize positive strides and try to boost lower self-concepts, which directly impacts academics. Maybe not every situation is an *angelic* one, but academic lessons that reach for the sky and acknowledge not only the content, but also the emotions and affects of the inclusive students, yield higher results!

The following assessments are two examples of how teachers and schools can obtain reliable baseline data to identify students' emotional, social, and behavioral needs. Using assessments such as these has classroom implications for preventions and interventions.

* Behavior Assessment System for Children–Teacher Rating Scales (BASC-TRS)

  Offers assessments of internalizing and externalizing behaviors
  http://ags.pearsonassessments.com/assessments/technical/basc2.asp

* Multidimensional Self Concept Scale (MSCS)

Social and emotional adjustments of students ages 9 to 19 are explored, evaluating self-concept issues regarding families, academics, affect, competence, and physical issues
    www3.parinc.com/products/product.aspx?Productid=MSCS

EMPOWERING ADOLESCENTS IN DEMOCRATIC INCLUSIVE CLASSROOMS

Democratic concepts began back in ancient Greece, in Athens many centuries ago, continued in England with the Magna Carta, and then spread its wings across the Atlantic delivering the Bill of Rights. Next, along came John Dewey in the early 20th century, considered to be a progressive educator, who believed that classrooms should also practice democracy. This democracy needs to extend to inclusive classrooms as well, offering adolescents opportunities to not only voice their needs, but also have those needs recognized with appropriate interventions. The next quote puts much of this into perspective and applies to inclusive classrooms.

One of the best ways of educating people is to give them an experience that embodies what you are trying to teach. When you believe in a democratic society, you provide a setting for education that is democratic. (Horton, Kohl, & Kohl, 1997, p. 227)

As shown in global arenas, many repressed citizens eventually revolt against tyranny. Also true is that repressed students in inclusive classrooms may sit quietly, yet not gain academic or social strides in tyrannical classrooms that do not value their voices, interests, strengths, and abilities. Dewey's argument, along with that of other educators who followed such as Jerome Bruner, a true advocate of discovery learning, is that students learn best when allowed freedom to construct their knowledge. Of course, educators must give appropriate guidance, but the students are the ones who are now more involved and empowered to learn.

Students with disabilities need these same democratic opportunities to become self-regulated learners who can voice and reflect upon their choices. Various researchers (Thoma, Nathanson, Baker, & Tamura, 2002; Wehmeyer, Agran, & Hughes, 1998) have written about how problems arise when self-management and self-determination skills are transferred and applied to the classroom. It is then difficult for students with learning variances to construct their knowledge if self-management skills are weak. Applying this to students with lower cognitive levels requires intensive practice and monitoring, and the strong belief that students with more severe disabilities are capable of learning how to manage their own behavior as self-advocates, affording them the same opportunities for democratic inclusive advancements.

Behavior modification programs with frequent repetition and application can target desired skills and allow students to develop at their own pace to establish more reflective behaviors that will lead to further growth as independent adults. Applied behavioral analysis is an example of a structured program that involves the collection of baseline data to reinforce desirable behaviors. Depending on the needs of individual students and staff configurations, this can be implemented in a range of settings, from one-on-one to smaller groups within a larger inclusion class. Once the behavior is established, more metacognition is possible. Some students may respond to abstract presentations with words and readings accompanied by monitoring and reinforcements, while other adolescents need additional visual prompts, oral readings, or concrete examples. Students with varying abilities across different classroom environments have successfully used self-management behaviors involving these outlined self-monitoring steps:

a. Determination if student is consistently on task and focused: *Am I present and involved every day?*

b. Self-evaluation to rate the level of performance: *Was I okay, or could I have done better?*

c. Self-reinforcement: *Was the end reward what I justly earned?*

Self-management promotes academic productivity, class attention, and socially appropriate behavior (Gilberts, Agran, Hughes, & Wehmeyer, 2001; Pierce & Schreibman, 1994). Without being self-regulated learners, students will have only made classroom gains, not lifelong ones that extend beyond the school setting.

Robert Sternberg (1996, 1997), a psychologist, outlined ideas about mental self-government under the categories of hierarchical, monarchic, oligarchic, and anarchic. This includes students handling multiple goals, prioritizing them, following rules, and solving problems. Also delineated were local and global styles, respectively centering on more specific and concrete problems as opposed to global and abstract ones. Sternberg identified two "scopes" of mental self-government: internal (working independently) and external (working cooperatively with others). These explain the different ways students complete tasks. He describes mental self-government thoughts as liberal, legislative, executive, and conservative ones, involving changing rules, conforming to rules, following them, or buying into them as your own. This model deserves attention in inclusive classrooms so as to assist adolescents in gaining more functional academic problem-solving skills.

Overall, this idea of a democratic classroom refers to educators allowing students to have learning choices or multiple ways to absorb knowledge, ones that match their instructional levels, interests, styles, and intelligences. This is evidenced when there is a selection of goal choices and activities, for example, students being drawn into a topic through problem-based learning, more questioning, and open discussion. Rather than expecting everyone to obediently sit in their chairs, with all eyes and heads facing forward, while a teacher spews out knowledge that the students are then expected to memorize for the test, what about valuing what adolescents are thinking, before you tell them what they should be thinking? Many students, when they hear that an item will not be on the test, simply stop listening, since it has no value to them. Learning *itself* should have value; that can be accomplished when students are treated fairly and democratically, allowed to cast their votes to customize their learning and realize how they learn best, with improvement of self-regulation systems accompanied by direct instructional strategies. Of course, I am in no way advocating that educators abandon curriculum standards, but just that they use those curriculum standards in a different way, a way that promotes democratic inclusive adolescent classrooms for students of all abilities.

To connect with the curriculum, view the motivating questions/topic openers on the next page, curriculum connections, and assignment/assessment choices for students, to entice them to be part of the learning process. Just the fact that there are choices has an element of *universal design* (a broad strategy that helps everyone, not just those with disabilities) built into the lesson. Now students are collaborating with others to complete final products, and are also self-accommodating by democratically choosing how they will discover more. Skills are embedded in the lessons, beyond the textbook, with problem-solving approaches that encourage adolescents to develop more connections with the curriculum, themselves, and both their school and home communities.

IEPS AND AYP: ADOLESCENTS, FAMILIES, AND SCHOOL SUPPORTS

Each student receiving special services has an annual individualized education program (IEP) that states his or her academic and functional levels of performance, along with appropriate objectives, goals, behavioral supports, modifications, accommodations, testing procedures, and ways of reporting progress to families. An important element of an IEP is the LRE (least restrictive environment) statement, which is the premise for this book—educating adolescents in inclusive environments, if that is determined to be the

Hypothetical Topic Openers/ Motivating Questions	Curriculum Connections & Skills	Assignment/Assessment Choices
Students are falling asleep in morning classes. How can teachers better connect to them more? Give specific examples.	Mathematics, Science, History, English, World Languages, Music, Art, Physical Education, and more!	Student written lessons Conducting questionnaires and surveys Interviews with teachers and students Dramatic skits or PowerPoints Sequencing ready-made photos of students
The library received a grant to replace the carpet. Investigate different options for the new floor covering and a plan to both rearrange and order more books.	Literacy genres, Geometry, Economics, Architecture, study skills	Different committees set up to contact, collaborate, and present findings with the following: a. administrative offices b. Board of Education (BOE) c. principal d. librarians e. students f. educators and other staff g. community Some students could count and sort books into categories.
People are fearful that high unemployment rates will lead to another Great Depression. What can the U.S government do to help the average family deal with the harsh economy? What can local communities do as well?	American History, Economics, Music, Art, Mathematics, diversity, research, World Politics	Interview community members and local politicians Graph and compare economic conditions then and now, e.g., item costs View and report on DVDs and movies Listen to music and view art from both eras
Students who are auditory and kinesthetic learners feel that there should be more music and movement in classrooms. Choose your least favorite subject and try to connect songs and moving activities with the concepts.	Mathematics, Science, History, English, World Languages, Music, Art, Physical Education, and more!	Connect songs with least favorite subjects by collaboratively doing the following: a. listing topics in the subject b. matching songs and pieces c. thinking of movement exercises d. creating your own lyrics e. clapping to beats and topics
Some students who are asked to do research papers copy information from sources online, without citing the references. How should teachers handle this situation?	Research & study skills, technology, character education, English	Student debates Interviews with students Interviews with educators Online research Library visits
A recent tornado devastated a local community. How can the town rebuild, deal with the damage incurred, and take more preparatory steps for future natural disasters?	Earth Science, Geography, Industrial Arts, Economics, research skills	Review of past tornadoes to see patterns Field trips to sites Community guest speakers, e.g., politicians, meteorologists, architects, homeowners

Hypothetical Topic Openers/ Motivating Questions	Curriculum Connections & Skills	Assignment/Assessment Choices
A local theater group is performing several Shakespearean plays this summer and would like to donate the majority of its profits to charity. Unfortunately, rising costs along with poor past attendance has hurt them. How can our students help the theater in this cause?	English, Home Economics, Industrial Arts, character education, Science, technology, organizational skills	Set up school committees for the following: a. Community coordination b. School volunteers, e.g., ticket collectors, ushers, set designers, artists c. Fundraising activities coordinated by the PTOs d. Groups to raise more awareness, e.g., write editorials to local and school newspapers, contact local radio and TV, make signs, create advertisements

least restrictive environment. Many school districts no longer place short-term goals and objectives in the IEPs of students in inclusive classrooms who may have less severe disabilities, because the GE curriculum is now considered to be their goals and objectives. Many staff members are also uncertain how differing goals and objectives will be assessed in an inclusive classroom. Some team members believe that placement in the general education classroom means that students must achieve the same objectives and pass assessments with grades comparable to their peers, or the inclusive placement is not the correct one. In those cases, the IEP should list more accommodations and modifications, for example, extra wait time, extended testing, do not penalize for spelling errors, grade on content of written work rather than appearance, Braille, assistive technology devices and services, and others as appropriate. It is imperative that a specific statement outlines how the student's disability affects involvement and progress in the general curriculum, and that preferences and interests are included that relate to transition from school to postschool outcomes.

Input regarding placement, services, and interventions is given by team members, families, and the students themselves—if their attendance at IEP meetings is appropriate. At this age, when some adolescents attend their IEP meetings, they are able to communicate what supports and services they believe will be necessary ones that are aimed toward future educational successes. Being privy to the game plan is different from just following along. This adolescent attendance then translates to a more self-regulated learner who is prepared to assist with and maximize his or her IEP goals. Of course, the level of IEP participation will differ, depending upon the ability level of each adolescent, but all students should be encouraged to be involved with their goals and desired outcomes. Even when students have more complex intellectual needs, they may not always be able to express their thoughts or wishes, but their presence at IEP meetings allows them to have more knowledge of this whole process, being sponges who absorb that others are thinking and caring about them. Being present at an IEP meeting allows the adolescent voice to be acknowledged and respected, so as to prevent the development of inappropriate goals and objectives that do not match students' interests or future plans. In short, student IEP participation promotes collaborative thinking and more self-regulated learners.

The next step is for these annual IEP goals to be implemented, monitored, and reviewed at quarterly periods during the school year and then subsequently reported to families whose input went into the initial formulation of the IEP document. Items such as an EYP—extended school year program—are also investigated to see if students need additional summer interventions or other appropriate programs if there is significant regression of learning or social strides expected. All school staff must read the IEP and comply with its content. If a student's placement or program changes, for example, moving from an inclusion class to a replacement program or the reverse, then parents must again be contacted for additional feedback, input, and of course signatures of agreement. If there is a disagreement between what the school system wants and parents' wishes, and if the issues cannot be resolved in the home or school setting, mediation by a third party or legal action with due process may be necessary. Zirkel and Gischlar (2008) point out the requirement of the Individuals with Disabilities Education Improvement Act (IDEIA) amendments from July 2005 for an informal dispute-resolution step prior to a due process hearing. This step is a way to confront adversarial situations with more mediation prior to legislation. In addition, parents need to request changes and express their wishes in writing to the school district. Reevaluations are scheduled every 3 years, or before that if necessary, with parents able to conduct independent evaluations if they disagree with school decisions. Consult Wright's Law at www.wrightslaw.com for more legislative insights here.

In addition, adolescents who are age 16 are mandated to have a transition statement in their IEP that lists their needs, strengths, interests, and skills, along with academic preparation, community involvements or partnerships, independent living objectives, and—if appropriate—functional vocational evaluations and services. Other areas that can be included in the transitional plan are counseling sessions, social services, occupational therapy, physical therapy, and speech and language services if these match the individual student's needs. This transitional plan is also included in a student's IEP before the age of 16, if the plan is deemed appropriate for that younger adolescent, depending upon his or her needs. The idea is to prepare for adolescents' futures, whether the students are college bound, entering a career, or in need of independent living skills after high school. Services listed in the transitional plan can range from help with making dental appointments to food shopping to scheduling appropriate prerequisite English writing courses if the student wants to be a journalist, or math courses if future plans include aspirations to be an engineer. Transitional determinations can be made by the following informal and formal avenues:

★ Adaptive behavior/daily living and functional skills assessments
★ Aptitude tests and informal assessments on preferred intelligences
★ Interest inventories that outline needs
★ Interviews and questionnaires to determine employment goals and maturity levels
★ Curriculum-based assessment (CBA), for example, observations, task analysis, work sample analysis, portfolio assessments, ecological analysis, or informal and formal criterion-referenced tests.

Consult the Division on Career Development and Transition for more insights, at www.dcdt.org/publications/index.html#fact.

The following student template helps adolescents with disabilities to self-assess their current and future goals and needs. This template is intended as a starting point for students to either talk with an advocate, guidance counselor, teacher, or family member, or to candidly write free-write responses to later share or self-reflect.

T.A.Y.: Telling About Yourself

1. Describe yourself in a few sentences:

   I am _____

   _____

   _____

2. Tell about your goals for the following:

   Now,_____

   _____

   Two years from now, _____

   _____

   Four years from now, _____

   _____

   My future plans include _____

3. Tell what help you need to achieve these goals:

   School help I need: _____

   Family help I need: _____

   Community help I need: _____

   Help I can give myself: _____

   _____

4. Overall, my future options include _____

   _____and I plan to

   _____to reach them.

Transition plans bridge high school to life, ensuring that students receive preparation to live productive adult lives as contributing members of society, fulfilling their maximum potential and taking advantage of their strengths and interests. Actually, every student, whether or not he or she is classified under special education services, would benefit from such proactive planning. However, students with special needs are required by law to have this directly stated in their IEP, under IDEA.

Another IEP issue that affects adolescents with disabilities in inclusive classrooms is the fact that at the age of 18, students are considered legal adults. This means that students who are 18 years old do not require a parent's signature or consent concerning IEP services and programs, unless it is determined by a court of law that a student is unable to appropriately make his or her decisions or advocate for himself or herself. This is called a transfer to students at the age of majority. Some students with disabilities who are age 18 choose to continue to have their parents present at IEP meetings, while other students elect not to have their parents involved.

Implementing an IEP for adolescents in inclusive classrooms is tricky because of their age-level characteristics in reference to cognitive, emotional, physical, and social arenas. Peers are very important people to adolescents in middle school and high school settings. Adolescents who are receiving services under their IEP care about what other kids think about them. Many adolescents with IEPs at this age do not want to be stigmatized by receiving accommodations or modifications that in their minds single them out as being different from or inferior to their peers. Teachers circumvent this issue by offering accommodations to the whole class, since this is an excellent way for students with all abilities to shine. Many general education students also benefit from accommodations such as study guides, graphic organizers, extra wait time to respond to questions, more teacher feedback and praise, or receiving extended time on classroom tests. Inclusion for adolescents means just that—academic and social benefits translate to all students, not just those with disabilities.

The following list highlights areas to be reviewed and addressed in IEPs:

Student's learning needs: Daily living and functional skills; rate of learning; memory; understanding abstract concepts; learning style (visual, auditory, kinesthetic/tactile); recommendations for individual, small group, whole class, cooperative learning; how to maximize the application and retention of skills and concepts; ways for multiple steps to be broken down; homework support; monitoring and feedback needed; technology supports

Social needs: Plans to improve relationships and interactions with peers; self-awareness and regulation strategies; school staff, family, and community involvement levels desired

Physical needs: Fine and gross motor movements, health, sensory needs

Environmental needs: Classroom arrangement, seating choices, home support and collaboration, material and resources, instructional assistants required (http://www.vesid.nysed.gov/specialed/publications/policy/iep/presentlevels.htm.)

It is also vital that middle school and high school personnel consulted include a combination of case managers, advocates, teacher mentors, general education teachers, special education teachers, instructional assistants, guidance counselors, and more. Educators, all staff, families, and students need to keep their eye on the ultimate goal, which is to design courses of study that prepare adolescents to graduate with appropriate diploma requirements (e.g., course credits earned, tests passed and ones required), with an expected graduation date listed. This helps the adolescent, his or her family, and school staff to consistently review what else is necessary in terms of accommodations, modifications, courses, and remediations to achieve the goal of graduation with the maximum transferable skills to postsecondary environments.

NCLB = No Child Left Behind (or for This Book's Purposes, NALB = No Adolescent Left Behind)

This federal law (NCLB), when first initiated, rightfully annoyed many administrators and educators. Stakeholders argued, how could schools be held accountable for students' lack of progress or be given sanctions for lower-than-acceptable student achievements? From my viewpoint, as someone in the special education field for over three decades, I was delighted that students with special needs were actually being monitored and were expected to achieve academic results with appropriate interventions. Although many state education departments will concur that the law needs fine-tuning with correct formulas and more appropriate time lines, no one would argue with the overall reasoning behind the fact that not leaving anyone behind is a way for students with disabilities to take *many steps forward!*

AYP = Adequate Yearly Progress

Achieving academic progress under NCLB is crucial for adolescents who will be entering the workforce, going on to college, or continuing with career training. Data from informal and formal standardized tests are reviewed and monitored to determine effectiveness of programs. When an adolescent consistently meets AYP requirements, this translates to realistic preparation for career training and future postsecondary decisions. This is achievable when adolescents' academic skills are sharpened and connected to job requirements and daily life activities.

Whether or not every stakeholder agrees with all of the rules and sanctions behind NCLB, every stakeholder is behind the premise that students of all abilities, races, cultures, and genders should continue to make achievements. The WebQuest that follows on page 110 offers educators and all staff an opportunity to research topics previously discussed and ones that will follow. Before we move ahead to the third section of the book, with response to intervention (RtI) and a focus on results, it's helpful to pause, review, and preview issues. Adolescents in inclusive classrooms sometimes need that chance to pause, too, to not only reach AYP, but LP—life potentials—too! Use this WebQuest to explore more.

Adolescent WebQuest	
Understanding how psychological principles help educators reach and teach adolescents	
a. Name some metacognitive factors that help to create successful learners. b. Identify specific positive and negative emotions that influence learning. c. How can educators encourage and support learners through interactive, collaborative instructional contexts?	www.apa.org/ed/lcp2/lcp14.html
Learning more about psychosocial, cognitive, and moral development theories	
a. How can e-mentoring/telementoring relationships benefit educators and students in adolescent classrooms? b. Identify the six pillars of *Character Counts*.	www.iearn.org/circles/mentors.html http:www.telementor.org http://charactercounts.org/defsix.htm www.thinkers.co.nz/telementoring
Exploring technology as a multimedia teaching tool	
a. Choose one of the virtual field trips and explain how it will appropriately relate to both the curriculum and the age-level characteristics of the adolescents in your inclusive classes.	http://www.field-trips.org/
Addressing gender bias in reference to adolescent differences	
a. Name five ways that teachers can avoid gender bias.	www.deebest.com/Teachertips.html
Applying behavioral learning theories and operant conditioning for adolescents	
a. Identify classroom ideas and reinforcers educators can implement to shape better performances from all learners.	http://tip.psychology.org/skinner.html

PART III

Focusing Upon Results

6

Meshing Research to Achieve and Surpass Standards in Adolescent Classrooms

This chapter includes an examination of how response to intervention (RtI), universal design for learning (UDL), differentiated instruction (DI), constructivist strategies (CS), cooperative learning (CL), understanding by design (UbD), and evidence-based practices (EBP) influence learning performances. It provides an overview of appropriate accommodations, modifications, assessments, and mentoring programs to enhance the academic, social, communicative, sensory, physical, and emotional experiences for adolescents in inclusive classrooms.

IMPLEMENTING THE TRIOS OF INITIALS

RtI and EBP: Effective Three-Tier Models

RtI is a data-based approach to decision making that can influence the following:

- The nature of instruction
- Early intervention
- LD determination (Strangeman, Hitchcock, Hall, Meo, & Coyne, 2006)

RtI's impact on these areas is the reason it is entering classrooms to shape lessons and connect with individual students' needs. RtI now influences whether or when a student receives an LD classification. Before IDEA 2004, there had to be a discrepancy between a student's tested level and his or her performance level in order for there to be a learning disability diagnosis. Now, with RtI, there is an additional way for students to receive a learning disability classification. If a student does not respond to appropriate, scientific, evidence-based practices or interventions, then with a parent's consent, the student can receive an evaluation to determine if a learning disability is present, and just what additional interventions may be needed. A discrepancy factor is now not the sole determinant for an LD classification. RtI allows for the postponement of labeling to see if the learning difficulties may be instruction related, rather than student centered. After a set period, the data is reviewed, and decisions are made whether to continue, tweak, revise, or reevaluate courses of intervention. With RtI implementation, it is possible that with the proper interventions, a student will progress in the inclusive general education classroom without an automatic label or pullout program being necessary.

Like many concepts still in their infancy, RtI and EBP still need more definition, clarification, application, and evaluation to determine their exact components, validity, and reliability in that often unscientific laboratory we call the classroom. Due to the variability of the students in inclusive adolescent classrooms, the *standard practices* for RtI and EBP cannot be uniform. Matching appropriate EBP designs to different populations and settings is not an easy task, yet it is one worth pursuing to ensure the quality of instructional practices. Prior experiences, teachers' educational training, instructional deliveries, multiple outcome measures, and data collection and interpretation influence positive and negative RtI results.

Overall, RtI has incredible future implications for adolescents in inclusive environments, but many of these details have still not been determined. Different levels of service, or tiers, involve the collection and interpretation of data, along with the monitoring and assessment of students' responses to scientific, research-based interventions. Individual teachers and team members problem solve together prior to the implementation of strategies to select an instructional approach from a range of options. Thus far, RtI has been implemented more frequently in younger grades than middle school and high school levels, yet the need for success before students become disillusioned during the older school years is crucial. More monitoring and accountability focused on achieving successful outcomes during these adolescent years require accurate testing with reliable evaluations and acceptable programs that have proven track records of success. The brightest part of RtI is that it can even catch the student who has been undetected until this point, for example, a student who is not a discipline problem, who completes homework, and who receives good grades. This student may be a sight-word reader, who memorized words in prior grades, but is still two to three grade levels below his or her peers in reading comprehension. This type of student has probably been quietly moved along from grade to grade, without the monitoring of his or her progress. RtI allows adverse educational scenarios to be recognized and viable educational interventions to be offered. RtI involves tiers, not tears! These *desalinated tiers* can include but are not limited to the following:

Tier 1: Research-based interventions and remediation are given in the general education setting to the whole class, individuals, or groups. This may include coteachers working together with research-based interventions, or general education teachers working alone, hopefully with frequent outside consultation and continual monitoring.

Tier 2: This tier includes more support with the implementation of research-based interventions by multiple teachers, team members, and additional staff in the general education class. This configuration can be given in smaller groups or individually as needed. Support here is more intense than in the first tier.

Tier 3: If the data says that a student with a disability has not achieved significant positive response to interventions from either tier one or two, then with prerequisite parental consent, this student can be given a comprehensive evaluation to determine eligibility for special education services. After that determination of specific skills, appropriate services are given either by special education teachers in the general education classroom or in smaller settings with intensive programs, for example, literacy, mathematics. Not all adolescents achieve success in inclusive environments, but the goal is to extend to all adolescents the maximum opportunities to reach their potentials in whatever environment best includes and matches their needs.

There may be additional tiers than those delineated or ones with different configurations. These tiers can be thought of more as waves, rather than as separate levels, since there may be back-and-forth movement among tiers, depending on students' needs. RtI is about students achieving outcomes that lead them in the direction of AYP. RtI is destined to succeed with the help of ongoing professional development and collaboration from coteachers, team members, support staff, families, and administrators. General education and special education staff then orchestrate lessons with interventions that target students' strengths, while monitoring their achievements or their responses to the interventions.

The main objective of RtI is to deflate frustrations and replace them with ways to help students achieve academic acumen within the general education classroom, with appropriate scaffolding of research-based interventions. Middle school students who *slip through the cracks,* with unnoticed learning gaps, then become high school students in danger of dropping out of school due to frustrations, unmet expectations, and what they may consider to be futile or self-deflating school experiences. Most important, RtI is about optimism. It cleverly tackles each unique situation and offers ways to improve adolescents' and teachers' outlooks by replacing apathy and unmet potentials with strategies that are designed for improved outcomes. Basically, RtI is a *meaty sandwich,* with assessments placed as the top and bottom slices of bread. Problem identification and interventions are sandwiched in between the pre and post assessments. It's a sandwich that all can *educationally* munch!

RtI Sandwich:

The "crust" of the matter includes assessment of student's needs, sandwiching in the next two layers.
Lettuce, means let us figure out, identify, and problem solve which interventions will best suit this student's current needs.
The meaty parts of the RtI sandwich are the implementation of scientific research-based strategies, appropriate instructional approaches, and plans.
Now, there are more assessments—back to the crust of the matter—determining if the interventions have produced acceptable results, and seeing if the interventions were appropriate ones. Otherwise, change concerning intervention methods is warranted. New sandwich meat is required!

RtI does not advocate social promotion, but targets students' academic needs to ensure that adolescents have the skills and subskills to proceed to the next level of learning, before a *snowball effect* occurs upon a weak learning foundation. RtI might mean that a student will double up on English courses, receive more intensive one-on-one mathematics instruction, or have additional study skill help across disciplines. RtI can assist adolescents to gain organizational skills, positive self-talk, additional social skills, more metacognition, and many other necessary academic skills.

More factors to consider concerning RtI involve students with cultural backgrounds that are different from the school norm, who are often inappropriately diagnosed as needing special education services when in fact there is no disability present, just *disabled instruction* that does not match students' diversity. This can include inappropriate methods of instruction, along with unfair assessments. Coutinho and Oswald (2004) confirm that when high school students are significantly lagging behind their peers, schools often guide these students into special education services, even if they do not actually have a disability. The tiers of RtI offer students a chance to respond to classroom interventions before classifications are assumed as automatically needed, along with their unwarranted labels.

UDL: Preplanning for Inclusive Successes With Universally Designed Lessons

Universally designed lessons allow students of many abilities access to curriculum materials in environments that expect, acknowledge, and give merit to their differences. This includes welcoming students with different strengths, cultural backgrounds, and prior learning experiences. UDL offers students visual, auditory, and kinesthetic-tactile preferences; instructional materials appealing to different reading levels and interests; and goals planned to address many cognitive, sensory, emotional, and physical abilities. It includes a classroom setup that does not wait for students to fail, but takes proactive measures to ensure their successes, ahead of time, before frustrations or misunderstandings present themselves. This can include, but is not limited to, students with visual needs; hearing impairments; or learning, sensory, physical, emotional, social, and behavioral differences. The following acronyms highlight some major principles of what is addressed in UDL.

GMMA = Give Me My Answers

★ Goals
★ Methods
★ Materials
★ Assessments

Recognizing Strategies Affectively = Three UDL Networks (based on neuroscience research at www.cast.org/research/udl/index.html)

★ Recognition network—*What's the content?*
★ Strategic network—*How does the learning process work?*
★ Affective network—*Why are emotions valued?*

E.C.M.O.W. = Every child makes out well!

E xpectations

C ontent

M ethods

O utcomes reach a

W ide range of students to maximize their strengths

It is no longer the scenario that adolescents exclusively gain knowledge through printed material in textbooks. Animated Web sites, computer graphics, visual aids, hands-on models, manipulatives, classroom discussions, videos, multimedia presentations, and more are now the norm, not the exception. Before lessons are designed, the audience of students must be considered. For example, knowing that a student has dysgraphia or attention issues, why not distribute an outline to the student on which he or she can just fill in the key concepts or vocabulary? That way, later on, the writing will be both legible and complete, with students' notes containing all of the necessary facts. Making advance course planners and outlines available for all students reduces writing and attention difficulties some students experience with auditory presentations. Students with visual impairments benefit from Web sites with text-to-speech and magnification capabilities. This allows students with blindness, low vision, dyslexia, and language differences the same access. When you cross the street, some traffic lights speak to you, tell you it is okay to proceed, while some museums even allow you to press a button and hear more about the exhibit. The classroom environment also requires these types of environmental sensitivities that clearly reach out to a variety of students.

In inclusive classrooms, UDL offers students with different abilities many options to express their learning. This can range from having visual dictionaries in classrooms; to taping your lessons and then having students play them back; to defining more difficult vocabulary with computer graphics and clip art, which allow students to listen to books on tape, or accommodations such as using line trackers. UDL refers to diverse materials, procedures, and assessments. Lessons that are delivered with the students' needs in mind are fruitful ones that yield exponential rewards to help students acquire learning in multiple ways with meaningful engagement.

The Center for Applied Specialized Technology (CAST), accessed at www.cast.org, affirms that UDL is necessary based on the fact that neuroscience research has identified different brain networks. These networks include a recognition network which is responsible for gathering, categorizing, and identifying learning concepts; a strategic network that determines how ideas are organized and expressed; and an affective network concerned with how students feel while they are learning, for example, whether they are excited, bored, or challenged. Classroom dynamics include purposeful writing, such as for the school newspaper, and applying rules of English, or using digital spinners to understand more about probability. More information about UDL can be accessed at www.cast.org/teachingeverystudent. Also, investigate http://bookbuilder.cast.org to place interactive and adolescent-friendly features in student- or teacher-created readings and writings.

As listed in IDEA 2004, the National Instructional Materials Accessibility Standard (NIMAS) has a provision that requires timely access to materials with alternate formats such as digital materials, Braille, audio, e-text, and large print for students with blindness and print disabilities in elementary and secondary schools. Inclusive adolescent classrooms that apply UDL principles allow the learning to be more accessible for all, thereby valuing diverse abilities with different instructional and assessment methods and approaches accompanied by a variety of goals and equitable materials.

Refer to these Web sites for additional accessibility insights:

National Instructional Materials Accessibility Standard (NIMAS)—http://nimas.cast.org

Bookshare—www.bookshare.org/web/Welcome.html

Daisy Digital Books—www.daisy.org/about_us/dtbooks.asp

Recording for the Blind & Dyslexic—www.rfbd.org

UT Library Online—www.lib.utexas.edu/books/etext.html

National Center for Accessible Media—http://ncam.wgbh.org/ebooks/comparison.html; http://ncam.wgbh.org/

The table on the next page offers lesson ideas that include appropriate UDL goals, objectives, motivations, procedures, follow-ups, and assessments. A blank template follows, for you to relate UDL concepts to your lesson plans, which allows students multiple options to express and engage in their learning within inclusive adolescent classrooms.

UbD = Understanding by Design

Sounding like it could almost be an architectural term, understanding by design involves teachers surveying both environments and their inhabitants. Educators first identify and then teach the essential knowledge and skills that encompass their disciplines. In inclusive classrooms, as Tomlinson and McTighe point out in their book, *Integrating Differentiated Instruction and Understanding by Design: Connecting Content and Kids* (2006), quality curriculum combined with quality instruction is valued. Concepts such as differentiation of instruction, flexible grouping, interest-based lessons, responsive environments, and appropriate instructional strategies ensure that each learner has the maximum opportunity for success. All of the *wh* questions are addressed (with the addition of *"how"*), such as the following:

What are you teaching? (curriculum objectives and concepts)

What support is offered at and between home and school? (family collaboration)

How are you teaching it? (DI, UbD, MI [multiple intelligences], cooperative learning, modeling, peer mentoring, discussion, multimedia presentations)

Where are you teaching? (classroom environment, school layout offering an availability of services in conducive settings, e.g., auto repair shops, places for cooking classes, science experiments, computer writing labs, drama clubs, exercise centers, extra help locations for tutoring services for different subjects)

UDL: Template to Preplan for Inclusive Successes

Lesson Goals & Objectives	Motivations & Procedures	UDL Options, Follow-Ups, & Assessments
Outline the big picture, before the minor details Include cognitive goals that accompany behavioral, social, and emotional ones. Mix higher-level with lower-level thinking skills. Value flexible goals that include mastery of learning vs. mastery of knowledge. Honor field-dependent and independent students. Share goals, objectives, and expectations with the students. Combine low-skill objectives yielding similar principles with rule-related ones that transfer to more learning. Include specific and measurable objectives with more general learner outcomes. Infuse generic study skill strategies with curriculum objectives across content areas, e.g., using an index, rubric, thesaurus, outline, Post-It Notes	High teacher expectation for mastery Empowerment with student choices across units Establishment of personal relevance of topics with analogous adolescent connections and interest-driven lessons, e.g., sports, music Increase in self-efficacy & intrinsic motivation Emphasis on self-regulation and transfer of knowledge Improvement of organizational skills, e.g., checklists for each step Mini lectures with guided practice, modeling and more discussion, Q & A Value adolescent expression Use of multiple examples, non-examples, relationships, comparisons, contrasts Collaborative peer groups, stations & centers, student team teaching Valuing of student contributions Technology for navigation, interaction, and composition, e.g., computer networks, telementoring Tiered activities Games & puzzles Virtual field trips	★ Preteaching of vocabulary ★ Direct instruction on how to paraphrase ★ Daily review, rehearsal, & support ★ Ongoing anchor activities based on units ★ Compact curriculum ★ Dissection of concepts ★ Chunk information in smaller amounts ★ Utilizing technology e.g., adapted keyboards, voice-activated sites, word prediction programs, multimedia programs ★ Modeling & guiding discovery ★ Reinforcement of time on tasks & efforts as well as achievements ★ Maintaining portfolios/learning logs ★ Keeping anecdotal notes & observations ★ Offering realistic and ongoing feedback ★ Raising successes; lowering frustrations ★ Delivery of oral/written tests & quizzes ★ Applying constructivist approaches ★ Scaffolding as needed, e.g., templates ★ Enlisting family support ★ Documenting of student work ★ Documenting teacher observations and lessons ★ Enlisting gender-sensitive approaches ★ Delivery of culturally appropriate content ★ Valuing global connections Multiple Intelligences: ★ Bodily-Kinesthetic (physical/hands-on activities, manipulatives, dance, motion, pantomime) ★ Visual-Spatial (graphics, concept maps, charts, drawings, videos, graphic novels, bubble dialogue, illustrations, animations) ★ Musical-Rhythmic (songs, CDs, DVDs, multimedia, hypermedia, sounds, background music, oral presentations, skits, role playing) ★ Verbal-Linguistic (lectures with guided note taking, class discussions, reading & writing workshops, debates, essays, literature circles, speeches, poems) ★ Logical-Mathematical (computers, number/time lines, chronological sequencing, problem solving, outlines, lab reports, open-ended deductive and inductive activities)

Lesson Goals & Objectives	Motivations & Procedures	UDL Options, Follow-Ups, & Assessments
	Adult mediation to help adolescents plan, focus, regulate, reason, and reflect upon learning goals, progress, and needs	★ Interpersonal (cooperative learning: think-pair-share, jigsaw, roundtable, flexible groups, centers, stations) ★ Intrapersonal (self-discovery, journals, reflections, charting progress, independent research, student self-assessment, K-W-L, interest-driven books, reflective surveys) ★ Naturalist (classifications, checklists, environmental cues) ★ Existentialist (value questions and open-class discussions)

Teacher: _____ Topic: _____

Subject: _____ Class: _____

Lesson Objectives	Motivation & Procedure	UDL Options	Follow-Ups & Assessments

Who are you teaching? (students of all abilities, ages, interests, cultures)

Who are you teaching with? (coteachers, support staff, grade-level teachers)

Who can you go to for extra help? (interdisciplinary teams, principal, librarian, supervisors, central office administration, school secretaries, guidance counselor, other special and general education teachers, support staff)

When are you teaching? (time of day, length of the period)

According to Wiggins and McTighe (2008), the mission of high school is to help students make meaning of what they are learning. This includes an enduring understanding of what is worth being familiar with. Basically, without transfer of learning, why bother with the instruction? All educators will agree that lessons are meaningless ones if students do not gain the required knowledge beyond regurgitation and are unable to apply the concepts. Ownership of the learning needs to be shared by teachers and then fully absorbed by the students. Using the content knowledge in authentic situations allows the learning to be better retained. In inclusive classes, UbD includes the following:

* Replacing direct instruction with more facilitation of learning
* Increasing student exploration in constructivist environments
* Valuing student discovery in interest-generated lessons
* Employing cooperative learning in heterogeneous groups
* Active problem solving across the curriculum
* Motivating learners to have a stake in their performance
* Previewing topics with students to determine interest
* Discussing learning, for example, Socratic seminars, debates
* Giving timely feedback on independent practice
* Revisiting the concepts for further retention
* Connecting goals with real-world applications

With UbD, you concentrate at the beginning on what you want students to do at the end of the lesson. Even in the game of Monopoly, everyone begins at the same spot; rolls the dice; and hopes to own property, create monopolies, charge rent to those who land on those properties, and eventually gain the most real estate. Now, classrooms can be compared to that very game, but it's not the teachers who should *monopolize the learning,* but the students who need to keep rolling their own dice and *making the decisions on what they are buying into.* It is essential that teachers keep the end goal in mind when they begin instruction across all curriculum areas. At times, many students with learning disabilities are at a loss about what they are responsible for knowing, or how facts connect to each other. With a UbD philosophy, students see the big picture before they can get lost in a maze of facts.

UbD is really not a program; it is more a type of *pedagogical thought* that empowers students to be dynamic learners as opposed to static ones, going nowhere! As a curriculum comparison, think of students as *endo-learners,* rather than *exo-learners,* since now the learning is permeating the inside of them, rather than just touching their outer surface. Inclusive educators need to challenge students to maximize their potential in environments designed for student absorption of meaningful content, rather than meaningless *skeletal* facts.

The bottom line of all education is successful outcomes to strengthen everyone's abilities, with RtI, UbD, and UDL involved at every stage. UbD instruction is therefore connected and matched with results and performances.

CONSTRUCTIVIST STRATEGIES FOR INCLUSIVE MIDDLE SCHOOL AND SECONDARY CLASSROOMS

Constructivism values teachers who do not teach isolated unrelated facts, but believe in the discovery of learning and effective problem solving. Jerome Bruner (1986) was a true believer in constructivist learning, with students actively involved in the *construction* or discovery of their knowledge. Basically, after students are given minimum instruction, for example, a motivating hook, background knowledge, or strategies modeled, students then construct and expand their learning. In addition, constructivist learning is grounded in real-life tasks and settings, with relevance to students' lives.

Inclusive constructivist principles for adolescents include the following:

* ★ Active engagement and exploration of learning processes and curriculum
* ★ Student investigations with teacher collaborations
* ★ Student ownership of the knowledge
* ★ Reflection on the importance of learning
* ★ Classroom management with smaller cooperative groups
* ★ More peer collaboration
* ★ Respect for diverse opinions
* ★ Expectation of high-quality student input
* ★ Organizational structure
* ★ Starting points and student investigations
* ★ Mnemonic devices: imagery, acrostics, loci
* ★ Book notes with reflections accompanying standard types of exams
* ★ Reflective journals across all curriculums
* ★ Episodic versus semantic memory

To *constructively* sum up this section, review the table on the next page.

INSTRUCTION THAT DIFFERENTIATES BUT DOES NOT SEGREGATE

As many middle school and high school teachers and families will affirm, students at this age are *extremely* conscious of what their peers think about them. Although differentiation of instruction that allows students to show what they know in multiple ways is a crucial ingredient for adolescents to succeed in inclusive classrooms, if students are singled out as being different from their peers, the benefits of the differentiation escape them. Most important is that students are able to concentrate on the lessons without interfering internal or external distractions. If the students are too busy watching who is watching them, or if they think that other students are looking down at them as inferior because their learning and content is watered down, then the egos of the adolescents supersede the differentiation. How can adolescents attend to and concentrate on the lesson if they are concerned with their appearances? Somehow, this differentiation needs to be achieved

Constructivist teachers . . .		
clamp learning to prior knowledge.	fill in learning gaps by engaging students' curiosity.	allow students to link and share ideas through discussion of hypotheses, prediction, and general points of view.
don't hammer in ideas, but allow students to learn by doing to pull out their strengths.	go beyond skill and drill.	cut out the nonessential memorization and regurgitation of facts.
plan fun activities that incorporate the academic nuts and bolts.	smooth out emotions by allowing ample wait time.	establish an environment that allows for *wrenching discoveries.*
long-term learning and help tighten ideas to students' long-term learning.	encourage students to bounce ideas off each other.	dig deeply to connect to learners.
actively staple learning to curriculum standards.	measure and then remeasure students' progress, efforts, and achievements.	have a toolbox filled with strategies for students to self-regulate and discover learning concepts.

Source: Karten, T. (2008). *Embracing disabilities in classrooms: Strategies to maximize students' assets.* Thousand Oaks, CA: Corwin Press.

without student stigmatization. Circumvent this *negative differentiation* by remembering this starred list:

★ Differentiation of instruction means that both general and special education teachers and support staff assist *all* students.

★ Inclusion itself does not translate to automatic achievement, unless it is given in an atmosphere that values differentiation for all students, those who are classified with special needs and those who are not.

★ Coteachers offer ongoing help to all students so as to develop more metacognition to understand personal strengths and needs, for example, rewriting notes; more practice and rehearsal; mnemonic devices; visual, auditory, or kinesthetic-tactile opportunities. Such assistance could also mean allowing a student with Asperger syndrome to use a word processor if fine motor skills are weaker, or providing a student with hearing issues more graphics and/or optimal proximity to learning stage

★ Develop appropriate communication systems with students, providing feedback that does not draw extra unwanted attention, for example, e-mail, teacher-student journals, private scheduled conferences with all students, hand signals, Post-it Notes, quieter praise, or written graphs that plot progress.

★ Allow students to release extra energy in an alternate setting or positive way, such as by having them return books to the library or deliver office memos.

★ Always challenge students to achieve their highest potential, encouraging undertakings with teacher and peer guidance.

★ Assist students to deal with frustrations, helping them not to shut down.

★ Apply step-by-step approaches that break up skills into subskills, teaching students to learn how to repeatedly do that for themselves so as to become more self-regulated learners.

★ Value MI connections such as using more visuals, acting out the concepts, using reflective journals, having cooperative groups, singing the curriculum, classifying concepts, encouraging mathematics, engaging in reading, connecting through writing, working on listening skills, advocating speeches, having debates and discussions, and more!

★ Develop learning contracts with students, negotiating types of proactive differentiation, for example, "If you consistently only complete 4 out of 5 homework assignments, the highest grade you can receive is a C–."

★ Teach all students that not everyone in this world is the same; hence, the accommodations some students receive are not to be mocked or to be jealous of, but are appropriate ones to match those students' unique needs.

★ Directly deal with bullies by firmly establishing a *zero-tolerance policy* about such behaviors.

★ Differentiate units across the curriculum, with grade-level teachers, coteachers, instructional assistants, and supervisors.

★ Include study skills with content lessons, for example, how to create an outline, scan a text for information, use an index, create acrostics, take notes, remember what is said, visualize concepts, create concept and mind maps.

★ Allow students to work in cooperative, heterogeneous groups.

★ Set up a *strategy box* or table with appropriate curriculum materials that all student have access to, for example, magnification pages, calculators, writing templates, lists of transitional words, headphones, pencil grips, colored overlays, highlighting tape, thesaurus, electronic and content-related visual dictionaries.

★ Always raise the *differentiation bar* to continually maximize students' potentials with high, yet realistic expectations.

The table on page 124 offers a graphic representation of some differentiation options. The following quote sums this subject up well:

Adolescent-centered differentiation anticipates and builds on students' learning strengths by offering varied, multiple, and flexible options to learn, to work together, and to succeed academically. (Crawford, 2008, p. 152)

Differentiation of Instruction: Planning Stage Examples		
1—Definite	**2—Worthwhile**	**3—Extra**
These are the learning objectives and goals that you have set for all students.	These are learning objectives that most students will accomplish.	These learning objectives will be accomplished by some of the adolescents.
90–100 percent of the class will achieve these goals	70–85 percent of the class will learn these goals and objectives, too.	15–25 percent of the students will achieve these more complex objectives or goals.
Differentiation of Instruction: Delivery Stage Examples		
anchor activities	varied curriculum texts	problem-based learning
cooperative & individual grouping & instruction	graphic organizers	tiered centers
multiple intelligences	discussion sessions	learning choices
Differentiation of Instruction: Assessment Stage Examples		
learning contracts	varied homework	independent study
digital portfolios	additional time allowed	student rubric
reflective journals	growth vs. achievement paradigm for grading	self-, peer-, and teacher-monitoring and observation

Approaches such as UbD and UDL that value the skills of individual learners offer multiple ways for adolescents to construct and expand their knowledge and potentials. Teacher facilitation with proactive planning not only has the curriculum in sight, but also respects the individual students. Inclusion then results in benefits for all students.

WHY COOPERATIVE LEARNING WORKS

What is cooperative learning? *Hmm* . . . cooperation. What an excellent way to prepare learners for life! This involves assistance, teamwork, support, problem solving, individual and group accountability, and of course the right attitude. Since adolescents value the opinions and thoughts of their peers, they are more willing to listen and learn together. Sharing common goals to investigate, explore, and expand knowledge through assigned tasks sends out strong messages that group efforts are not only valued, but can also achieve productive results. Research shows that with cooperative learning, students spend more time on task learning from each other (D. W. Johnson & Johnson, 2003).

When peers spend time on task together, the results include academic benefits across multiple subjects, increased thinking skills, and social skill advancements. The next table gives both examples and non-examples of cooperative learning.

Non-Examples of Cooperative Learning	Examples of Cooperative Learning
Competing with each other or cooperative teams to achieve a goal	Working within a cooperative team to achieve a class, school, or community goal
Achieving only personal outcomes	Achieving shared outcomes
Reaching exclusive personal goals	Reaching mutual team goals
Working in whole-class instruction	Working in smaller groups
Completing tasks individually	Completing tasks together
Maximizing one's own potential	Maximizing group and class potential
Sharing little responsibility with group members	Sharing much responsibility with group members
Constructing projects without knowing contributions of each member, with little accountability	Constructing individual accountability for assigned cooperative work
Distributing participation to only the smartest or most capable	Distributing participation equally to maximize everyone's abilities
Encouraging negative dependence	Encouraging positive interdependence
Interacting with the task at different times, with some relaxing or being idle, while others are more productive	Interacting simultaneously and productively with engaging assigned roles
Valuing personal successes exclusively	Valuing the successes of others
Structuring lessons and groups with ancillary materials unrelated to curriculum objectives with undetermined outcomes	Structuring lessons and groups based on specific curriculum materials, objectives, and desired outcomes
Diagnosing and observing whole-class needs without looking at students' needs	Diagnosing and observing individual students' needs
Intervening infrequently and haphazardly	Intervening frequently and purposefully
Highlighting individual successes	Highlighting group successes
Connecting with unrelated learning	Connecting prior related learning
Sharing few responsibilities and only haphazard goals with the students	Sharing the majority of the responsibilities and specified goals with the students
Employing students as competitors	Employing students as cohesive partners
Engaging in sedentary activities	Engaging in active learning
Functioning independently without a group mentality	Functioning as a cohesive group with a rewarding group mentality
Increasing student boredom with mundane activities	Increasing student motivation with purposeful activities
Arranging homogeneous groups	Arranging heterogeneous groups

(Continued)

(Continued)

Non-Examples of Cooperative Learning	Examples of Cooperative Learning
Collaborating only occasionally as a group or class	Collaborating consistently as a group and class
Reflecting without critical review or making changes	Reflecting upon learning with changes made
Teaching students to disregard peers as teachers, devaluing their contributions	Teaching students to learn together through active discovery of each other's findings
Promoting growth only for students with special needs	Promoting academic learning and emotional and social growth for all students

Reducing competition while valuing cooperation is a way to increase time on task, attention, retention, and, of course, individual growth. Higher-order thinking skills with multiple intelligences replace mundane individual learning. Assessments now involve reviewing tangible, concrete finished products cooperatively produced; grading personal reflective journals; or rating positive social interactions. Students are given different cooperative roles such as reader, recorder, materials manager, focuser, checker, timer, artist, discussion leader, and more. Literature and curriculum cooperative circles include roles such as a passage/text paraphraser, interpersonal connector, intrapersonal connector, visual translator, musical interpreter, curriculum connector, logic expert, and other content-related cooperative players. Group members collectively and creatively absorb fiction and nonfiction genres in classes such as English, Science, History, Mathematics, and Spanish. If conflicts arise while working within cooperative groups, it is a purposeful way to teach adolescents appropriate emotional, social, and behavioral skills. Some cooperative configurations include, but are not limited to, the following:

Jigsaw—As Slavin (1995) describes, an assignment, comparable to a jigsaw puzzle, is divided into its pieces or components, with each person in the group responsible for mastering his or her part and teaching it to the others in the group, for example, each person reads a different page in a text chapter.

Think-Pair-Share—Students are involved in a three-step process to first listen to and reflect upon a question or problem, next discuss and collaborate with a peer for more thoughts or solutions, and then share findings with the class.

Roundtable—As described by Kagan (1994), a roundtable has students working in teams to write answers to a question or offer comments to process information and to stimulate further discussion.

Numbered Heads Together—After being assigned numbers, for example, 1 to 5, students whose number is called are accountable for a response to a particular question so as to promote positive interdependence.

Send a Problem—Students create questions and write them on index cards, which are then given to another group to answer.

Sources: http://www.pgcps.pg.k12.md.us/~elc/learning1.html; http://www.co-operation.org/pages/cl.html.

The next table offers a cooperative checklist and ratings scale to further enhance individual accountability with cooperative assignments. Share this rubric and its outlined descriptors with adolescents before they begin the assignment so that they know exactly what is expected of them as an outcome. It promotes a UbD design, since the outcomes and final products are influenced by the criteria outlined in the assessment. If desired, teachers and adolescents can fill out the form together to help all students develop increased reflections, metacognition, communications, and positive collaboration. In addition, input gathered from cooperative peers within each student group or from peers in other groups adds social and behavioral accountability and encourages peer interactions.

Teacher/student directions: Cooperative ratings can be checked off as either a yes or no, or for more individual accountability, scored on a 1–5 scale, with 5 being the highest achievement, equivalent to an A, while a 1 would be the lowest possible rating, equivalent to a failing grade for that descriptor. Afterward, if a 1–5 scale is used, the individual descriptors are averaged together for a final grade. The N/A category means that the descriptor is nonapplicable.

Student: _____

Names of other group members: _____

_____

Date assignment given: _____

Completion date: _____

Cooperative Descriptors	Definitely	Somewhat	Not at All	N/A
1. The student helped the group to achieve the cooperative goal.				
2. The completed product was exemplary.				
3. Evidence of effort is shown.				
4. All requirements of given directions were fulfilled.				
5. Student was an integral part of the group, both leading and following.				
6. Creativity was evidenced.				
7. Positive interdependence was shown.				
8. Excellent social skills were displayed within the group.				
9. Student displayed a collaborative, noncompetitive attitude.				
10. _____ _____ _____				

When students learn from each other, motivation is increased without negative competition. At times, direct instruction to properly monitor groups is required, as are gentle reminders. In addition, be *spontaneous cooperative teachers.* For example, once when my sixth-grade students were assigned individual landform reports in social studies that had three requirements—written outline, class presentation, and a visual representation—it turned into a collaborative class report. Each student independently completed his or her landform assignment, for example, archipelago, glacier, geyser, valley, but as the inclusion teacher, I then collected all of their pictures and, with a group of students, organized the collection into a class collage of the landforms. We labeled each collage with a letter corresponding to an answer key that explained what each picture represented. This geographic collage hung in class all year long, and the students got to see how their independent assignments became a cooperative one, yielding one finished product. Cooperative spontaneity is not a difficult concept to achieve, if you turn independence with individual accountability into productive peer collaboration. This yields the message that it's not about what each student can produce, but how students can join together to form not just many landforms, but the *formulation of positive interdependence.*

Building and maintaining *cohesive climates* means that students with different abilities in inclusive classrooms are not singled out, but are an integral part of their group, class, and school. When adolescents value each other and share goals, many curriculum strides are achieved. The table on the next page expands this cooperative concept across the curriculum to outline roles, connections, and skills.

ACCOMMODATIONS AND MODIFICATIONS TO CREATE ENTHUSIASTIC LEARNERS

Inclusion involves adaptation as well as acceptance. Adolescents require modifications and accommodations that appropriately allow them to access, express, and expand their learning. These should always challenge adolescents to achieve their highest potential. Dilution of content without thinking about individual student needs automatically assumes student incompetence. That is why accommodations should be the first avenue looked at, before modifications or changes are made to the curriculum. The first option is to accommodate the student, then if necessary modify the lesson content or expectations. However, even when accommodations and modifications are used, gradually weaning students off these supports creates more independent, self-regulated learners. Most important is that teachers are IEP compliant, by offering the students the specifications outlined in their IEP, while working to make the students themselves more aware and independent.

If educators have high expectations, the learning bar is raised, with adolescents guided to expand their knowledge. Many students who are classified with different types of disabilities that affect areas such as learning pace, stamina, memory, attention, language, and the ability to understand abstract reasoning require necessary accommodations and modifications to work toward both content and self-mastery. Adolescents with specific learning disabilities—ADHD, Asperger syndrome, autism, sensory impairments, physical and emotional differences—are now in the general education mix. Many times, they do not learn or process information the same way as their peers without disabilities. If that is the case, how can teachers be expected to teach and reach those students with disabilities, without accommodating or modifying the

Cooperative Lessons That Grab Students' Attention

Catchy Names/ Cooperative Roles	Assignment for Teen Connections	Subject Connections & *Hidden* Skills
Hard Rock Café Roles: Menu Designer, Rock Star, Appetizer Planner, Entrée Person, *Desserter*	Create a restaurant menu that describes appetizers, entrées, and desserts, such as igneous, sedimentary, and metamorphic sandwiches; other rocky platters; or even lava á la mode that your group will offer as the owners of this restaurant.	★ Physical science/research ★ Computer tools ★ Literacy skills ★ Graphic design/art ★ Interpersonal skills
Accounting Figures Roles: Calculator, Interior Designer, Researcher, Itemizer, Personal Shopper	Pretend that you have $2,500 to spend to redecorate the school. What layout would your group use? Research and itemize the cost of the items your group will purchase, including tax. Find local businesses where you will shop. If you have money remaining, tell which charity you will donate the money to and explain why.	★ Mathematical computations ★ Geometry ★ Measurement ★ Accounting/bookkeeping ★ Life skills ★ Architecture ★ Community connections ★ Character education ★ Interpersonal skills
American History Idol Roles: Collector, Song Writer, Judge, Melody Writer, Lyricist	Identify your group's favorite *stars* from American History. What songs would they sing if they were on *American Idol*? Pick historical judges and share their comments. Your group could use a tune or melody from today and rewrite the lyrics or create your own. Creatively find a way to collect votes, e.g., e-mail, survey.	★ Music ★ Technology ★ Historical research ★ Data analysis ★ Discrete mathematics ★ Interpersonal skills
Musical Math Roles: Hip-Hopper, Number Rocker, Subject Chooser, Connector	Cooperatively create a song using your favorite style, e.g., hip-hop, rock, rap, country, jazz, heavy metal, that tells about some of the concepts, theorems, and formulas you learned about in geometry and algebra, e.g., adapt a song by Breaking Benjamin, Adema, KoRn, Carrie Underwood, Amy Grant, Alabama, Beatles, Billy Joel, Jonas Brothers, and more.	★ Algebra ★ Geometry ★ Music ★ Interpersonal skills ★ Literacy skills
Surfing on the Web Roles: Animator, Graphic Artist, Web Designer, Product Researcher	Create a Web site that promotes a hygiene product that your group will use often, e.g., hair gel, shampoo, suntan lotion. Include an appealing design with appropriate text, pictures, and animation.	★ Economics ★ Life skills ★ Consumer education ★ Technology/graphic design

(Continued)

(Continued)

Catchy Names/ Cooperative Roles	Assignment for Teen Connections	Subject Connections & *Hidden* Skills
Life Lessons Roles: Movie Critic, Plot Connector, Book Reviewer, Copy Editor	Choose a character from a recent book your group has read or a movie that all of you have seen, and describe the thinking of the protagonist or antagonist, giving specific personal and physical character traits with relevant plot connections. Vividly describe how the settings influenced the characters.	★ Biology ★ Brain research ★ Literacy skills ★ Intrapersonal thoughts
Worldly Wonders Roles: Cartographer, Translator, Travel Agent, Musician, Artist	Your group has just won a trip to visit all of the continents. What sights will you choose to see? Create a map, giving the latitudes and longitudes and distances of your choices. Research the music and art you will hear and see at each stop. Practice some handy phrases in different languages that you will need to know.	★ Global connections ★ Geography ★ World history ★ World languages ★ Computer skills ★ Music/art
Dancing With the Stars Roles: Dancer, Researcher, Galactic Investigator, Fact Finder, Astrologist	Working as a group, create a kinesthetic way to remember facts about the solar system. Include research from text and other sources. You can pantomime, dance, juggle, create a sports connection, or move as you choose.	★ Astronomy research ★ Physical education ★ Study skills ★ Interpersonal skills

students' workload requirements, their methods of acquiring the knowledge, and/or the means of assessment?

Not all accommodations or modifications need to be complex, just appropriate. These adaptations may involve helping students to follow directions, assisting them in attending to tasks, or encouraging more classroom participation. If there are two teachers in the classroom, then the inclusive and general education teachers can both offer ongoing coaching and support with the content of lessons as well as the strategies that need to be applied. Once, during a science lesson, the students just could not comprehend the difference between intrusive and extrusive rocks. When I constructed a table in a word processing document, which was displayed on a SMART Board, suddenly the students understood the difference. This graphic organizer was not a complex one; it merely helped students to visually see the difference and provided better comprehension through a more organized note-taking system. Other simple accommodations involve breaking directions into steps, for example, using cue words such as first, next, and after. When teachers proactively provide models, offer choices, outline quality work criteria, guide social interaction, allow for creative expression, and offer consistent feedback, then individual accommodations are universal for the class and assist all adolescents toward higher outcomes.

The adjective *appropriate* has a different definition for each student. Even if an adolescent shares the same classification with another student, that does not mean that every student with the same classification will require the same accommodations or modifications. Adolescents with hearing impairments, blindness, learning differences, or emotional, social, or behavioral disorders are not all the same within or across their labels. Suppose your friend asks you to purchase a box of cereal at the store, but neglects to tell you what kind of cereal. Now, here you are in the cereal aisle, faced with a dilemma: Just what will you purchase, when there are shelves upon shelves of different kinds of cereal boxes to choose from? They all share the name or category of being *cereal,* yet one with marshmallows certainly differs from one with raisins. Adolescents with disabilities are the same way. No two are alike, with or without disabilities, yet all deserve *palatable* ways to show what they know.

The table on page 132 offers some appropriate accommodations to help adolescents be the best that they can be, under the guidance of educational staff, families, and their own regulatory systems. Various scenarios are shown, yet please keep in mind that the accommodations or modifications listed in IEPs are not optional but required, as they were mutually agreed upon by families, school support staff, and the students when appropriate. In addition, general educators need to decide whether these very same accommodations could also benefit other adolescents in the classroom who are not responding to conventional means of instruction or assessments. It is important to consider—even though they do not have an IEP— whether other students could benefit from similar learning adjustments.

The last column, Weaning Plans, has been added to remind educators and students that many of these accommodations do not need to be permanent, but can eventually be phased out as students' skill levels are raised. If that happens, there is a loud and clear message that more responsibility for learning is taking place. That does not mean that a student with blindness is not always offered a Braille transcription or a student with deafness will not be given a sign interpreter, but it does mean that students should be consistently challenged with learning on their instructional or independent skill level. Accommodations and modifications are basically designed to remove frustrations and replace them with adolescent achievements. Reflect upon these accommodations, and appropriately offer your own across curriculum contents to create enthusiastic learners who are not frustrated by what they cannot do but are honored for their abilities.

Accommodations differ from modifications, since the former do not change the learning objectives or outcomes. Modifications offer students opportunities for changes such as alternate settings, different expectations, and fewer curriculum objectives. Most important is that all accommodations and modifications are developmentally age appropriate and that they do not enable or frustrate students, but challenge them to be adolescents who will one day turn into productive and independent adults, taught to capitalize upon their potentials, strengths, and interests. All adolescents are capable of diverse achievements when trained and sensitive educators astutely honor their abilities.

This next table offers teachers a chart to document accommodations given and assessment grades achieved for units and topics in courses. These accommodations may be IEP generated or ones that educators deem necessary to maximize student achievements. The chart can be filled out by both the general education and special education staff for each marking period and then shared with all staff, students, and families to reflect upon adolescent efforts, achievements, and ways to modify instruction and programs.

Adolescent Scenarios	Accommodations	Weaning Plans
Academic **English class scenario:** Student with a learning disability has decoding issues with multisyllabic content-level vocabulary, which hinders student's comprehension. The student's verbal expression and oral comprehension are excellent, but written expression and encoding skills are weaker. Student is sensitive to this oral reading weakness and prefers not to orally read in class.	Allow student access to visual, manual, and talking electronic dictionaries to pronounce difficult, unfamiliar words and to break up words into syllables. Omit oral reading in front of class. Provide student with a digital tape recorder to record notes and express thoughts. Allow a word bank or text for correct spellings. Grade on content; do not penalize student for spelling errors. Provide a writing frame and a list of transitional words for organization. Pair student with a peer to check written work and scribe notes. Allow student to demonstrate knowledge in other ways, e.g., drawings, PowerPoint presentations. Use books on tape (www.rfbd.org). Use high-interest, age-appropriate novels on alternate reading level.	Teach student how to use the word processing tools for spelling corrections. Provide student with scored writing samples and rubrics to review to see graded writing pieces. If coteacher is available or if time and logistics permit, offer both individual and group instruction within the classroom to guide all students on direct skill practice with syllabication. Praise student's improvements and gradually hold student more accountable for weekly content-related spelling lists. Be certain that if student fills in words on a writing frame, the student then manually rewrites the entire writing frame to gain additional skills in written expression.
Behavioral **Algebra class scenario:** Student has extreme difficulties sitting still in longer lectures, and often misbehaves, drawing attention to herself and distracting others from concentration on lessons. Student's strongest intelligence is musical-rhythmic.	Excuse student from longer seated lessons by offering the whole class cooperative tactile opportunities to complete identical assignments in shorter clips, e.g., working with algebra tiles. Allow her and other students opportunities to independently complete guided computer assignments, while listening to their favorite (teacher-approved) music on headphones. Offer more brain breaks and movement, e.g., kinesthetically demonstrate human equations. Acknowledge self-control efforts in an outlined behavioral contract or plan that offers agreed-upon incentives.	Share details of student's functional behavioral assessment (FBA) with both the student and family, so positive behavior is self-monitored, continued, and improved in all environments. Encourage graphing of daily moods to detect patterns; use redirection and channeling to more positive outlets. Establish a self-control system. Schedule private conferences to discuss improvements and future behavioral plans, e.g., changing time on task. Replace concrete reward system with more intrinsic rewards.
Perceptual **Spanish class scenario:** Student cares a great deal about the subject, but is continually failing Spanish quizzes and	Increase size of the font and spacing with uncluttered, student-friendly formats on worksheets and tests, e.g., test divided into sections, more graphic organizers. Allow student to use a magnification page to enlarge print. Permit comparison of notes	Honor this student's learning style with varied instructional methods and assessments to send a clear message to this caring student. If you pair this student with a class or homework partner, then gradually reduce the number of times per week

Adolescent Scenarios	Accommodations	Weaning Plans
tests due to poor attention to visual details, weak fine motor skills, and low vision. Student is definitely an auditory learner.	with peers' notes or teacher's outlines. Offer student an opportunity to orally respond to questions. Have a *strategy table* in the room, equipped with slant boards, pencil grips, different size writing implements, templates, Spanish books on tape, and orally available lessons.	that the student meets with his or her mentor. Offer a checklist, rubric, and graph to self-monitor progress. Encourage student to employ multimedia computer programs to gain additional Spanish skills.
Developmental Delay **Chemistry class scenario:** Student is unable to grasp abstract concepts presented in course text. Student often perseverates on own interests and does not exhibit social reciprocity. Student has strong mathematics skills.	Increase amount of models, visuals, multisensory presentations, graphic organizers, vocabulary flashcards, and study guides. Develop a private signal with the student that encourages appropriate social interactions. Give frequent praise for strides. Acknowledge student's strengths and interests by paralleling chemistry facts with math concepts. Offer more Web sites for reinforcement of concepts.	Rehearsal techniques with practice and variety are required here to both retain chemistry concepts and increase appropriate social interactions. Capitalize upon the student's mathematical strength in cooperative group assignments by assigning a role that allows peers to view student's capabilities. Increase self-evaluation skills across academics and social areas.

Student:	Teachers/Staff:		
Subject:	**Topic/Unit/Marking Period:**		
Student Data Documentation			
Circle, highlight, or add instructional strategies.	**Test/Quiz Grades**	**Informal assessments/ Observations & comments— Student strengths & interests List specific classroom, small-group, or individual interventions.**	**Dates**
Linking to prior knowledge			
Preteaching			
Reteaching			
Multisensory lessons			
Concrete presentations			
Providing outline/notes/advance organizers			
Additional breaks			
Family support			

Student Data Documentation			
Circle, highlight, or add instructional strategies.	Test/Quiz Grades	Informal assessments/ Observations & comments— Student strengths & interests List specific classroom, small-group, or individual interventions.	Dates
Modeling			
Step-by-step directions			
Study guide			
Lessening requirements			
Reducing reading			
Acting out concepts			
Self-esteem builders			
Cooperative learning			
Extra time or wait time			
Preferred seating			
Homework modified			
More visuals/graphics			
Less writing			
Peer support			
Color code			
More auditory cues			
Additional technology			
Quiet setting			
Student metacognition			
Frequent monitoring			
Coteaching/collaboration			
Focus on positives			
Manipulatives			
Variety of assessments			
Alternate task			
Other			

Source: Adapted from Karten, T. (2008). *Embracing disabilities in the classroom: Strategies to maximize students' assets.* Thousand Oaks, CA: Corwin Press.

APPROPRIATE ADOLESCENT ASSESSMENTS

Dilemmas concerning assessments for adolescents emerge, diverge, and converge. Student failures in inclusive classrooms may stem from unprepared students or teachers, lack of student or teacher motivation, too much curriculum material, incomplete student prior knowledge, poor instructional delivery, unfair or invalid assessments, the trickling down of administrative demands, parental demands, inappropriate placements, and more. In this *assessment-frenzy age,* test preparation often takes priority over content. As a result, many adolescents are more concerned with grades received than the knowledge gained. When students ask, *"Is this going to be on the test?"* The translation is, *"I'll only listen to this stuff if I will be graded on it. Otherwise, I just don't care!"* In order for assessments to be successful, they must be received by accepting adolescent audiences.

Assessment options help secondary learners by empowering them with choices. Choices allow adolescents to be an integral part of the learning process as *student drivers* in their education. Of course, the teacher is still the ultimate instructor who facilitates the delivery of the curriculum and ensures that *traffic delays, road blocks,* and *detours* do not *sway adolescents off the road,* by missing the lesson's objectives. The major benefit of options is that teachers now no longer dictate or spew out knowledge; rather, they demonstrate how learning can be processed and *played with,* in fun yet meaningful ways.

With both self-selected and mandated requirements, assessment options can increase time and attention on task, with higher levels of productivity, accuracy, and mastery. For example, the choice to work cooperatively rather than independently honors the interpersonal vs. the more intrapersonal learner. Learners with issues such as oppositional defiant disorder (ODD) respond better when assessment choices are offered to allow them empowerment, with an increased stake in their learning. One art teacher recently voiced concerns over three choices she offered to a student who then refused all of them. As a suggestion, I recommended that she offer the student four choices—three positive choices and one negative one—and then see which one he picks. That way, he is deciding not to be punished with a negative choice, and just might realize that those first three choices were not such bad ones. Sometimes, it's the presentation that must vary. The teacher is still the ultimate overseer who moves about the classroom helping individuals and groups to better understand the concepts as they process the information in multiple assessment formats.

Some students experience tremendous anxiety concerning tests. Joseph Casbarro's book *Test Anxiety and What You Can Do About It* (2005) elaborates ways that students, teachers, and families can address this anxiety, by targeting physical, emotional, and cognitive anxiety symptoms. He encourages students to do many of the following:

Look over the whole test before they begin.

Underline key words.

Pace themselves.

Eliminate incorrect choices.

Use visualization.

Organize ideas with graphic organizers.

Review and reread.

Casbarro (2005) advocates that parents look for teachers who exhibit the four Cs: compassion, caring, competence, and communication. Families and schools help adolescents reduce their test anxiety with strategies such as positive self-talk, study skills, more proactive organization, and increased preparation.

Sharing the knowledge with students about how they are assessed with outlines and rubrics is a critical way for adolescent learners in inclusive classrooms to know what is expected of them. Rubrics take the mystery away from just what constitutes an acceptable or exemplary finished product. The following are examples of assessments in mathematical and literacy lessons that have creative, analytical, and practical applications. These motivating lessons connect to multiple intelligences with students' interests being honored. These choices allow and address individual cognitive, social, emotional, sensory, communication, and behavioral differences. The first assignment asks students to bring in their favorite recipe and then cooperatively halve and double it, while the next one has categories for ordering items from a menu and creating word problems. The last one is based upon an oral presentation for the retelling of a novel.

Rubric for the Math Recipe Project
Cooking for More or Less

Choose your favorite recipe and then cooperatively halve or double the ingredients. The maximum amount of points you can receive if you accurately fulfill all of the requirements for each of the five categories is listed and will total 100% for all.

SCORING CATEGORIES	TEACHER COMMENTS POINTS EARNED	STUDENT COMMENTS AGREE/DISAGREE
1. ACCURACY All facts were accurate. (30 points)		
2. COMPLETION All requirements and directions with the assignment were followed. (30 points)		
3. ORGANIZATION Information was neatly and clearly presented. (20 points)		
4. BEHAVIOR Used time efficiently and worked cooperatively with peers. (15 points)		
5. INITIATIVE Showed ability as a peer leader to help others. (5 points)		

Eating Out With My Friends	Ways I will be graded	Points earned
Choose one of the menus from the class pile, and join three of your peers to decide what you will order. Remember to add a _____% tip and _____% for tax. Give the total cost with tax and tip. Then cooperatively create two other word problems involving percentages. The maximum points you can receive if you accurately fulfill all of the requirements for each of the five categories listed is 20 points to equal a total of 100 points	Class presentation	
	Accuracy	
	Consistency of the group's written responses	
	Word problem creativity	
	Collaborative group behavior	
	Comments:	Total Points:

After some assigned readings on ancient Roman civilization, I allowed students to complete one of the following choices to answer the focus question. As you will notice, students are asked to compare Roman knowledge to a prior Egyptian unit to maintain and reinforce earlier learning and honor higher critical, comparative thinking skills.

Focus Question: What achievements do we have today for which we owe thanks to the ancient Romans and/or Egyptians?

After completing the assigned readings, you may choose one of the options below to answer this question. You can work independently or with a partner.

★ Write an essay that compares and contrasts the achievements of the civilization of ancient Rome to that of the early Egyptians. (maximum 250–300 words)
★ Create a captioned illustration or bubble dialogue of an Egyptian slave speaking with a Roman citizen about their respective cultures.
★ Make a Venn diagram comparing ancient Rome or Egypt to society today.
★ Create and perform a musical song or dance about both of the civilizations.
★ Make time lines of the Old, Middle and New Kingdoms and one of ancient Rome from the Roman Republic to the Fall of the Roman Empire.

What a test format looks like and contains influences the performance of some adolescents and often determines whether the responses given will be meaningful ones. A format that includes ways to maximize successes rather than having students set up for frustrations or failures is measuring what the students know. Appropriate formats extend beyond the written question to honor students' competencies. Factors such as universal design and fairness apply to all groups across abilities and cultures.

CATEGORY	Well done 8–10	Great efforts 5–7	Needs more 2–4	Missed goal 1–3
Collaboration With Peers	Almost always shares with, listens to, and supports the efforts of others in the group. Tries to keep people working well together	Usually listens to, shares with, and supports the efforts of others in the group. Often a team member	Sometimes listens to, shares with, and supports the efforts of others in the group but is not always a good team member	Rarely listens to, shares with, and supports the efforts of others in the group. Rarely is a good team member
Content of Skit	Shows a full understanding of the book's content	Shows a good understanding of book's elements	Shows somewhat of an understanding of parts of the book	Does not seem to understand the book very well
Enthusiasm	Facial expressions and body language show a strong interest in and enthusiasm about the topic	Facial expressions and body language sometimes show interest and enthusiasm	Facial expressions and body language are used to try to show enthusiasm, but seem fake	Very little use of facial expressions or body language
Posture and Eye Contact	Stands up straight, looks relaxed and confident. Establishes eye contact with everyone	Stands up straight and establishes eye contact with some	Sometimes stands up straight, but establishes little eye contact	Slouches or does not look at people during the presentation
Stays on Topic	Stays on topic all (100%) of the time	Stays on topic most (80–90%) of the time	Stays on topic some (70%–80%) of the time	It was hard to tell what the topic was
Preparedness	Student is completely prepared and has obviously rehearsed	Student seems pretty prepared but might have needed a couple more rehearsals	The student is somewhat prepared, but it is clear that rehearsal was lacking	Student does not seem at all prepared to present
Volume	Volume is loud enough to be heard by all audience members for more than 90% of the presentation.	Volume is loud enough to be heard by all audience members for more than 80% of the time.	Volume is loud enough to be heard by all audience members at least 60–80% of the time.	Volume is often too soft to be heard by all audience members.
Listens to Other Skits	Listens intently, without making distracting noises or movements	Listens intently but makes some distracting noises or movements	Sometimes does not appear to be listening but is not distracting	Sometimes does not appear to be listening and exhibits frequent distracting noises or movements

Source: Adapted from template found at http://rubistar.4teachers.org.

This next sample Grade 7 mathematical item brings to mind that modifications of testing items need not be complex, but certainly must be appropriate. A comparison of the original mathematical item to the modified example shows that when extra verbiage and one answer is eliminated, opportunities for success are supported through the assessment. Directly including appropriate formulas where they need to be applied, instead of having students lose focus with other distracting items on the reference sheet, also increases successes and focuses students on the problem at hand rather than figuring out what the problem is asking. Overall, the second choice sensitively scaffolds students to display their optimum competencies.

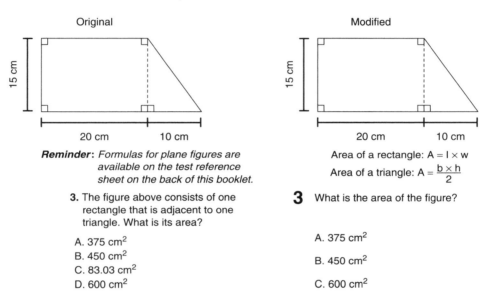

Sample Grade 7 Mathematics Item

Original

15 cm

20 cm   10 cm

Reminder: *Formulas for plane figures are available on the test reference sheet on the back of this booklet.*

3. The figure above consists of one rectangle that is adjacent to one triangle. What is its area?

A. 375 cm²
B. 450 cm²
C. 83.03 cm²
D. 600 cm²

Modified

15 cm

20 cm   10 cm

Area of a rectangle: $A = l \times w$

Area of a triangle: $A = \dfrac{b \times h}{2}$

3 What is the area of the figure?

A. 375 cm²

B. 450 cm²

C. 600 cm²

Source: Beddow, P. A., Kettler, R. J., & Elliott, S. N. (2008). TAMI: Test Accessibility and Modification Inventory. Nashville, TN: Vanderbilt University. Used by permission of the authors.

Peter Beddow, Ryan Kettler, and Stephen Elliott from Vanderbilt University designed the *Accessibility and Modification Inventory* (TAMI), which can be accessed at http://peabody.vanderbilt.edu/Documents/pdf/LSI/TAMI.pdf. This site outlines how existing tests and test items can be improved in reference to increased accessibility, appropriate level of content, relevance, and difficulty. If we are assessing students, shouldn't the outcomes reflect fairness for all students to display their optimum competencies? These developers are aware that items such as readability, use of idioms, bold letters, distracting versus pertinent visuals, essential versus nonessential information, amount of choices, layout, ample white space, usage of margins, font size, and more mitigating factors determine adolescents' levels of performance.

To close this unit about assessments, how about a quiz? Review the following 21 questions and decide whether the statements are true of false, and keep in mind there are no *TFs*—those are the *trues* that look like *falses* and the *falses* that look like *trues*. Place your answers in these boxes.

T or F	1.	2.	3.	4.	5.	6.	7.	8.	9.	10.
11.	12.	13.	14.	15.	16.	17.	18.	19.	20.	21.

Assessment Quiz

1. Realistic and relevant performance tasks help adolescents to value learning.

2. Past failures and newer achievements should be weighed equally.

3. Ongoing assessments only serve to create increased adolescent anxieties.

4. Assessments support instruction.

5. Practice and rehearsal of sample questions create critical thinkers.

6. Standards often confuse students.

7. Teacher comments on tests are unnecessary.

8. Classroom discussions stimulate higher-order thinking skills.

9. A thought-provoking question can lead to more understandings rather than a quantity of questions.

10. Exit cards (with learning tasks to complete as students leave class) are unfair assessments.

11. Results on standardized tests are indicative of students' understandings.

12. Tests sometimes reveal disabilities, not knowledge gained.

13. UbD means U (you) better do it!

14. Sharing a test's format with students hinders their growth.

15. Digital portfolios can be employed across content areas.

16. Scaffolding skews the validity of grades.

17. Summative assessments are the best learning indicators.

18. Extra-credit assignments are valuable ways to boost students' grades.

19. Reflections are more necessary for students than teachers.

20. Adolescent successes and failures indicate the level of educators' competencies.

21. Adolescents with disabilities who are instructed in inclusive classrooms are sometimes unfairly assessed.

So would you like immediate feedback? Look at the answer key and grade your paper for a numerical score. Write the number of questions correct over the total number of 21 questions to figure out your grade. That's the same way I offer grades to my students, in all subjects, to strengthen their skills in converting fractions into percentages across all subject areas, by connecting math to other disciplines.

Answer Key to Adolescent Quiz

Now you can stop here and walk away with just a numerical grade, or you can review the more detailed explanations that follow to gain additional insights about assessments. Offering adolescent learners similar feedback helps them to value the learning, rather than exclusively the amount of points scored as a grade. Many adolescents and their families place that grade upon a throne, rather than acknowledging the learning. Yes, grades are overrated, and at times, learning is simply *underscored!* Inclusive classrooms should loudly and clearly delineate the message that *there's more to school than just achieving grades!*

T or F	1. T	2. F	3. F	4. T	5. F	6. T	7. F	8. T	9. T	10. F
11. F	12. T	13. F	14. F	15. T	16. F	17. F	18. F	19. F	20. F	21. T

Detailed Explanations of Quiz Answers

1. Realistic and relevant performance tasks help adolescents to value learning.

   Explanation: True. Learning that relates to adolescent lives sparks the sensory register to attend, thereby increasing motivation.

2. Past failures and newer achievements should be weighed equally.

   Explanation: False. When students with learning difficulties first learn concepts, they frequently experience a level of discomfort, combined with confusions that interfere with their processing of unfamiliar concepts that are not within their prior knowledge. If students demonstrate improvements within the same unit, weighing progress will send a strong message that student effort is recognized and given more credence than past failures.

3. Ongoing assessments only serve to create increased adolescent anxieties.

   Explanation: False. Formative feedback stops misconceptions from spiraling and allows student reflections and instructional feedback, which permits teachers to adjust and tailor lessons to better address students' levels before the larger unit test.

4. Assessments support instruction.

   Explanation: True. Teachers can change instructional gears when they review students' achievements and errors through a valid assessment lens.

5. Practice and rehearsal of sample questions creates critical thinkers.

   Explanation: False. Concentrating exclusively on practice and rehearsal promotes regurgitation of facts and strict memorization of answers, and it devalues critical thinking skills.

6. Standards often confuse students.

   Explanation: True. The wording of the standards is written by professionals for professionals, not the students. Quite often, these standards need to be reworded into language and vocabulary that link them to learners in inclusive classrooms.

7. Teacher comments on tests are unnecessary.

   Explanation: False. Although offering comments is often a time-consuming task for teachers overwhelmed by paperwork, it is time well spent and serves to promote critical thinkers—for examples, explanations given for this assessment quiz!

8. Classroom discussions stimulate higher-order thinking skills.

   Explanation: True. Adolescents attend to their peers and value their thoughts. Students with learning issues sometimes require step-by-step explanations, but they are also entitled to presentations that nurture and develop their higher-order thinking skills by participating in stimulating classroom discussions.

9. A thought-provoking question can lead to more understandings rather than a quantity of questions.

   Explanation: True. Sometimes less is better when the quality of the question is evidenced, specifically not spoon-feeding the learning to adolescents, but leading them to self-discoveries. For example, rather than saying, "Open your textbooks to pages 55 and complete problems 1 through 12 on equivalent fractions," how about asking a question such as, "Can you identify more than one fraction between 1/3 and 1/4?"

10. Exit cards are unfair assessments.

    Explanation: False. Exit cards can reveal student focus and circumvent weak learning foundations. As students leave the classroom, teachers require them to complete a learning task, for example, list three things they learned during the period, or respond to a specific question such as "Explain cell respiration." This benefits students with attention difficulties and processing disorders by helping them to be more accountable and to increase their metacognition. Exit cards would be unfair assessments if they were the only kind of assessments used, without valuing multiple representations.

11. Results on standardized tests are indicative of students' understandings.

    Explanation: False. Standardized tests do not always reflect students' understandings, nor are they indicative of future school successes. These tests are sometimes just a snapshot of a student on a given day. Student performances are influenced by nonacademic factors as well, for example, anxiety, motivation. In addition, if students do well on standardized tests, they might just be good test takers or trained to respond to rehearsed questions that are mimicked on the test without actually achieving deeper levels of understanding.

12. Tests sometimes reveal disabilities, not knowledge gained.

    Explanation: True. Inclusion classrooms that have students with dyslexia, language disorders, visual and hearing differences, and alternate prior knowledge and cultural experiences are sometimes *disabled* by the test's format and expectations.

13. UbD means U (you) better do it!

    Explanation: Of course not. UbD means understanding by design, and sharing with students just what knowledge and concepts they are responsible for knowing on upcoming assessments at the initial phase of instruction. It avoids surprises and often organizes a disorganized student with ADHD or a student with Asperger syndrome who requires this informative type of structure. UbD helps all students by outlining the learning expectations at the onset, and it assists teachers to preplan their instruction with specific learning outcomes in mind. It keeps successes as the primary objective.

14. Sharing a test's format with students hinders their growth.

    Explanation: False. Sharing the format alleviates student fears and anxieties and values student preparation.

15. Digital portfolios can be employed across content areas.

    Explanation: True. Dated digital portfolios document advancements with evidence in all curriculum areas, for example, math explanations, literature journals, lab reports, student-scanned quiz and test corrections, history projects, videotaped debates, and more. Adolescents value technology as a medium for both instructional deliveries and assessments.

16. Scaffolding skews the validity of grades.

    Explanation: False. As noted by cognitive researcher Vygotsky (1978), instruction in the zone of proximal development (ZPD) avoids learning frustrations for both educators and adolescents.

17. Summative assessments are the best learning indicators.

    Explanation: False. Formative assessments are more revealing about the stages of the student learning process. Informal and even ungraded quizzes along with observation are reflective pedagogical tools that educators in inclusive classrooms often use to gauge, fine-tune, or redirect instruction.

18. Extra-credit assignments are valuable ways to boost students' grades.

    Explanation: False. Extra-credit points given frequently do not indicate understandings. It is not always just about the grade. If students do poorly on a test and then they self-correct or retest, this serves as a more valuable indicator of their unit knowledge.

19. Reflections are more necessary for students than teachers.

    Explanation: False. Reflection is a two-way, three-way, and sometimes multiway highway that all players need to travel down!

20. Adolescent successes and failures indicate the level of educators' competencies.

    Explanation: Of course not! Educators cannot be held responsible for a student's lack of achievements if the makeup of the inclusive class has students with varying prior knowledge, motivation, familial support, and more. Educators can reflect upon their instructional delivery and try to give more detailed step-by-step explanations, appeal to student diversities with multiple intelligences, use cooperative learning, add more technology, and make use of visual-auditory/kinesthetic-tactile learning opportunities, but test results are certainly not sole indicators of teachers' competencies.

21. Adolescents with disabilities who are instructed in inclusive classrooms are sometimes unfairly assessed.

    Explanation: Yes, this is true! That's the bottom line!

Check out these sites for additional information about rubrics and assessment options:

Student Project Assessment—http://eduscapes.com/tap/topic53.htm

New York Performance Standards Consortium—http://performanceassessment.org

Exemplars Rubrics—www.exemplars.com/resources/rubrics/index.html

RubiStar—http://rubistar.4teachers.org/index.php

Additional assessment insights with formative, summative, and kinder tests and evaluations are offered in Chapters 7 and 8.

INCLUSION MENTORING FOR PEERS, EDUCATORS, AND FAMILIES

Inclusive mentors are analogous to the following occupations:

Stock Analyst: Just as an analyst recommends which stocks to buy or sell, an *inclusive analyst* focuses students on which courses to take and how to invest their time to better learn and retain concepts. With the economy as it is, it's not always an easy task!

Camp Counselor: Just as a camp counselor arranges a meaningful social experience for all campers, *inclusive counselors* ensure that adolescents understand the hidden curriculum, display appropriate age-level behavior, and establish productive relationships with peers in inclusive settings.

Tour guides help travelers to plan their trips and navigate unfamiliar terrains, while *inclusive tour guides* assist staff and students with lesson plan deliveries and understandings as they navigate unfamiliar environments and courses.

Tutors assist students with subjects ranging from music to Spanish to calculus.

Trainers in gyms develop workout programs and challenge their clients to stretch, tone, and strengthen. *Inclusive trainers* stretch minds, tone strategic practices, and strengthen learning by exercising both bodies and minds!

Coaches are people who encourage and train athletes to perform their best through regimented practices, discipline, and teamwork. *Inclusive coaches* also value structure, discipline, and collaboration with staff, administration, peers, and families.

Gurus, acting as conduits, offer spiritual insights to their followers and lead them toward increased self-realizations and more proficiency. *Inclusive gurus* are also conduits, guiding adolescents toward more self-realization and proficiencies as self-regulated learners.

Pilots are the ones who lead passengers and cargo through sometimes turbulent weather to predetermined destinations, while *inclusive pilots* guide students to preplanned learning destinations in diverse inclusive climates.

Teachers are the ultimate professionals who can be found in any setting, but those in inclusive classrooms specifically educate students to academically and socially shine!

Extensive research was conducted in Australia and New Zealand with peer mentor programs, tracking over 2,000 adolescent learners. This research (see www.yess.co.nz/PeerMentor.html) supports many positive effects on school communities as a result of programs that value teamwork, friendships, trust, self-awareness, making decisions, effectively using resources, and more through the use of Youth Empowerment Seminars (YES!).

Caring adults, families, and peers are strong catalysts who create, foster, and promote positive academic and social experiences for adolescents in inclusive environments. Most crucial, though, is the training involved to complete this task. Just the way a pilot would not fly a plane without having put in the proper flight time hours, or one cannot teach a lesson without first outlining the proper motivation, procedure, and assessment, mentors need training as well. These mentoring programs can range from helping students with autism model appropriate body language and more social reciprocity to teaching a student with dyslexia to sharpen his or her reading skills, or assisting a student with hearing impairments or dysgraphia to effectively take notes. Some of the mentoring skills include the following:

Knowing the adolescent, including his or her present levels and strengths, for example, academic, behavioral, social, emotional, perceptual, sensory, communication

Defining and describing desired objectives and outcomes

Determining if there is a better match with the adolescent, whether it is a family member, peer, or other staff member, to avoid *oil and water relationships*

Detailing and outlining specific skills and subskills required to best deliver the content across subjects

Setting up a realistic time frame with specific dates listed to accomplish the goals

Ongoing communication of progress with a third objective party to determine intermittent progress of the mentoring program and additional guidance needed, rather than waiting until too much time has passed

Reflecting on results achieved for mentors and inclusive adolescents

Deciding to revise, continue, or abandon mentoring program

The following mentoring chart is designed as an aid to graphically expand and relate the above points to specific adolescents. Space is offered for additional thoughts and continuous reflections.

Effective Mentoring Components to Cooperatively Review With Adolescents
Present levels and strengths outlined
Desired objectives and outcomes
How to match personalities, needs, and strengths between mentors and adolescents
Specific skills and subskills required
Time schedule planned
Progress check and monitoring
Reflections given by all
Revisions necessitated
Other thoughts

Peer collaboration is a valuable tool for students. It can include classwide peer tutoring and cooperative learning configurations. Peer tutoring assigns mentors or involves the whole class with divisions into halves, thirds, or quadrants to assist each other to process, understand, apply, review, and retain curriculum concepts. Adolescents with disabilities are often hesitant to share responses or display behavior that indicates misunderstandings in larger groups, but dividing a class into smaller, more manageable, less threatening groups often alleviates and diminishes these adolescent hesitations. Peers are important to adolescents with and without disabilities. The bonds formed in collaborative groups foster a team mentality that has the goal of all its members in mind. Teachers are then free to facilitate and guide these groups as necessary. Research indicates there are many benefits of implementing such programs (DuPaul & Henningson, 1993; Greenwood, Terry, Utley, Montagna, & Walker, 1993).

Many times, families also need psychological and academic guidance to effectively mentor their adolescents. When educators offer ways to connect the academics to home environments, then this type of collaboration fosters more growth for all parties. Connections can be accomplished through face-to-face conferences, phone calls, e-mails, and teacher or district Web sites that offer specific educational strategies, resources, and parenting tools to continually validate the school learning in home environments. Community connections are vital ones that need to be capitalized upon. Quite often, it is not that families are unwilling to offer their assistance; rather, they are just not sure what the appropriate mentoring components are, for example, how to begin, continue, and connect with their adolescents. Educators can help train families to be their collaborative inclusive partners who reinforce the school's objectives.

Mentoring programs also help newer teachers entering the special education field who are sometimes overwhelmed by administrative, bureaucratic, instructional, curricular, and family demands. Weekly scheduled meetings proactively prevent situations from escalating, with kind ears and watchful eyes easing transitions. Teachers help other teachers gain many skills through continual mentoring and an exchange of ideas. Newer teachers gain skills from more experienced ones, while veteran teachers are exposed to fresh and innovative, creative enthusiasm offered by younger professionals.

In general, school and home support groups, whether they are composed of teachers, peers, or families, who offer additional emotional guidance or academic tutoring, yield powerful social and academic dividends. Trained mentors offer encouragement, compassion, strategies, and discipline to adolescents. Teachers in inclusive environments can wisely capitalize upon all types of these positive collaborations.

7

Classroom Dynamics That Enhance Learning and Retention

This chapter concentrates on valuable and applicable ways to build competencies, way beyond skill and drill. The emphasis is on flexible lessons that increase student absorption of concepts, acknowledging both the curriculum and diverse students' needs. In addition, the chapter examines multiple curriculum representations that take adolescents into interdisciplinary lessons and thematic units that value literacy, numeration, social studies, science, technology, poetry, music, art, and manipulatives with ongoing, energizing middle school and high school lesson activities.

Many students view the achievement of good grades as the most important thing about their school experience. Yes, a good grade is often indicative of successful mastery of the content. But do students remember or apply the knowledge beyond the test? Inclusive classrooms consist of students with varying learning needs, who observe and emulate their peers. The fact that adolescents are in inclusive classrooms motivates them to attend to learning, putting more value on both instruction and assessments. Adolescents also have the need to fit in and not be looked upon by their peers as different or inadequate. This means that many adolescents, when placed within inclusive environments rather than self-contained settings, put forth more effort to be academically on par with their peers. Another important point is that inclusive classrooms offer increased curriculum exposure. Prior separate special education classrooms often did not mirror the breadth of knowledge given in the general education curriculum.

Even when students are taught replacement instruction in separate environments such as the resource center, one way to include them with the same course of study is to require that they learn the concepts from the same text that their peers in the general education classroom use. Adapt the scope and sequence to match their prior knowledge, but use the text as their reference tool. When students complete classroom and homework assignments from the same textbook their peers use, that in itself raises their confidence level, since they do not view their assignments as inferior or *babyish*. Quite often, reading levels will differ, but in this age of technology, comparable supplemental literature selections and resources can be offered with the added support of books on tape, videos, and appropriate guided instruction to increase decoding skills, vocabulary development, and comprehension. Additional manipulatives with alternate and more concrete presentations can accompany the lessons and text concepts, but the desired goal is to expose the students to the same breadth of knowledge so as to ultimately allow those who are prepared with the academic skills and competencies to return to the inclusive classroom. I love when students in replacement subjects transition to an inclusive classroom. In my opinion, every student belongs in that *regular* classroom if the proper supports are proactively in place to help him or her succeed.

Adolescents in inclusive classrooms often need assistance to process information. This may involve helping them attend to, recognize, and transform presented learning stimuli into understandable representations that they can relate to better. Meaningful learning basically occurs when organized material is joined together with prior stored knowledge. The following list offers some adolescent classroom dynamics for teachers in inclusive classrooms to incorporate on a daily basis.

VALUABLE AND APPLICABLE THINGS TO DO THAT BUILD COMPETENCIES

1. Establish prior knowledge and metacognition, by activating the desire to learn as mature adults.

2. Preplan lessons with structured objectives and elements of backward design, by thinking ahead with instruction to parallel desired outcomes that will be measured in valid assessments.

3. Give merit to creative adolescent expressions with authentic curriculum links.

4. Proceed from the simple to the complex by using discrete task analysis, with dissections and then adolescent connections.

5. Use a step-by-step approach, with much practice and repetition for only those students who need it, while offering enrichment and advancements to others.

6. Reinforce abstract concepts with concrete examples, for example, identify the area of classroom geometric shapes, survey and graph peer responses, relate forces of motion to daily activities, compare and contrast protagonists to people you know.

7. Think about possible accommodations and modifications that might be needed, for example, a digital recorder for notes, graphic organizers, advance planners, and outlines to proactively apply UDL principles.

8. Incorporate sensory/technological elements—visual, auditory, kinesthetic, and tactile—to process information, allow for individual differences, and honor varying learning styles; for example, use multimedia presentations.

9. Teach to strengths to help students compensate for weaknesses, for example, by creating world history plays, or by demonstrating plate tectonics to show the Earth's movements.

10. Concentrate on the strengths of individual adolescents, not their syndromes or labels; for example, always use *people-first* language.

11. Challenge students to reach their maximum potential and highest cognitive level.

12. Provide opportunities for success to build self-esteem and self-efficacy, by offering realistic feedback that accentuates the positives before negatives.

13. Understand that learning is influenced by how adolescents feel about themselves and how they think others view them at this critical age.

14. Encourage more peer collaboration with smaller, heterogeneously designed cooperative learning groups working together to achieve goals and to increase time on task.

15. Have modeling of concepts and appropriate behavior with both teachers and peer mentors; then continually direct peers to help each other and make compromises, thereby decreasing adolescent egocentrism.

16. Vary types of instruction and assessment, for example, multiple intelligences and constructivist approaches for meaningful learning and thinking skills.

17. Relate learning to adolescents' lives using interest inventories to honor and match important emotional, social, behavioral, physical, and cognitive differences, for example, literacy choices, environmental issues, interest-generated articles.

18. Remember the basics such as teaching students about nutrition, exercise, hygiene, persistence to stay focused to master tasks, social skills, respecting others, effective listening, reading directions on a worksheet, and employable work ethics.

19. Establish a pleasant classroom environment with active discussions that promote multiple points of view.

20. Encourage students to ask questions as critical thinkers, and to become stakeholders in their learning.

21. Increase students' self-awareness to create self-regulated learners who are ready to explore productive postsecondary options.

22. Communicate, interact, and collaborate as a team with families, students, colleagues, and administration while smiling: it's contagious!

Source: Adapted from Karten, T. (2005). *Inclusion strategies that work!* Thousand Oaks, CA: Corwin Press.

KILL THE "SKILL AND DRILL": DEVELOPING HIGHER-ORDER THINKING SKILLS ACROSS THE CURRICULUM WITH PROBLEM-BASED LEARNING

Special education in inclusive classrooms involves differentiation, acceleration, accommodation, and modification to increase comprehension and competencies. Yes, students must gain information, but adolescents will not accomplish this if the learning activities do not encourage higher-order thinking skills with more metacognition that promotes better learning, retention, and relevant application. Rehearsal alone, without a variety of thinking skills, devalues critical and independent learners. Basically, aren't all students capable of exhibiting exceptionalities? Creativity, curiosity, and problem-solving skills are applicable for all learners in inclusive classrooms, whether adolescents are considered to be gifted, to have learning disabilities, or to be twice exceptional. Some students who are twice exceptional may be highly imaginative, have an excellent vocabulary, and be good problem solvers, but may possess weaker organizational skills or have difficulties with social interactions. Overall, the development and refinement of thinking skills benefits the whole child, which gives merit to the cognitive, physical, perceptual, behavioral, and social strengths of learners of all abilities.

Critical thinking skills instruction should thus not be limited to those with the highest academic skills, but must be developed and nurtured in all learners. Instruction involves solving problems through careful analysis and rearrangement of stored knowledge with newly gained facts. When this process is introduced in inclusive classrooms, educators need to start at baseline levels that allow students to gradually increase the complexity of their thought processes. When adolescents accomplish problem solving in cooperative groups, then the added element of collaboration with peers combines cognitive thought with social components to achieve further academic success. Students in inclusive classrooms thrive in environments that promote elevating concrete learning to more abstract levels through guided scaffolding and relevant learning tasks. Rather than drudging through textbooks with page-by-page guided instruction, motivating activities with alternate texts and references—for example, online, primary ones—are used as sources for information to solve problems. Adolescents gain many strides when they construct their own learning experiences under a teacher's auspices and facilitation.

Web sites offer many ideas for adolescents to explore topics such as natural resources, biology, geography, Braille, exploring for Arctic oil, solving quadratic equations, or forecasting an earthquake. Interactive instruction is then capitalized upon when students share their findings in smaller group discussions to practice critical thinking skills. In addition, keep in mind Benjamin Bloom's verbs asking students to actively demonstrate their understandings. Bloom and his followers, for example, Forehand (2005), offer ways to expand students' critical thinking skills, with educators addressing their planning, instructional delivery, and assessment choices in cognitive, psychomotor, and affective taxonomies.

The next two tables sum up some of these cognitive concepts.

Benefits of a Problem-Solving Approach				
student responsibility	constructivism	independence	acquisitions	self-direction
descriptions	connections	motivation	prioritization	collaboration
application	challenges	decisions	creativity	applicability
solutions	exploration	demonstrations	elaborations	revisions
involvement	interactions	understandings	informative	resolutions

Blooming Verbs					
remembering	understanding	applying	analyzing	evaluating	creating

Source: http://projects.coe.uga.edu/epltt/index.php?title=Bloom%27s_Taxonomy.

The following outlines more about Bloom's Taxonomy and suggests classroom curriculum applications for developing better critical thinking skills through active problem solving and cooperative approaches. Students choose a topic or issue to be discussed, and if possible resolved, following delineated steps. Students in cooperative groups are allowed a given period (days or weeks) to plan together to complete this long-term, teacher-approved project. Intermittent review and guidance given by the teacher ensures understandings, eliminates off-task behavior, and monitors progress toward the desired outcomes. Students meet, plan, collaborate, and complete requirements in class, in the library, online, and through other home communications and school meetings. The following outline and sample topics are just a few that establish societal adolescent relevancy through a problem-based learning (PBL) approach.

Exploring Problems

Possible Topics/Problems to Explore

Why is the Dead Sea shrinking, and how can scientists address this problem?

Many people argue that in this increased age of terrorism, many civil rights are sacrificed, how can the United States government address this issue?

With decreased amount of farmland replaced by housing developments and shopping malls, many animals such as deer and bear are misplaced, with their environments shrinking. How can we help to create a better balance for their ecosystem?

A large department store is being built in a rural town. Quite a few local businesses are protesting, claiming that local jobs and town proprietors will suffer harsh economic losses. What should be done?

Remembering:

1. Identify and describe your topic or problem.

2. List materials and resources.

3. Define vocabulary.

Understanding:

1. What are you doing to find out more?

2. List and summarize the steps:

   First . . .

   Next . . .

   Later . . .

   After . . .

   Finally . . .

Applying:

1. Connect to the information.

2. Record, classify, and calculate research:

   What is known?

   What must be discovered?

3. Classify the information.

Analyzing:

1. Think about the implications of your solution.

2. Break it up and explain it more.

3. What are your conclusions?

Evaluating:

1. Were you satisfied with the solution to the presented problem?

2. What did you learn?

3. Criticize or defend your solution.

Creating:

1. Produce a picture, graph, model, chart, diagram, poem, song, dance, news article, or PowerPoint presentation about the problem.

2. List some predictions about what would happen if you changed any of the variables.

3. Generate an idea for related topic/concept.

4. Reorganize the data, research, or procedures to obtain different or similar solutions, results, or patterns.

Source: Adapted from Karten, T. (2008). *Embracing disabilities in the classroom: Strategies to maximize students' assets*. Thousand Oaks, CA: Corwin Press.

Using curriculum-related Web sites, texts, newspapers, online sites, student-generated topics, and more, students identify multiple perspectives on issues in problem-solving lessons that incorporate constructivist approaches. When adolescents in inclusive classrooms are given more unconventional approaches to comprehend abstract concepts, then attention, retention, and student engagement is increased, as evidenced by teacher observation of increased time on task.

Explore these Web sites to discover more about problem-based learning:

http://www.pbli.org/pbl/pbl.htm

http://www.udel.edu/pbl/problems

http://www.mcli.dist.maricopa.edu/pbl/info.html

RULERS, RUBBER BANDS, AND SPONGES

Although structured inclusive environments offer frameworks for the deliverance of curriculum, flexibility is a necessary ingredient to help students absorb concepts. Hence, you need rulers for classroom structure, rubber bands to expand and to be flexible teachers, and sponges for students to soak up the knowledge. Therefore, although rulers may measure the progress students attain, inclusive teachers also need to have flexible minds, like the elasticity evidenced in rubber bands, to allow students to demonstrate their knowledge with multiple curriculum opportunities. That's why educators need a *mental supply* of *rubber bands, rulers,* and *sponges*. The plethora of strategies is then disseminated to help students achieve objectives in multiple ways. Review the following questions and apply them to a curriculum area, offering students opportunities for appropriate structure, flexibility, and absorption.

LITERACY, NUMERATION, AND MUCH MORE

By the time students become adolescents, it is expected that they have achieved a certain level of proficiency in reading, writing, and mathematics. Without these prerequisite skills, adolescents face a tenuous path toward mastery of the curriculum. Literacy and numeration skills are connected to many learning skills across the curriculum, and of course are directly related to postsecondary decisions and opportunities. A report from the National Assessment of Educational Progress (NAEP) in 2005 showed a decrease in the proficiency level of reading scores for 12th graders in the years indicated below.

Reading Proficiency Levels	1992	2005
Twelfth graders	80% proficiency	73% proficiency

Ways to Apply Structure, Flexibility, and Absorption to Inclusive Classrooms		
Rulers	**Rubber Bands**	**Sponges**
How will the learning be structured, measured, assessed, reported, e.g., formative, summative, portfolios, progress, efforts, achievements, conferencing, self-monitoring?	What accommodations and modifications will be offered, e.g., extra time, pacing, more praise, seating preferences, behavioral plans, breaks, extra help, anchor activities, revisitation opportunities?	How will students absorb the learning, e.g., cooperative groups, discussion, technology, peer mentors, multiple intelligences, VA/KT* opportunities?
Some curriculum thoughts:		
Rulers	**Rubber Bands**	**Sponges**

*VA/KT = Visual-Auditory/Kinesthetic-Tactile

The U.S. Congress is addressing the fact that middle school and high school students need to improve their literacy skills with the Striving Readers Act. Many colleges and employers are also noting that students entering either postsecondary education or the workforce have inadequate literacy skills involving both reading and writing. Globally, the United States has decreased its share of college-educated students from 30 percent to 14 percent in the past few decades (National Council of Teachers of English [NCTE], 2007). This leads to the fact that students need better direction in secondary schools on how to critically read and write more proficiently. These alarming statistics cross genders, disabilities, and cultural backgrounds.

Students with disabilities are faced with increased conundrums, directly related to weaker literacy and numeration skills that impact mastery of the curriculum. For example, it is more difficult for a student with dyslexia to tackle a list of Spanish words when he or she is reading English two to three grade levels below proficiency. A student with dyscalculia who still has difficulty telling time or opening his or her locker may very likely be frustrated when asked to find the distance, midpoint, or slope of line segments when given two points. Interpreting results from science laboratory experiments would be a harder task for a student with attention or processing difficulties when his or her reading and math levels are lower than those of the student's peers. If a student with Asperger syndrome does not fully understand the nuances of figurative language and idioms, then interpreting reading passages, completing writing assignments, conducting research reports, or translating verbal or symbolic information into algebraic expressions may be assignments that are asking that student to operate at a frustration level, rather than an independent or instructional one.

Sample Lesson Plan Template

Topic: _____

Lesson Concept: _____

Objective: _____

Desired Goals: Social/Academic/Emotional/Behavioral/Social/Physical/Cognitive:

_____

Baseline Knowledge: _____

Motivating Activity: _____

Visual/Auditory/Kinesthetic-tactile_____

Sensory Elements: _____

Critical/Creative Thinking Skills: _____

Interpersonal Activity/Cooperative Roles: _____

Curriculum Connections: _____

Possible accommodations: _____

Parallel activity: _____

Anticipated Roles of:

General Educator_____

Special Educator_____

Instructional Assistant_____

Student_____

Peers/Family/Specialists/Related Services/Administration:

_____

Adult/Peer/ Self Assessments: _____

_____

Closure: _____

Revisitation dates: _____

Source: Adapted from: Katen, T. (2004). Inclusion strategies that work! Research-based methods for the classroom. Thousand Oaks, CA: Corwin Press

Research shows the following:

★ The learning of content can be improved with informal writing (Boscolo & Mason, 2001).
★ Teachers are not tapping students' prior literacy skills, and unless direct teacher effort includes and draws out those skills, they will not be evidenced in the classroom (Moje, 2002).
★ If students are not acknowledged as having constructive literacy, they are less apt to respond to school-based literacy (Lenters, 2006).
★ Clearly visible reading and writing approaches have social and intellectual dimensions (Moje et al., 2004).
★ Adolescents need *enjoyable texts,* not always teacher-selected ones (Moje, 2007).
★ Classroom environments that provide student choices and real-life connections build student confidence and increase student engagement, using mistakes as opportunities for growth (Kamil et al., 2008).

★ There's a relationship between student motivation and engagement when teacher support, respect, and the promotion of interactions are increased (Ryan, 2001).

★ "Teachers need to cultivate greater self-awareness of the ways they select texts, establish expectations for classroom discourse, and pose questions to students surrounding texts as a way to jockey for authority" (Lesley, 2008, p. 184).

★ Critical literacy manipulates texts as sparks of discussion and conversation between teachers and students to explore multiple meanings to either reject or accept (Bean & Moni, 2003).

★ Classroom communities need to encourage students to make contributions to the text and to be part of the story (Moje, 2000; Santa, 2006).

★ Adequate processing speed enables learners to perform basic tasks such as word reading or math computation without conscious effort, thereby allowing the learner to focus . . . attention on the more complex tasks of comprehending text or solving math problems. (Benner et al., 2008).

★ Students require fluent word recognition to achieve deeper comprehensions and command of basic facts to focus on more difficult problem solving and complex algorithms (Fry & Hale, 1996).

★ Academic processing speed involves visual processing, working memory, long-term memory, and executive functioning that is required to produce accurate responses to reading, mathematical, and written language stimuli (Berninger & Richards, 2002; Woodcock, McGrew, & Mather, 2001).

★ It is important for educational services to investigate both the reading and arithmetic skills of children referred for learning disabilities (Dirks, Spyer, Lieshout, & Sonneville, 2008).

★ Many students receiving special education services are not receiving enough science instruction to be considered in line with national standards documents (Melber, 2004).

★ Educators should examine students' error patterns and mathematical misconceptions in graphic representations (Scheuermann & Van Garderen, 2008).

Even though adolescents are in higher grades, do not assume that they possess the prerequisite rudimentary rungs of the academic ladders to succeed in middle schools and high schools. For those who do not, it does not necessarily mean that they were never taught these concepts; lower skills in various reading and numeration areas can also be indicative of poor motivation; weaker long-term or short-term memory; attention and processing issues; and many other cognitive, emotional, social, behavioral, sensory, physical, and environmental factors. If students were sight-word readers, then they need to be aware of linguistics, knowing and categorizing different syllable types. Math concepts and computations also need to be strengthened through direct and explicit instruction to close numeration gaps.

Teachers can informally outline which students require additional interventions in these areas and then solicit support from school personnel such as building-level and outside administration, colleagues, and team members. Proactively addressing these very issues increases students' comprehension of curriculum concepts, which in turn influences academic performances on both informal and formal assessments. The ultimate goal is to reverse students' lower self-concepts resulting from lower academic skills and performances.

In addition, teachers need to review and analyze student errors across curriculum areas from sample works, informal and formal testing, and observations. Brain-based research advocates that when educators are aware of students' strengths and keep individual profiles, it helps students to learn. Some students may perform at a slower pace, or possess attention issues, sequencing and spatial deficits, poor memory, language issues, or social or higher-order cognition deficits (Levine & Barringer, 2008). Prepared educators who expect these traits to be evidenced pro-actively include accommodations that are designed to increase attention, retention, cognition, communication and perception skills in their lessons.

Curriculum-based measurement (CBM) can address some of the issues outlined by brain research. CBM was designed to assess and build academic processing speed with automaticity in academic tasks involved with reading, writing, spelling, and mathematics (Deno, Fuchs, Marston, & Shinn, 2001). Sometimes, going back to basics is not a step backward, but yields many steps forward. This Web Site offers resources, programs, and trainings for assistance in mathematics and literacy: www.interventioncentral.org/htmdocs/interventions/cbmwarehouse.php.

The intention of the table on page 159 is to begin the process of improving students' literacy and numeration abilities by rating student needs based upon multiple sources such as informal classroom assessments, observations, quizzes, tests, essays, reports, oral and written performances, homework completion, and other assignments. This portfolio snapshot-like rating is then shared with other personnel to more formally diagnose issues and offer specific classroom interventions.

Students in inclusive classrooms require opportunities to experience successes so as to master grade-level standards and objectives, based on their current levels, needs, and IEP goals. The next table (see pages 160 through 164) offers some ways to dissect the curriculum into its components, examining goals, study skills, vocabulary, motivation, classroom activities, and assessment options to address varying literacy and numeration levels. If teachers in inclusive classrooms proactively consider learners' needs and varying levels during unit planning, then frustrations are diminished for students, teachers, and families, while conversely, more achievements are evidenced.

Refer to page 199 for reading programs, publishers, and online sites that offer appropriately leveled literature materials to help older readers with phonetic skills, fluency and comprehension across the disciplines.

POETRY, MUSIC, AND ART FOR ADOLESCENT EYES, EARS, MINDS, AND SOULS

As delineated in prior chapters, many adolescents with and without disabilities in inclusive classrooms face internal and external crises that often do not have *simple, next-day solutions*. Poetry, music, and art offer solace as healthy outlets for adolescents to shine. They can help students to do the following:

Work through identity confusions

Relate better with peers and adults

Increase motivation and attention

(Text Continued on page 165)

Students	Word Decoding/Encoding/Syllables	Reading Comprehension	Reading Fluency	Written Expression	Verbal Reasoning/Receptive Language	Basic Math Facts	Number/Algebra Sense	Problem-Solving Skills

Rate students' abilities with the codes below; then solicit help from learning consultants, colleagues, supervisors, administrators, basic skills instructors, and independent research on in-class strategies and recommended programs to implement. Be certain that these issues are also addressed in students' IEPs, or make revisions as necessary. If extra support is needed, the IEP needs to reflect that, too.

Codes

AA—Above Average

SO—Skills Okay

RN—Remediation Needed

Course: English

General Goals: Students will improve literacy interpretations of textual, factual, functional, and recreational passages.

★ **Unit Objectives:** Students highlight the main idea, draw conclusions, determine cause and effect, distinguish fact from fiction, outline literacy elements, identify supporting details, decide sequence of events, and create personal literacy connections.

Time Frame	These literacy goals are ongoing ones that will be continually reinforced throughout the year with a variety of genres ranging from biographies to nonfiction, poetry, fiction, and fantasy.
Lesson Content **Accommodations** **Modifications** **Support**	Students orally, silently, and cooperatively read assigned text passages, short stories, essays, newspaper articles, informational writings, written directions, periodicals, and poems to reach above literacy goals and objectives. Students with dyslexia, dysgraphia, and other reading/writing issues are distributed photocopied passages to take notes or highlight key terms to decrease written requirements and visually emphasize concepts, e.g., underlining or highlighting the main idea, numbering or sequencing details, content-related visuals. Readings will be available on tape, with students using headphones. Teacher will have a supply of passages at varying reading levels to allow students to demonstrate their competencies with the skills and not be unfairly graded due to reading at frustration levels, e.g., www.studyisland.com. Teachers and support staff circulate about to assist with comprehensions. Ongoing anchor activities are available to students who accurately complete work more quickly, e.g., classroom newspaper, cooperative poetry project.
Strategy Lessons	Direct group and independent instruction to illustrate examples of figurative language and analogies. Logic lessons and cause-effect examples are modeled with think-pair-share cooperative assignments before independent readings.
Vocabulary	fiction, nonfiction, context clues, cause, effect, deductive reasoning, logic, sequence, propaganda, conclusions, opinion, main idea, supporting details, arguments, analogies, syllabication, prediction, chronological, symbolism, generalization, transitions, setting, plot, conflict, climax, resolution
Motivation	Comprehension skills will be related to adolescents' lives: ★ Connections to other subjects, e.g., comparing comprehension skills to art such as step-by-step drawings to extract details ★ Menus from local restaurants ★ Circulars from favorite businesses or stores ★ Interest-generated articles, passages, interviews, advertisements, e.g., sports figures, cooking, skateboarding, video games, history, music ★ High-interest but age-appropriate reading selections ★ Group discussion on life application of reading skills in careers and daily living requirements
Activities	As appropriate, students will work in cooperative groups to think-pair-share collaboratively as duos and through whole-class discussion, computer assignments, individual monitoring, conferencing, and constant student reflections of progress, e.g., graphing dated scores on comprehension with metacognitive snapshots, reviewing feedback, sharing progress.
Assessment Options	Rather than answering assigned comprehension questions, some students will be allowed to fill in a graphic organizer, e.g., one that highlights the characters, plot, setting, climax, resolution. Students will be graded upon improvements in comprehension skills rather than norm-referenced achievements.

Organizer to Fill in Story Elements	
Characters **Protagonist** **Antagonist** **Major characters** **Minor** **Characters**	
Setting **Where & when**	
Plot **Sequencing of details in order**	
Climax **(exciting part)**	
Resolution **(ending)**	
Themes	
My opinion/ Personal connections	

Course: Environmental Sciences **General Goals:** To increase understandings of the effects of human impact on our environment **Unit Objectives:** Students will investigate and share insights on environmental practices and laws in reference to air and water quality, other natural resources, and global climate.	
Time Frame	Unit will be completed within a 3-week time period.
Lesson Content Accommodations Modifications Support	Focus on the four Rs of rethink, reduce, reuse, and recycle, with students working in cooperative groups to conduct online research to reveal tangible examples for each *R*. Mini lessons and packets of background information will be distributed with reference to economics, agriculture, fossil fuels, ecology, interactions of atmosphere and oceans, global warming, and current and impending National Environmental Policy Act (NEPA) legislation (www.epa.gov). Visual science dictionaries will be used and access to additional Web sites made available to further explain and reinforce terms and concepts. Students with more intellectual needs will concentrate on the interactions of living organisms just within their immediate community, or only one *R*. Peer mentors will be assigned to circulate and assist cooperative groups to capitalize on each other's strengths and interests. Support will be given to students with visual and auditory needs to better absorb concepts with additional graphics, magnification pages, larger print, preferred seating, and removal of extraneous distractions. Additional scaffolding will be used as required through teacher observation, review of written and oral responses, student and family requests, and conferencing.
Strategy Lessons	Study skill organization on completing long-range assignments with intermittent check and reinforcement of student progress. Using www.inspiration.com, students will be given an advance organizer detailing the unit of study, review of terminology before the lesson with some of the words broken down into syllables, and teaching of structural analysis with prefixes and suffixes.
Vocabulary	ecology, physical, chemical, biology, resources, climate change, contamination, pollution, atmosphere, global warning, carbon dioxide, extinction, deforestation, fossil fuels, emissions, ecosystems, biodiversity, depletion, conservation, consequences
Motivation	★ The class will review the site www.myfootprint.org and take the environmental quiz together, using collective input to explore the human factors affecting the environment.
Activities	Assignments build upon multiple intelligences as cooperative groups gather together to compile a class list under the categories of rethink, reduce, reuse, and recycle. Students will share findings through songs, dances, chart, graphs, speeches, visual time lines, collages, poems, crossword puzzles, www.puzzlemaker.com, concept maps, outlines, A–Z lists, and student-created WebQuests.
Assessment Options	Students receive separate grades based upon completed activities: a. Social: working collaboratively as part of their cooperative group b. Academic: completing multiple choice, fill-ins, and open-ended responses on a written test, read orally to some c. Classroom projects based upon model rubrics distributed: www.rubrics4teachers.com, www.teach-nology.com/web_tools/rubrics

Course: Algebra

General Goals: Learning about how symbols represent numbers, with increased knowledge of variables, constants, expressions, and how to solve equations

Unit Objectives: Students will do the following:

- ★ Translate words into algebraic equations
- ★ Combine like and unlike terms
- ★ Solve equations with the operations of addition, subtraction, multiplication, and division using whole numbers, fractions, and decimals
- ★ Demonstrate knowledge of signed numbers, both positive and negative

Time Frame	Three-week unit plan divided into 15 weekly 45-minute classes. Will continue review of concepts with daily do-now activities throughout the year
Lesson Content **Accommodations** **Modifications** **Support**	Lessons will guide, model, and instruct students on how to solve equations and inequalities, apply the order of operations, add and subtract polynomials, and multiply and divide polynomials. Each student will define vocabulary words with concrete visual examples. Through observation and informal assessment, some students experiencing difficulties will be given additional instruction by peer mentors and support teachers. Students operating at or above grade level, who quickly master the content, will be given additional instruction to factor polynomials and to solve quadratic equations. Weekly communication sheet will be given to students and sent home to families to increase reflections.
Strategy Lessons	Coteachers and instructional assistants will monitor note taking to be certain that notes are well-organized, sequential, and legible. Students will be asked to intermittently paraphrase understandings of lessons. Some students will require reinforcement of skills involving fractions and decimals without algebraic concepts present before they proceed further. Students with more cognitive needs such as those with Down syndrome will sort algebra tiles and connect Unifix cubes to create a concrete number line as a parallel activity.
Vocabulary	variables, binomials, polynomials, equation, inequality, like and unlike terms, expression, coefficient, order of operations, positive and negative signed numbers
Motivation	Algebra will be related to students' lives with the following connections: ★ Comparing temperature below and above zero ★ Using football games where athletes gain and lose yards ★ Making interest-related teen connections, e.g., inserting Hannah Montana or Ryan Sheckler as characters into algebraic word problems
Activities	After 15 minutes of guided instruction, heterogeneous cooperative groups are asked to solve word problems to demonstrate their understandings of given algebra goals and objectives. Teachers and support staff circulate to assist as needed. Students are given entrance and exit cards with sample problems to obtain snapshots of understandings.
Assessment Options	Double-sided math journals with personal reflections and sample questions are completed and graded to increase student self-reflections on progress and to gauge lesson pacing. Informal quizzes are given with prompt feedback and comments. Summative unit test is compared to informal quizzes to gauge and factor in improvements. Class participation and effort are monitored.

Course: Global Awareness

General Goals: Increasing students' knowledge of what it means to be a global citizen

Unit Objectives: Students research and share understandings of the problems that many of the citizens in these locations face: Americas, Africa, EU, Middle East, Indian subcontinent, Asia, Oceania, China.

Time Frame	Unit will be an interdisciplinary one, reinforced with activities in each marking period with social studies, English, mathematics, world languages, and science connections.
Lesson Content **Accommodations** **Modifications** **Support**	Students are divided into cooperative groups to jigsaw assignments a–e as per interests; then assessment choices will be given from the options below. Some students with more learning needs will have abstract concepts explained with additional concrete examples to expand prior knowledge, e.g., geography skills, understanding vocabulary words with personal connections. Students with visual needs and kinesthetic learners will use relief maps. Some students with attention issues will be allowed to listen to Web sites with headphones. Students with varying writing and reading levels will be given options to dictate letters to peer scribes. Lessons will capitalize upon students' strengths and interests.
Strategy Lessons	Writing templates, outlines, and rubrics will be offered to students for essays and letters. Guided instruction will be given for world geography, map skills, and how to create charts. Glossary of vocabulary terms will be created and shared before assigned readings.
Vocabulary	citizen, local, national, global, fair trade, discrimination, ethnicity, poverty, child labor, gender equality, sanitation, exclusion, inclusion, nutrition, immunization, health care, conflict, vulnerability, government, politics, corruption, social action
Motivation	The following statistic is the catalyst for class discussion: *More than 1 billion children in the world suffer from one or more extreme forms of deprivation in adequate nutrition, safe drinking water, sanitation facilities, health care services, shelter, education, and information.* *Source:* UNICEF. (2006). The state of the world's children. http://www.unicef.org/sowc.
Activities	a. Technology application: using the sites http://youth.unicefusa.org/ www.freethechildren.com, www.ymca.net/ international, www.nylc.org, www.oneworldyouthproject.org, students will read and view stories, pictures, and actions to help students around the world living in less fortunate situations and then list actions warranted to remedy these conditions. b. Journal writing activities will be included with entries from the perspectives of students in selected countries around the world. c. Map skills will be increased as students explore at least two countries on each of the continents that demand global action to improve existing conditions. d. Art, music, science, and mathematics skills will be investigated as students explore the present and past contributions of worldwide citizens. e. Students will paraphrase perspectives of invited speakers, e.g., politicians, families, community members.
Assessment Options	★ Students collect data to create graphs that compare and contrast conditions of citizens according to given criteria. ★ Through Internet research and contact with several world organizations, students create a pictorial world map with people and resources. ★ Persuasive essays are written to world leaders to improve existing practices in countries. ★ Assigned fiction and nonfiction books are critiqued through literature circles, panel discussions, debates, and skits.

Gain appropriate recognition

Address their interests and strengths

Cathartically affirm their sense of belonging

Improve literacy skills

Enhance academics

Connect to the curriculum

Enhance self-esteem

Develop discipline

Turn frowns into smiles

Whether these arts are created or appreciated, they represent personal avenues of imagination and creative expression, which often replace feelings of depression, loneliness, disconnection, and inferiority. Poems, songs, and other art forms allow adolescents to question beliefs through visual and auditory rhythms, by soothing their ears, eyes, minds, and souls. Students with attention issues can often focus more, while students with behavioral or social issues enjoy curriculum presentations that have the arts integrated. I've used the arts to help students pay attention to visual and auditory details, organize thoughts, remember facts, and assess knowledge, and to deliver and assess instruction. The arts are not superfluous parts of adolescents' days, but—when used appropriately—integral ways to tune teens into learning.

Poetry units range from assignments requiring students to write limericks, haikus, diamantes, and ballads to understanding iambic pentameter in one of Shakespeare's plays. Skills can be modeled by teachers, while more difficult passages are read together. Reading poetry is also a way to improve literacy skills by understanding simpler and often shorter literary pieces that contain symbolism, rather than trudging through longer reading passages or texts. When students write poetry, encoding and decoding skills are strengthened, for example, finding rhyming words or words with a defined number of syllables. One of my students frequently shared her poems with me, which she illustrated with abstract watercolors. Taking me into her confidence, she wanted to share a part of herself. Rather than feeling ignored, through poetry adolescents can feel validated with purposeful writing. Poems offer a way to release adolescent turmoil or may even create levity in curriculum areas. Poetry units can incorporate student-written poems or those by contemporary or period artists. Poems can be used as primary sources for increasing historical knowledge, for example, have them read "I Never Saw Another Butterfly," written by children in a concentration camp during World War II, as part of a Holocaust unit.

As shown with the next poem, "Being Me," writing poetry is a form of expression that releases inner abstract thoughts onto paper and transforms those abstractions into concrete thoughts for others to read, appreciate, identify with, and learn from.

Being Me

Being me

Being a teen

Betwixt and between

Watching, growing

Scared to show

What you don't know

Texting, dancing

Ready to expand

Handling each demand

Juggling, timing

Finding out each day

How to learn another way

Revealing, concealing

Hearing the inner voice

To make the right choice

Knowing, wishing

Can't you see

Just how tough it is

Being me?

—T. Karten

The following are poetry Web sites for additional insights:

Types of Poetry—www.types-of-poetry.org.uk. This site outlines an array of poetry and explains poetic terms to help students write their own poems, offering examples of many of the styles offered.

Poetry 180: A Poem a Day for American High Schools—www.loc.gov/poetry/180. This site encourages high school students to read a different inspirational poem each school day.

Showcases students' poems–http://teenpoetry.student.com/

Melting With Music

My son is no longer an adolescent, but when he was, he would often sit in front of the computer to listen to and watch music videos. Whenever I walked into the room, the site would of course be automatically minimized, and he would kindly verbalize something to the effect of "There might be some words that you might not want to hear, Mom." I appreciated his warning, and left the room. In retrospect, I probably should have listened more to the music and lyrics and offered my own interpretation—not that it was requested! Now, this same son also played the saxophone in his high school marching band and at concerts throughout middle school and high school. Although he was not equal to the caliber of a musician like Charlie Parker or John Coltrane, I think that playing an instrument enriched his life and school experience. It taught him discipline, the importance of adhering to a schedule, the reward of performing for others, collaboration, and more. His wise band leader never believed in musical competitions, but offered the students momentous occasions to perform at nursing homes, amusement parks, and even the United Nations.

In research studies (e.g., Rauscher, Shaw, & Ky, 1993), music has been linked to performing better in school and to increasing abstract and spatial reasoning. For a time, the *Mozart effect* was even the rage for many parents who played classical pieces for their infants, with hopes to improve their mental skills. The musical score from a movie accompanies a script and elicits a range of emotions from fear to calmness. Classrooms can also *score* with music that creates pleasant classroom climates and teaches content through lyrics. Billy Joel's song "We Didn't Start the Fire" has endless potential classroom connections, as do many other songs. I once witnessed a sixth-grade student with expressive language difficulties happily sing along while the science teacher played a Sponge Bob CD as background music while the class investigated invertebrates. Auditory learners and those students with stronger musical rhythmic intelligences appreciate these types of presentations.

The National Association for Music Education (MENC), at the Web site www.menc.org, offers many standards for music, including improvising melodies; performing on instruments; reading notations; and connecting music to history, culture, and other arts and disciplines. As adolescents search for their identity, music is often a path they choose to travel along. When related to the curriculum, music offers numerous lessons for adolescents. The Web site www.edu-cyberpg.com/Music/classres.html delineates ways for adolescents to enhance their emotions and understandings across the curriculum, from war songs to rap, folk, and hip-hop. Music can also be used to teach English as a second language as indicated by this site: www.songsforteaching.com/esleflesol.htm.

Carl Orff, a 20th-century composer and music education theorist from Munich, Germany, valued exploration, improvisation, and composition. He combined movement, music, and dance to get students to branch out. Middle schools and high schools still make use of Orff's theories today. Studying music notation, historical connections, theories, and cultural musical contexts is important from the early grades and up into adulthood. Bands, choirs, and orchestras perform for their peers, families, and communities at assemblies, plays, scheduled concerts, football games, and more with classical, jazz, and contemporary pieces. Whether adolescents study Billie Holiday, Bob Dylan, Miley Cyrus, Chris Brown, Rihanna, David Banner, Bow Wow, Kanye West, the Jonas Brothers, or Mozart, they are gaining additional skills across the curriculum and their lives.

Musical principles such as meter, rhythm, tonality, intervals, chords, and harmonic progressions are explored through the analysis of music in environments ranging from schools to garages. MP3 and CD players, along with many other multimedia tools, rhythmically enhance learning. Some adolescents experience stress at this time in their lives, which music often alleviates. Other students in inclusive classrooms whose least favorite intelligence may be verbal-linguistic and who may have lower reading or writing strengths are given opportunities to understand more curriculum concepts through a musical-rhythmic mode. Overall, music is an outlet that sometimes tells a story with a guitar, voice, or other instrument, to honor and connect with students' passions and strengths.

The following Web sites offer additional musical adolescent insights:

www.cornerstonemedia.org—Commentaries on the 12 worst teen-selected annual songs, *The Dirty Dozen*. Has clips to promote further discussion and musical reflections.

http://kidsmusic.about.com/od/kidsmusicforages1013/Kids_Music_for_Preteens_and_Teens_Ages_Eight_and_Older.htm—Children's music listed by genre and style. Also includes music reviews.

www.rocknlearn.com/html/ Site teaches multiplication using rap music, country music, and more.

http://www.teenmusic.com—Teen Music

Artful Connections

Many adolescents in inclusive classrooms artfully doodle along during lessons. These types of learners—myself included—enjoy pictorial representations of the abstract. That does not necessarily mean that doodlers are not listeners. Quite often, I will draw symbols to represent what is being said during lectures and speeches. Walking around inclusive classrooms, I've witnessed even the brightest of learners multitasking by doodling, beading, or crocheting. Art is basically a medium of expression that enhances students' curriculum understandings and also serves as a way to release emotions, extra energy, and stress.

Art therapy is a combination of art and counseling to help students and adults deal with traumatic experiences, resolve problems, increase self-awareness, and nonverbally express emotions. This involves using media such as watercolors, clay, charcoal, pen and ink, and more. Students in inclusive classrooms need not produce pieces of art to be displayed in museum cases or framed and placed in galleries— although that is a possibility, it is not a necessity. Art sometimes just lets students nonverbally express themselves.

A colleague of mine—an art teacher—was in a deep frenzy. He was assigned to teach art to students with autism. Committed to his discipline, eager to help the students, but in an absolute panic over what his lessons would look like, he was scrambling for ideas. He wanted his students to learn but felt ill prepared to address their learning needs. As we processed this together, I offered suggestions on taking smaller steps to dissect more complex lessons into their components and then teaching those subskills to students in the class. I also reminded him that students with autism need life skills connections with functional academics. Art was a way to accomplish that, such as with lessons that had students better recognize their names by tracing them and then functionally conversing and interacting with peers and adults to develop more language skills. When teaching about shadows, students could view real-life photographs of their community. Complementary colors could be investigated through traffic lights, road signs, and school signs by using manipulatives such as scented markers, coffee filters, brushes, and water. I also offered the art teacher some sources to investigate to increase his understandings about students with autism (www.autism-society.org, www.autismspeaks.org, www.autism.com/index.asp).

One school year, many students in class had perceptual issues, frequently reversing their *b*'s and *d*'s, rushing through assignments, and not attending to written details and directions. That year, my coteacher and I incorporated art options as anchor activities for these students as well as the rest of the class. Students replicated a small-scale picture with larger proportions on graph paper by concentrating on each box's specifications. Students chose their favorite picture, cartoon, or advertisement and then painstakingly graphed coordinates to reproduce a larger version. They gained insights on mathematical ratios and proportions and the value of concentration to details. Another time, students wrote a biography of an artist to improve literacy skills, and then reproduced that person's artwork through 2-dimensional pictures or 3-dimensional sculptures. No matter what dimension they chose, the learning obtained was *multidimensional!*

Art can be tactically raised to help students with many disabilities gain balanced access to the principles and beauty. Adolescents with visual impairments or blindness can *see* the art, too. A wonderful bound resource, *Art and the Alphabet: A Tactile Experience,* offered by the Metropolitan Museum of Art, has textured masterpieces for students with blindness and visual impairments to appreciate the reproductions. Museum audiotapes offer more explanations to students with visual and reading difficulties to absorb the written words by the showcase displays and exhibits. Students with physical disabilities and limited use of their hands have held paintbrushes and pencils in their mouths or toes to create work of incredible quality. Often, a click of a computer mouse or a differently held stylus can access and reproduce art as well. Art Beyond Sight: Yellow Pages, accessed at www.artbeyondsight .org/sidebar/yellowpages.shtml, also has many resources worth exploring. Inclusive classrooms can offer access to museum programs ranging from exhibits in Africa to those in the United States through virtual online experiences, such as those accessed at http://icom.museum/vlmp.

Art also increases insights across the curriculum for students who respond well when visuals accompany and explain more difficult vocabulary and concepts in physics, chemistry, history, literature, and other disciplines. Curricular art connections can range from interpreting political cartoons from World War I to exploring social issues by viewing Picasso's *Guernica* to understand more about the Spanish Civil War. Art offers students skills to understand not only realism, but the abstract, too.

Art can be use to enhance comprehension when adolescents

★ visualize geometric principles such as circumference.
★ illustrate sequences of events in stories, passages, and poems.
★ research architecture and artifacts in various civilizations, for example, Greek sculpture, Great Wall of China, Rosetta Stone.
★ understand more about inferential skills by interpreting political cartoons.
★ draw pictures and models of the atoms of elements in the periodic table with media such as markers, ping pong balls, golf balls, clay, or Styrofoam.
★ create graphs to demonstrate central tendency.
★ Illustrate vocabulary words from literature, science, social studies, or mathematics.
★ create hieroglyphics that mirror Egyptian writings.
★ reproduce picture writings of Native Americans.
★ investigate artistic works representing historical periods, for example, from the Stone Age to the Age of the Enlightenment, Civil War, Holocaust, and Civil Rights Movement.

The following Web sites and organizations *artfully* illustrate more:

National Institute of Art and Disabilities—www.niadart.org

A *New York Times* Learning Network Lesson Plan Unit—www.nytimes.com/ learning/teachers/lessons/visarts.html

The Getty Museum—www.getty.edu/artsednet

ArtsEdge—http://artsedge.kennedy-center.org/teach/standards/standards_58.cfm

NGA Classroom for Teachers and Students—www.nga.gov/education/classroom

Art in the 21st Century—www.pbs.org/art21/education/onlinelessonlibrary.html

Pictures for Learning—www.pics4learning.com

IDEAS FOR MULTIPLE CURRICULUM REPRESENTATIONS

Prepared teachers often know what curriculum standards to target during a lesson or unit, but are hesitant about just how to deliver those standards to an inclusive class of adolescents. How can the very same curriculum reach a class of very different students whose prior knowledge, cognitive, motivational, perceptual, sensory, physical, language, and interest levels vary across a wide spectrum? Here's where innovative teachers avail themselves of many different resources that appeal to the varied population of students being taught.

For example, suppose the class was beginning a unit on the American Civil War. Why couldn't teachers heterogeneously group students and jigsaw the concepts with multiple curriculum representations? First off, the teachers need to give everyone accurate background knowledge before the unit of study begins, explain just what a civil war is, and even connect it to present times, by describing countries that are in turmoil today within their own boundaries. The concepts delivered then need to be the same, whether the inclusive classroom is in Alabama, where the Confederate flag was born, or in Delaware, which was a Union state. *Experiencing the American Civil War*, by Hillstrom and Hillstrom, offers teachers a wide selection of curriculum opportunities to use. These representations include the investigation of novels, nonfiction books, short stories, poems, plays, movies, songs, and Web sites. Students collaboratively investigate a book like *Across Five Aprils* by Irene Hunt, the film *Glory*, or the song "The Night They Drove Old Dixie Down" by Robbie Robertson to share their findings and insights. Curriculum representations could include a battle reenactment of what happened at Gettysburg or the delivering of the peace treaty at Appomattox. Some students may write their own curriculum plays, songs, interactive letters, American Civil War Jeopardy review, or visual time lines, or may even moderate a debate among Grant, Lee, Davis, and Lincoln. The point is that the curriculum is the same, but the constructive, student-produced representations appeal to learners' diverse interests, intelligences, and learning levels.

A unit on World War I would necessitate talking about the world at the turn of the 20th century, locating countries on maps, comparing present-day countries to the ones that existed then (to avoid later confusions), and creating a time line of events before and after the war so that it is not viewed as an isolated event, but can be seen in a larger context. Many students with learning disabilities that I have instructed have difficulties understanding *the big picture*, by focusing too much on minor distracting details that interfere with their comprehension and application of concepts. That's why a unit such as World War I needs to be grounded in time, not taught as an isolated event. Student assignments can range from investigating propaganda posters to analyzing *A Farewell to Arms* by Ernest Hemmingway or paraphrasing Wilson's Fourteen Points. Collaborations would be those that give merit to adolescent strengths and support from students, teachers, families, communities, libraries, and more.

Curriculum representations that are well organized will proactively reach a diverse inclusive class of adolescents. Always allow adolescents to see how the curriculum connects to their lives. A simple columned chart as shown below has huge merit, whether the class is learning about 20th-century musicians, the history of mathematics, life sciences, or how economies operate.

Topic: _____ Names: _____ Date: _____		Connections:
Summary of what I/we read:	**Materials:** **Text pages** **Web sites** **URLs** **Other Sources**	**What this makes me/us think about in my life/our lives:**
		Performance project chosen: **(Choices: written, verbal, visual, kinesthetic-moving about, independent, cooperative, other teacher-okayed design)**

In addition, students need to synthesize how some topics, concepts, or vocabulary relate to one another so as to better self-gauge comprehensions and misconceptions. For example, just knowing definitions of isolated political curriculum words such as *autocracy, democracy, monarchy,* and *totalitarianism* helps students to match words with their meanings, but does not offer the critical thinking skills to make analogies between the words or to write essays comparing concepts. Unless the students fully understand that all of these words fall under the big umbrella that *opens up* to types of government, the concepts are lost.

Vocabulary and concepts need to be nourished in all *inclusive biomes,* whether they are coniferous or deciduous classrooms. We can help students see the differences of the many trees in the forest, literally and figuratively. Constructing a chart such as the following one, together with the class, teaches learners how to extract abstract main ideas from informational text and represent them in charts. The lesson on biomes is then accompanied by a strategic lesson on how to create study guides to develop more self-regulation and retention of the curriculum. This chart highlights major points and helps more concrete learners by removing extraneous text. It visually appeals to learners because the bigger ideas are delineated. Some students in the class investigate more comparative details about the two forests, such as learning about taiga or boreal forests, while others move on to investigate additional biomes. Afterward, the class gathers together as a whole with groups collaboratively presenting their findings to peers.

Tulips, roses, and sunflowers are all flowers, but in no way are the three of them identical. Pointing out subtle differences to learners helps them to gain more meaningful knowledge of the curriculum. For example, if you began the lesson with the words *thorns, seeds,* and *Holland,* then students would not just focus on the flowers, but the differences that the flowers possess in terms of their appearance and in what geographical areas they are found. The ability to classify according to attributes is a skill that can be expanded upon with infinite curriculum representations.

In addition, some students gain better understandings when words or concepts are not defined but instead shown as nonexamples. The curriculum example on the next page offers a *shapely one* accompanied by visuals to better understand that a square qualifies as a rhombus, but a rhombus cannot be categorized as a square.

Adolescents in inclusive classrooms gain further curriculum connections using representations such as Geometer's Sketchpad, yarn, graph paper, and 3-dimensional wooden shapes that give value to tactile and technological approaches. Explore multiple curriculum possibilities by filling in the next chart.

ENGAGEMENT: BRING BACK THE MANIPULATIVES!

Just what are bacteria? We cannot see bacteria with the naked eye, yet we must wash our hands to remove the harmful effects of bacteria. Even though they are a kind of germ, they can have good qualities, too, for example, bacteria that help make cheese, yogurt, and medicines. So how can students understand more about bacteria, otherwise known as *prokaryotes?*

How about using a manipulative, such as modeling clay, to represent bacteria? Students of course would omit a nucleus, creating a simple, single-celled replication of this organism. Maybe other students could create replications of antibiotics, while some students investigate bacteria's harmful effects using online and text studies of strep throat, tetanus, gangrene, diphtheria, anthrax, Lyme disease, and pneumonia. Some students could investigate the research of scientists such as Sir Alexander Fleming and Carl Woese.

Could adolescents understand more about scientific concepts such as bacteria, mitochondria, or electrons if these concepts were represented with clay models? Could manipulating pattern blocks, tangrams, or Geoboards help increase mathematical understandings? What about examining algae from marine environments or studying

Coniferous Forests	Deciduous forests
Type of biome	Type of biome
Evergreen trees, cone-bearing	Oaks, maples, beeches, shed leaves
Trees never lose leaves	Leaves fall off in fall and winter
Leaves always green	Leaves turn colors
Found in colder climates, more north	Usually found in more southern areas
Needles and thick sap hold onto moisture	Located in areas with more moisture

Unit: Geometry

Topic: Quadrilaterals

Objective: To compare characteristics of a square, rhombus, and parallelogram

Square	Rhombus	Parallelogram	To sum it all up:
quadrilateral	quadrilateral	quadrilateral	All three figures have four sides, which makes them all quadrilaterals. They are also all parallelograms since all three have opposite sides parallel. However, the square is the only shape that qualifies under all three categories, being a rhombus and a parallelogram.
opposite sides parallel with equal lengths for all sides	opposite sides parallel and all sides have equal lengths (equilateral parallelogram)	opposite sides parallel, but not necessarily equal	
four right angles	different types of angles	different types of angles	

Check Your Understanding

Directions: Read these statements and decide if they are true or false:

1. A square, rhombus, and parallelogram are all quadrilaterals. _____
2. A rhombus is also a square. _____
3. A square is a rhombus. _____
4. A rhombus is a parallelogram. _____
5. A parallelogram is a square. _____
6. A square is a parallelogram. _____
7. I like squares, rhombuses, and parallelograms. _____

Unit:			
Topic:			
Objective:			
			To sum it all up:

a replication of a human heart? What about using clear Jello or a Ziploc bags to recreate a cell's environment? Wouldn't celery be a good representation of a cell wall, and couldn't shaving cream be used for a cell membrane?

Using a variety of instructional materials helps students learn, whether the learners are in primary or older grades. Quite often when students reach middle school and high school classrooms, teachers abandon using as many manipulatives, yet that's when they are needed even more, to concretize the spiraling abstract concepts in courses that are often filled with intricate details and facts not solidified within an adolescent's prior knowledge. Enlisting a wide range of manipulatives motivates adolescents to attend to lessons and gives them kinesthetic-tactile opportunities to touch and be touched by the concepts. The standards are then introduced and concretized by curriculum-related manipulatives such as atlases, globes, raised relief maps, microscopes, jump ropes, calculators, photographs, algebra tiles, and more.

For example, a student with Down syndrome will not fully understand proper hygiene unless he or she physically brushes his or her teeth and hair. Would you ever deny a student with communication needs a form of augmentative communication such as pictures attached by Velcro to a felt board or technological supports? Reading a map is meaningless when it is strictly shown on a workbook page, unless it's reinforced and accompanied by a real map within an adolescent's world, for example, one of the school, local mall, or a concert venue. While reading a book with the class on the Holocaust that mentioned ration cards, I brought in an actual ration book, purchased at a flea market on Portobello Road in London. I did not have to ask students to imagine or visualize what the ration book looked like; they saw the separate pages with the stamps and different food groups and products. Hence, *brushing up on concepts* means sometimes actually allowing students to hold the brush! Manipulatives must also not be *rationed*, but just as maps take us to our predetermined destinations, so do classroom manipulatives. Think of ways to bring back the manipulatives across the curriculum!

Unit: _____ Concepts/Topics	Manipulatives	Learning Activities

SAMPLE ANCHOR ACTIVITIES AND ONGOING STATIONS

Classroom Scenario

Adolescent A: I'm finished with the assignment. What should I do now?

Adolescent B: I don't understand the assignment. Can you help me?

Adolescent C: How much time do I have for the assignment?

Adolescent D: Can I finish this at home?

Adolescent E: Not sure what to do next!

Adolescent F: He's being too loud. I can't concentrate.

Adolescent G: I left my book at home!

Adolescent H: I have to leave class early for chorus practice.

Adolescent I: I really don't like this subject!

Adolescent J: I really don't like you!

Adolescent K: I really don't like him!

Adolescent L: I really don't like myself!

Adolescent M: School is exciting!

Adolescent N: School is boring!

Adolescent O: When is the class period over?

Adolescent P: How will we be graded?

Adolescent Q: I love my cooperative group!

Adolescent R: I'm tired of being the only one who knows what she's doing!

Adolescent S: That kid is cool!

Adolescent T: That kid is weird!

Adolescent U: Glad I got a good night's sleep!

Adolescent V: My afterschool job is exhausting.

Adolescent W: I plan to ask my mom for help.

Adolescent X: I wish that I had someone at home who could help.

Adolescent Y: I can't wait to go to college!

Adolescent Z: Who cares about college?

These statements involve issues such as student apathy, self-esteem, prior knowledge, extracurricular activities, attention, motivation, home environments, outside pressures, and more. Rather than waiting for students to express some of the negative statements, why not proactively have ongoing assignments set up around the room that engage students in academics with increased positive social interactions and collaborative teamwork under your auspices? Yes, there is curriculum to *cover*, but more gains are *uncovered* when students motivationally *discover!* Learning stations and ongoing anchor activities are conduits for additional academic and social gains to occur. Every adolescent does not need to be doing the same thing at the same time on every given day in order for learning to take place. When the *all heads facing forward* approach is replaced with an *all heads digesting* approach, then students will even come back for more servings!

Anchor activities and stations initially involve more plans, preparation, collection of materials, and—most important—a teacher's release of the lesson to the students. Placing the lesson in students' hands allows them to digest the concepts in ways educators never dreamed possible. Digestion itself involves many processes, including the breakdown of food, which then yields more energy. Digestion begins in the mouth, moves onward to the stomach and small intestine, and then flows into the large intestine. Helpers include the enzymes and juices in the liver and pancreas, which add enzymes and juices to aid in this process.

Here's the inclusive connection: Activities and stations are bodily-kinesthetic ways for adolescents to channel excess energy to break down the concepts. Just as food moves along to different organs, students also move along to different stations. The enzymes and juices that assist students with the centers and stations are peers who can act as mentors, cooperating teachers, and collaborative grade-level teachers who value interdisciplinary approaches. Anchor activities and stations empower adolescents to think, pace, control, regulate, and tailor their learning. Teachers and support staff circulate about the classroom, acting as facilitators, ready to support, acknowledge, redirect, and praise as appropriate to help students *ingest* and *digest* their learning.

The table on page 178 offers some ideas for anchor activities and stations across and between disciplines to support adolescents with their *digestion* of concepts.

The centers you design should be based upon your curriculum areas. Customize these to the needs of students in your inclusive classrooms using the planner/outline (a–f) and listed Web sites to help you begin.

Station/Center Directions

Create your own curriculum-related stations or centers for adolescents to constructively explore many topics within and across disciplines. Choose one of the following titles, or design your own station/center.

Living the Math

Literature Teams

Technology Plans

Connecting With Bloom

Our Nation's History

Famous People

Interdisciplinary Lessons

Global Lives

Scientific Scenarios

_____

a. List topics and concepts that are cooperatively explored by students.

b. Write a specific measurable objective for students to achieve.

c. List the materials needed at that station.

d. What competencies would you be assessing in a rubric? Include cognitive, behavioral, communicative, and other appropriate ones.

e. Remember to tell how you will include the elements of cooperative learning:

P = positive interdependence

I = individual accountability

E = equal participation

S = simultaneous interaction

Anchor Activities/Materials	
Language Arts English Literacy Skills	Word walls; brain quests; analogies; personal stories; joke/anecdotal corners; classroom/school newspapers; online reviews; classroom libraries with short stories, graphic novels, and poem selections; reading & writing corners; available high-interest books at an assortment of reading levels
Geometry	Interactive flashcards, cooperative reviews, creation of geometric classroom collages on bulletin boards, tessellating shapes on the computer and free hand, math personification stories, 3-D shapes
Algebra	Thought-provoking questions, word problem cards, math journals, WebQuests, pattern corners, online practice, algebraic software
Calculus	Boxes of irregular cardboard shapes, tutorial Web sites, graph paper, measuring corners, student-created visual dictionaries with captions to define terms, e.g., differential, integral, slope
Discrete Math	Sudoku, puzzles, journal writing, dice, class surveys, vertex edge problems, assortment of activities to apply algorithms and deductions
American History	Creating and completing class crossword puzzles, word searches with vocabulary and concepts defined, published and student-created skits & plays, replications of primary sources, e.g., treaties, speeches, diaries, maps, debates
World Civilizations	Time lines, music and art investigations, vocabulary word webs, cooperative reviews, student-designed tests, historical maps and globes, student-created artifacts, online sites, student-created games, art corners, trading posts
Economics	Stock market games, circulars, local and school menus, coupon corners, monitoring a mock classroom store, newspapers, currency corner, activities involving global economies
Biology	Lab centers, creating diagrams, science journals, observation charts, plant and animal microscope slides, life connections
Chemistry	Higher-order questioning, reflective group discussions, science journals, lab investigations, biography corner on scientists, balancing chemical equations station, independent and cooperative research
Physics	The Rollercoaster Game, technology corner, e.g., ranging from cellophane to computers, then creating a classroom techno/invention scrapbook; PBL physics connections with topics of electromagnetism, acoustics, thermodynamics, and more
World Languages/ Cultures	Creating travel brochures, designing postcards, translating children's books and simple prose, picture books in different languages
Music/Dance	Listening to and creating curriculum-related lyrics, e.g., rap, country, hip-hop; choreographing movements for curriculum concepts, e.g., plate tectonics, photosynthesis, archaeology, tessellations
Art	Visuals, http://icom.museum/vlmp, curriculum classroom scrapbooks, scented markers, colored crayons, curriculum visuals
Physical Education/Health	Stretching activities, meditation, brain breaks, nutrition-related activities, food and exercise diaries, yoga, relaxation corner

Station and Center Planner
a. Title of Station/Center
b. Topics/Concepts
c. Measurable Objective
d. Materials
e. Competencies/Assessments
f. How I will include PIES

Center/Station Ideas for Adolescents in Inclusive Classrooms	Topics/Concepts Objectives	Individual Student Concerns/Classroom Management	Constructivist Approaches & UDL Designs

Stations/Centers for Inclusive Adolescent Classrooms	Web Sites for Professional Curriculum Supports, Lessons, and Strategies
Living the Math	www.nctm.org http://eduscapes.com/tap/tapmath.html www.mathforum.org/library www.allmath.com www.aplusmath.com www.agnesscott.edu/lriddle/women/women.htm www.math.hmc.edu/funfacts
Literature Teams	www.webenglishteacher.com/esl.html http://teacher2b.com www.onlinemet.com www.ncte.org www.reading.org www.novelguide.com www.wilsonlanguage.com www.ortonacademy.org www.rfbd.org www.poets.org
Technology Plans **Study Skills** **Lesson Plans**	www.4teachers.org www.mindtools.com/memory.html http://eduscapes.com/web/teacher.html www.lessonplans.com www.iteaconnect.org/Resources/tewebsites.htm www.teach-nology.com www.techlearning.com www.cast.org www.inspiration.com http://teachers.net/lessons
Connecting With Bloom	www.apa.org/ed/new_blooms.html http://projects.coe.uga.edu/epltt/index.php?title=Bloom%27s_Taxonomy
Interdisciplinary Connections	www.menc.org http://artsedge.kennedy-center.org/connect/ctc.cfm
National & Global Lives **Multicultural Education**	www.tolerance.org/teach/resources/index.jsp www.ncss.org http://historymatters.gmu.edu www.timeforkids.com www.economist.com www.pbs.org/wgbh/globalconnections www.nameorg.org www.tramline.com/cross/world
Scientific Scenarios	www.nsta.org www.teach-nology.com/teachers/subject_matter/science www.sciencenewsforkids.org www.thecatalyst.org www.aapt.org www.rsc.org/education/eic

Stations/Centers for Inclusive Adolescent Classrooms	Web Sites for Professional Curriculum Supports, Lessons, and Strategies
Scientific Scenarios	http://kids.niehs.nih.gov http://biology.about.com/od/biologylessonplans http://kids.earth.nasa.gov www.sciencedirect.com http://highschoolace.com/ace/science.cfm
Learning more about different ABILITIES	www.cec.sped.org www.nichcy.org www.adl.org www.whatworks.ed.gov www.behavioradvisor.com www.asperger.org www.ldinfo.com www.thearc.org

CURRICULUM GRAPHIC ORGANIZERS (CGOS)

Study guides and graphic organizers focus students on learning before and during the task (Bender, 2002). Advance organizers help both teachers and students to organize related concepts and provide a way to understand both similarities and subtle differences between topics. Using graphic organizers may be the accommodation some adolescents need to better understand intricate relationships among concepts, themes, vocabulary, and disciplines, thereby replacing confusions and frustrations with more concrete visual representations. Adolescents who are inundated with a slew of concepts often experience *curriculum overload*. Graphic organizers basically take the curriculum and *graphically organize* it; hence, the name! The following starred list highlights that CGOs do the following:

★ Establish prior knowledge
★ Extract main concepts
★ Classify and organize facts
★ Identify relationships
★ Visually please learners
★ Delete the unessential
★ Assist with note taking
★ Increase thinking skills
★ Summarize understandings
★ Act as study guides
★ Give merit to reflections

One of my students really owned her graphic organizers. Now let me explain this statement further. I routinely distributed a two-page study guide in this visual format with questions written in the boxes on one page and the answers written on the corresponding boxes on the next page. This helps students to focus on pertinent curriculum questions and also allows many pages of notes to be placed on just two pages, which helps the disorganized student not to be overwhelmed by an abundance of information, or frustrated by his or her illegible notes. One student creatively redid these study guides in her own format with flip charts, columns with matching vocabulary, and her own visuals. The first time she did that, she sheepishly asked, "Is this okay, Mrs. Karten?" My response was, "No, it's not okay; it's great!" My guide had guided her to be her own guide!

Before I distribute study guides to students, which may very well be a listed accommodation requirement in their IEP, I consult with my collaborating teacher, and together, we decide which other students would benefit from such a tool. If I had my druthers, the whole class would receive the guide. Some years they do, some years we construct the study guides together, and some years certain students only receive the question sheet with a blank answer guide or indicated text pages and sources where the answers can be located. The following tables depict a world history study guide to learn more about ancient Egypt, with the first table containing the questions and the second with the corresponding answers.

Ancient Egypt Study Guide

Vocabulary: a king of ancient Egypt	Vocabulary: triangular-shaped deposits at the mouth of a river	Vocabulary: ruling family	Vocabulary: reed that grows by the marshes of the Nile, from which paper is made
Vocabulary: soil carried and mixed with water	Vocabulary: Egyptian spirit of each individual	Vocabulary: Egyptian burial places	Vocabulary: Ancient Egyptian form of writing
What type of math was started by the Egyptians?	Describe the Sahara's climate.	What did Egyptian farmers build to control floods?	Who was part of the Egyptian ruling class?
Why was the Rosetta Stone discovery important?	How did studying the stars help Egyptians?	What did the archaeologist Carter discover?	Describe what the ruler Menes accomplished.
What is the kingdom of Kush called today?	What did Egyptian farmers give their rulers?	Why did Egyptians preserve their dead bodies?	What sea does the Nile River flow into?

Answers

pharaoh	delta	dynasty	papyrus
silt	Ka	pyramids	hieroglyphics
geometry	hot and dry	dams	priests
It explained Egyptian writing.	It helped Egyptians develop the calendar.	Tutankhamen's tomb	He united Upper and Lower Egypt
Sudan and Ethiopia	They gave them crops to pay for the land.	It was for happiness in the afterlife.	Mediterranean Sea

The preceding vignette points out the value of graphic organizers as a tool to create more self-regulated learners with increased metacognition and ownership of the study guides, as well as how they learn. Nobody expects a house to be built with haphazard architectural plans, shoddy building materials, or inept workers. The schoolhouse requires the same care, patience, and delivery. Many graphic organizers have been included throughout this book; the next comparative one on page 184 visually highlights some differences and similarities between autism and Asperger syndrome, two conditions that are often confused and lumped into one category. Inclusion strategies are offered in one column of the graphic organizer to better address the needs of students with autism and Asperger syndrome to help students succeed in middle school and secondary inclusive environments.

Students with learning, behavioral, attention, and developmental variances are not ready to become independent learners without the proper scaffolding to help them organize, generalize, and personalize the curriculum concepts to achieve increased academic successes. Good teaching strategies help students become more self-regulated in general education classrooms to not only keep pace with the information presented, but also to absorb and retain the concepts. Graphic organizers offer help before, during, and after lessons. When they act as advanced organizers, students are able to preview the concepts and see just how the *big ideas* fit into general categories as the lessons progress. Study guides minimize rather than magnify differences, improve organization, and increase student engagement with the curriculum. Boyle and Yeager (1997) confirm that study guides can be used as a review prior to the presentation of new information, during a lesson to maintain student engagement, or after a lesson as notes. Schloss, Smith, and Schloss (2001) talk about the merits of content enhancement that helps students to be more actively involved in order to better comprehend relationships between abstract concepts and to distinguish what information is important versus unimportant.

Examples of additional CGOs follow.

	Understanding Autism and Asperger syndrome	
Remember that each child is different; these are some characteristics of autism and Asperger syndrome that may be evidenced, but they will be specific to individual students and displayed in varying amounts. Also, remember there is a one-letter difference between *autistic* and *artistic* and no one has a monopoly on the best or only way to view the world.		
Abilities & Strategies	**Autism**	**Asperger syndrome**
Social Areas	Social impairments affect how students with autism relate to and are accepted by others; students with autism respond to guided and structured social scenarios to improve eye contact and facial expressions. Students with high-functioning autism are not always interested in social relationships; students with autism with more cognitive needs are at times unaware of specific social rules and do not actively seek enjoyment or interactions with others. Students benefit from step-by-step ways to increase peer relationships and to improve emotional and social reciprocity	Students with Asperger syndrome have social impairments, e.g., poor eye contact, difficulty maintaining friends, inappropriate facial affect, cannot always understand other students' and adults' perspectives, and usually want to fit in with peers, but students are sometimes uncertain of the rules and ways to make friends, how to engage in conversation, and just what comments are appropriate ones. Practical applications of social rules across various settings and rooms help students develop more social strengths and acumen in natural settings.
Inclusion Strategies: Students respond to organization and structure; establish and reinforce routines, announce changes ahead of time, structure free time. If a paraprofessional is shadowing the student, let it be inconspicuous. Directly teach and model social skills, be aware of bullying and the internalization of negative feelings or possible depression, try to help the student develop a higher realistic self-image, and use intrinsic and extrinsic rewards. Explain the reasons for social rules and acceptable behavior with role models, social stories, behavioral plans, and reinforcement with praise for appropriate social interactions or eye contact; increase guided emotional and social reciprocity with peers and adults.		
Routines & Interests	These students prefer rigid routines and respond best to step-by-step explanations with discrete task analysis. Schedule changes can be a source of discomfort. Students may be unaware of or disinterested in other people's schedules, likes, or dislikes.	Transitions need to be explained to students with Asperger syndrome. Students are often preoccupied with own thoughts, have lower coping skills, frustrate easily. Students love to talk about own interests and subjects that they are well versed in; they display good interest in and curiosity about the environment.
Inclusion Strategies: Replace perseverations with other activities; be consistent in routines, yet explain changes; give advance notice of schedule variations when known; teach calendar skills, and how to keep personal agendas; guide student to achieve more self-regulation; offer visual and written posted schedules with photos that show the student following a schedule if more cognitive needs require the abstract to be concretized; acknowledge interests, but gradually add other focuses, to wean students off rigid or inflexible routines; help students branch out to obtain broader interests and add diverse yet age-appropriate experiences to their own personal choices.		

Abilities & Strategies	Autism	Asperger syndrome
Communications and Language Skills	Language delays evidenced before age 3 with words and phrases; verbal and nonverbal communications not always expressed or understood; augmentative communication is sometimes needed, e.g., pictures with Velcro, communication boards to replace lack of spoken language; receptive language is often better than expressive language; some echolalia may be evidenced. Those with higher language skills may need more instruction and prompting to engage in conversations.	Students exhibit communication difficulties, e.g., trouble with semantic pragmatic language, understanding nonverbal cues; body language, gestures, conversation skills are weaker; idioms and sarcasm are difficult to understand; developmental language delays usually not evidenced with normal language, with words spoken by age 2 and phrases by age 3.

Inclusion Strategies: Directly teach language skills, e.g., have students listen and respond to others in structured, rehearsed, or scripted conversations; value cooperative learning, peer interactions, buddies, social stories, role-playing, facial recognition programs, and comic strip stories with bubble dialogue as ways to improve communication and language skills; provide appropriate language phrases to students with guided, face-to-face practice or taped sessions; value metacognition of appropriate communication skills to create more self-regulated communicators; establish verbal behavior programs to help students verbalize or express needs with guided instruction.

Cognitive/ Academic Skills	Academic skills and cognitive thought will vary, but those that relate to functional life skills will be most valuable for students with autism who have more intellectual needs; students with high-functioning autism (HFA) may have average to above average IQs.	Students typically have average to above-average IQs, but understandings of inferential thoughts and more abstract concepts at times need additional remediation and explanations. Good self-help skills are usually evidenced with curiosity about the environment and a desire to achieve academic acumen within inclusive environments.

Inclusion Strategies: Capitalize upon students' stronger visual intelligences by offering more graphics, photos, advance organizers, outlines, and curriculum clip art to illustrate vocabulary and concepts; intermittently ask the student to paraphrase his or her understandings; offer concrete and semi-abstract presentations to reinforce unfamiliar concepts; move ahead with the curriculum, but review prior learning to reinforce and maintain academic skills; break up the learning into its components to offer partial mastery of skills and steps, rather than requiring 100 percent proficiency.

Abilities & Strategies	Autism	Asperger syndrome
Fine/Gross Motor & Sensory Skills	Students with autism typically have affinity for tactile stimulation, visual, and concrete experiences; movements may be awkward with weak gross motor and fine motor skills, e.g., gait, sports, handwriting.	Students may display fine/gross motor delays with more handwriting needs; some difficulties with sports activities in physical education classes; may be drawn to kinesthetic-tactile modes of presentations, e.g., math manipulatives, models, moving about to learn concepts.

(Continued)

(Continued)

Abilities & Strategies	Autism	Asperger syndrome
Inclusion Strategies: Allow the student to replace laborious written responses with verbal ones; increase technology, e.g., word prediction programs, keyboarding skills; assign peer assistant or mentor to help with note taking or act as a scribe; give student copies of your outlines; e-mail or post assignments on teacher Web sites; offer writing templates; lessen written requirements; educate instructional assistants, physical education, music, and art teachers about students' strengths, likes, dislikes, and preferred modalities.		
Organizational Skills	May be highly sensitive to too much stimulation, e.g., unstructured environment with noise, such as the school lunchroom, fire drills; prefers organization and routine	May concentrate on minor details rather than overall organization; difficult for student to organize and retrieve materials for short- and long-range assignments and reports
Inclusion Strategies: Offer quieter rooms and acceptable places to learn or cool down in calmer environments; teach adolescents how to monitor their reactions and notice improvements; reinforce appropriate behavior; color code loose-leaf folders and materials needed for AM vs. PM classes; teach calendar skills and ways to organize backpacks, homework, and short- and long-term assignments using sectioned notebooks, accordion files, and subject-separated spirals; give mini lessons on main idea vs. supportive or extraneous details.		

Clouds		
Main Idea	**Details**	**You**
Clouds are made from condensed water or ice and are formed from rising moist air. Vocabulary word: condensation—when a gas changes to a liquid	When humid, moist air rises, it condenses and then the droplets form clouds. 3 kinds of clouds: a. cirrus—feathery (streaky looking), rain or snow may be coming, highest in the sky b. cumulus—puffy heap, usually fair weather, may become a thunderhead c. stratus—layers, rain clouds, fog, lowest in the sky Steps in cloud formation: 1. Water evaporates when sunlight hits ocean surface. 2. Warm, moist layers of air are formed. 3. Humid air rises. 4. Water vapor condenses and forms clouds.	Have you ever looked up in the sky and predicted the weather that will follow? Describe a foggy day. Have you ever been caught in a thunderstorm? How does the weather in a movie or TV show set a mood? What does the expression *everything seems cloudy* mean?

Sequencing chart: How to subtract a fraction from a whole number

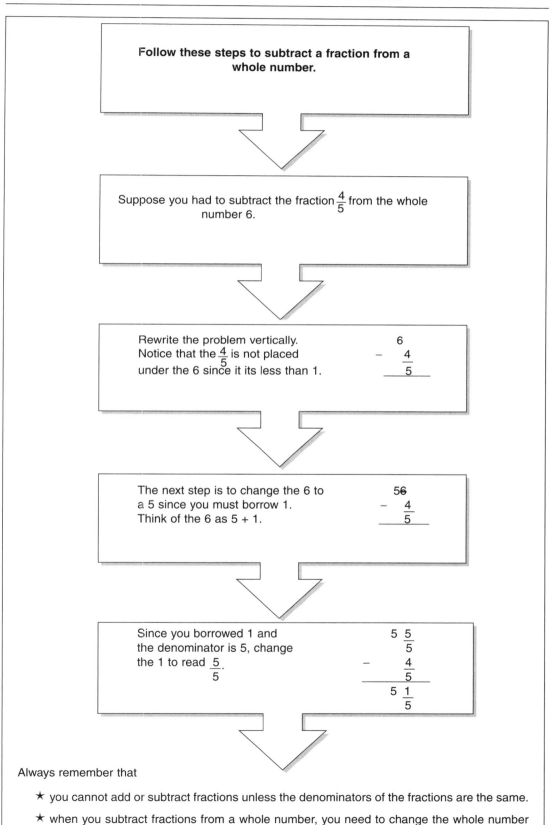

Follow these steps to subtract a fraction from a whole number.

Suppose you had to subtract the fraction $\frac{4}{5}$ from the whole number 6.

Rewrite the problem vertically. Notice that the $\frac{4}{5}$ is not placed under the 6 since it its less than 1.

$$6 - \frac{4}{5}$$

The next step is to change the 6 to a 5 since you must borrow 1. Think of the 6 as 5 + 1.

$$5\cancel{6} - \frac{4}{5}$$

Since you borrowed 1 and the denominator is 5, change the 1 to read $\frac{5}{5}$.

$$5\frac{5}{5} - \frac{4}{5} = 5\frac{1}{5}$$

Always remember that

★ you cannot add or subtract fractions unless the denominators of the fractions are the same.

★ when you subtract fractions from a whole number, you need to change the whole number to a fraction.

"To Be or Not to Be . . ."
A Storyboard About *Hamlet* by William Shakespeare

Setting

Where: Elsinore Castle in Denmark
When: Dark winter night
Written in late 16th century

Main Characters

Protagonists:

- ★ King Hamlet
  (deceased—ghost/spirit)
- ★ Prince Hamlet (King Hamlet's
  son and Claudius's nephew)

Antagonists:

- ★ King Claudius(King Hamlet's
  brother, Prince Hamlet's uncle)
- ★ Polonius (lord who is
  Claudius's advisor)
- ★ Laertes (Polonius's son)

Other Characters:

- ★ Queen Gertrude (was
  married to King Hamlet, then
  married Claudius)
- ★ Ophelia (Polonius's daughter
  and Laertes' sister)
- ★ Rosencrantz (Hamlet's friend)
- ★ Guildenstern (Hamlet's friend)
- ★ Ostrick (courtier)
- ★ Horatio (scholar—Hamlet's
  best and most loyal friend)
- ★ Fortinbras (Norwegian prince)

Plot: Hamlet avenges the death of his father whom he believes was killed by his uncle, Claudius.

Climax: Interaction between Hamlet and Claudius in Act III

Resolution: Tragedy for the royal family

Themes:

  a. ambition
  b. greed
  c. sin
  d. corruption
  e. madness
  f. loyalty

Questions for Discussion:

1. What role does the supernatural have in this play?
2. How did the setting affect the events?
3. Paraphrase the meaning of "To Be or Not to Be."

Connections to Today:

1. Can you compare Claudius or Hamlet to any famous political people today?
2. Was Hamlet a teenager in conflict? If so, explain.

Cooperative Group Assignments to Jigsaw:

1. Recreate the Shakespearean set.
2. Write a modern-day soliloquy from Hamlet to his mom.
3. If Hamlet were in a band, describe or play his music.
4. Write a letter to one of the characters.

Conceptual Organization

Directions: Concept maps such as these outline and connect facts, which gives the learner a chance to view and study information at a quick glance.

Although different abilities have many overlaps and may be visually represented in a variety of configurations, this is one offering that attempts to visually display connections and relationships among the many abilities that are evidenced in inclusive classrooms. Additional layers can most certainly be added to expand the outer divisions here even further.

Organizational Chart About Chemical Elements

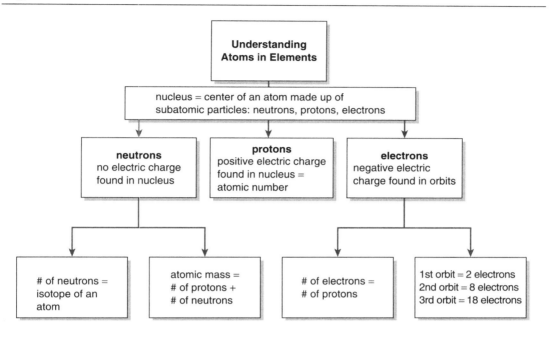

Concept Map About Vertebrates

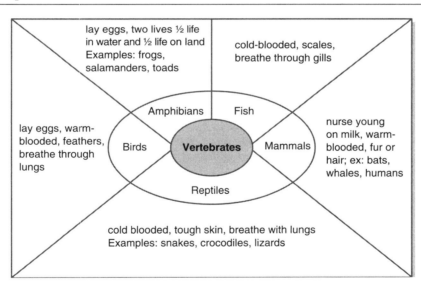

INTERDISCIPLINARY LESSONS AND THEMATIC UNITS

The best way to define the adjective *interdisciplinary* is to say that this particular word pertains to life. Interdisciplinary describes the life of a parent, student, educator, teacher, chef, businessperson, plumber, journalist, administrative assistant, sales representative, and more. Nothing that people do on a daily basis in today's society is simple. No one lives life in a vacuum, separated from his or her other roles and

Concept Map About Differences

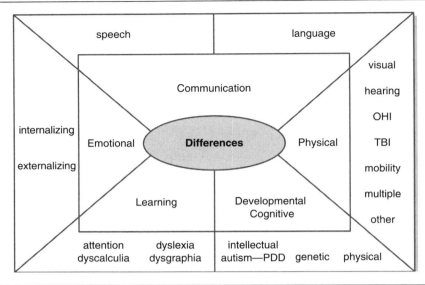

OHI = Other Health Impairments

TBI = Traumatic Brain Injury

PDD = Pervasive Developmental Disorder

responsibilities, unconnected to other people, situations, or disciplines. In order to be successful, isolation of skills is usually not an option. Yes, specialization has its place, with people being considered experts in their fields, but without uniting life's disciplines, isolation distracts from accomplishments.

To further illustrate this point, consider the following scenario: Your doctor is an expert in her field, but she lacks people skills and is unable and often unwilling to communicate and collaborate with her colleagues in an operating room or talk to patients and their families about proper pre- and postoperative care. Would you recommend this doctor to a friend? Will you remain her patient or switch to an alternate doctor? Okay, now let's connect this medical scenario to an educationally inclusive one.

Many teachers are also experts in their fields, but they lack the skills to effectively deliver the curriculum to their students, will not or cannot share strategies with colleagues, and may find collaboration and communication with colleagues and families to be difficult tasks to accomplish. *Uh-oh!* Would you recommend this teacher to another student? Would you as a student want to remain in this teacher's class? Middle schools and high schools are sometimes fragmented, with teachers who are qualified experts in their disciplines but who often do not communicate with their peers. Unlike the medical scenario, it's not always that teachers refuse to deliver the curriculum or are unwilling to collaborate; rather, sometimes, there is just not enough time for such planning sessions to be built into the schedules. In addition, their preservice training may not have properly prepared them with needed inclusive strategies to move beyond the mere dissemination of the curriculum.

For example, some middle school mathematics teachers think that simply giving a student with a learning disability extra time or reducing the number of problems on the page qualifies as the only accommodation the student needs.

Specific knowledge that journal writing, explaining, critiquing, justifying, and discussing solutions, as well as making kinesthetic connections and understanding the big ideas, are also crucial strategies and interventions (DeSimone & Parmar, 2006; Steele, 2002).

Putting the standards into practice in science classrooms is also difficult to achieve, which is why performance indicators for some students are necessary. Achieving understandings in science classes, from physical science to life science, requires students to be observers who are cognizant of the properties of animate and inanimate objects. Knowing and categorizing characteristics of objects and organisms in environments is essential. Earth science and technology requires a knowledge base that ranges from understanding what is in the atmosphere to knowing what is natural or human-made (Melber & Brown, 2008; Spooner, Ahlgrim-Delzell, Kohprasert, Baker, & Courtade, 2008).

The dilemma arises when scientific connections are not linked to students. Requiring students to rotely regurgitate principles that will not have lasting intrinsic value or application to their lives does not maximize instructional time. Classifying living organisms can be paired with daily living skills; valuing topics such as caring for a pet; or practicing good health, safety, and nutrition. Understanding how to manage and effectively use household technology such as a washing machine or a can opener or how to access daily information such as a weather report from a computer are important scientific performance indicators for students with cognitive disabilities. Students who require more functional performance indicators benefit from teachers who honor and match the science standards and other disciplines to students' lives.

Here's where the benefits of interdisciplinary lessons reinforce all subjects. As I began this section, I mentioned that life is just a tad complicated these days. If life is not about isolated subjects, but is connected to many disciplines, shouldn't schools prepare students to multitask across subjects as well, to prepare them for any job or career? So much more is gained when students connect algebra skills to logical thinking and deductive reasoning in reading comprehension exercises, or when an art or music teacher reinforces the social studies curriculum by sharing a culture's achievements. Science is about organization and observation. Isn't the same thing true about many disciplines? Chemical elements connect to form compounds and mixtures, primary colors when combined create secondary ones, and then primary and secondary colors create a tertiary one. Spanish culture connects to global studies, revolutions and rotations connect to physical movements and meteorology, and on and on! The point is, as the world keeps spinning and rotating, teachers need to keep the subjects spinning and rotating across the disciplines as well!

I fondly remember a school assignment that my son had to complete in eighth grade. Seven of his teachers magnificently collaborated to connect their disciplines of art, science, social studies, English, Spanish, music, and math. Each student in the class was then assigned a country to investigate. Students either chose their countries, or they were randomly assigned. Adolescents then worked cooperatively in class, and they were given independent time to complete this assignment. The multiple options matched the multiple subjects. The assignments and inter-disciplinary connections as remembered, with some embellishments, are indicated in the next table. Other objectives are offered, along with possible lesson adaptations. By the way, my son's assigned country was Luxembourg, and my personal favorite fact that he found out via online sources was in response to the following question:

What do they wear in Luxembourg?
Online answer: Clothes!

This interdisciplinary unit shows that teaching adolescents about differences is a valuable lesson for inclusive classrooms as well as more inclusive worlds. Offer adolescents choices and appropriate accommodations or modifications to complete this unit.

Many academic and social gains are achieved when learning experiences are connected to other subjects, life outside the classroom, and students' individual levels. That translates to S.O.S. for students as shown with this acronym:

S = Subject connections

O = Outside lives

S = Students' levels

Interdisciplinary Country Unit Assignments
English
Write a letter to someone from that country. Write a poem that describes the weather of that country.
Science
Identify an animal that inhabits that country and classify it with binomial nomenclature.
Mathematics
Write and solve an algebraic word problem that involves the setting and historical figures from the country you've chosen. Design a time line highlighting major events from that country.
World Languages
Design a card for a holiday celebrated in that country and then translate it into the language you are studying.
Music
Find a composer or musical artist who came from that country and share the score or lyrics from one of his or her compositions or songs.
Art
Construct a toy that a child from that country could play with. Investigate a famous artist from that country and create a replication of one of his or her works.
Social Studies
Create a political map of the country. List some facts about that country's history, geography, and government.
Character Education
With teacher approval, write to an online penpal from that country to find out more facts (see www.internationalpenpals.net).

INTERDISCIPLINARY UNIT GOAL: To learn more about other countries				
Objectives	Subjects and skills included & connected Other accommodations that may be needed	Students who may need additional help to focus	Students who need mini lessons	Anchor activities for more advanced learners
To compare, contrast, and translate word relationships in different languages	Literacy Skills, World Languages Help with word meanings in English first	Rita Y. Read	Ima Lost	Classroom newspaper design Poetry unit
To list the attributes of different world governments	Global Connections, Economics, Politics More background knowledge given with longer words broken into syllables	Wanna Watch	A. Pathy	Continent stations with WebQuests
To identify dependent and independent variables in experiments and the contributions of world scientists	Biology/Chemistry/Physics Help with research skills, e.g., giving specific guided questions, visual glossary of terms	Merry Smiley	Vary Able	Collaborative, research-based experiments valuing individual and cooperative interests
To complete a WebQuest about a country in each hemisphere	Research skills, Literacy, Cultures, Geography review Review computer procedures, positive social/behavioral expectations outlined and praised, behavioral contract if warranted	Lottie Talker	Cyber Less	Virtual field trips www.tramline .com
To use logical reasoning to solve word problems involving map skills and currency within given countries	Mathematics, Economics Step-by step map skills, e.g., reading a legend, using a scale of miles, concrete currency to manipulate, modeling of sample word problems, hundreds chart to refer to, direct social skills instruction with character education rules enforced	Bill Bully	Can't Count	Cooperative problem solving Map Corner Newspapers
To understand how competition is affected by collusion	Economics Preteach vocabulary; relate concepts to students' lives to increase motivation; assign cooperative roles with individual accountability.	Mucho Friendly	Wanna Leave	Stock market watch Research on global conglomerates

INTERDISCIPLINARY UNIT GOAL:				
Objectives	Subjects and skills included & connected Other accommodations that may be needed	Students who may need additional help to focus	Students who need mini lessons	Anchor activities for more advanced learners

In addition, informal experiences that give merit to inquiry across subject areas loudly state that like life, subjects are connected. For example, current event assignments yield literacy gains, with critical thinking skills valued beyond the subject of social studies. Students can understand the concept of the *tone* of a written piece by examining an editorial or newspaper article of interest in their communities (Pescatore, 2007).

As stated in prior chapters, UDL is a way to increase academic achievements across all subjects and prevent barriers from interfering with the deliverance of quality objectives in educational settings. Educators and researchers who at the

Options for Interdisciplinary Unit Assignment on Disabilities
English Read the short essay, *Welcome to Holland,* by Emily Perl Kingsley to discover how a disability impacts a family. Explain the analogy presented. www.our-kids.org/Archives/Holland.html
Science and Technology Describe how cochlear implants work. Create a technological invention that would ease the life of a person with a disability. www.nidcd.nih.gov/health/hearing/coch.asp
Mathematics All students learn differently. At times, students with and without disabilities do not understand algebraic concepts and need a step-by-step approach to better grasp the concept of how to solve an algebraic equation. Tell how you would teach someone to solve the following equation, using a step-by-step approach: $5x + 3 = 43$. Be certain to define these terms first: *variable, coefficient, balancing, equations, reciprocal, linear equation, inequality.* http://mathforum.org/sum95/ruth/alg1.html
World Languages Defend or refute why American Sign Language (ASL) should be offered as a middle school or high school world language. Try to sign a sentence with ASL, using this site: www.aslpro.com. Write a sentence to someone using Braille cells. www.brl.org/simbraille.html
Music Identify 10 songs by Stevie Wonder and then create your own lyrics, in any style that you prefer, that you'd like to sing to him one day to honor his accomplishments. http://steviewonder.free.fr
Art How has technology helped people with disabilities gain access to appreciate and produce the arts of different mediums? Create a collage of accessibility symbols. www.disabilityworld.org/index.htm www.acb.org/accessible-formats.html
Social Studies Investigate why Franklin D. Roosevelt did not want to be photographed while seated in his wheelchair. www.ur.umich.edu/0304/Oct27_03/19.shtml
Character Education Explain what is meant by *people-first* language. www.disabilityisnatural.com/peoplefirstlanguage.htm

onset look for ways to include diverse groups of learners are better able to deliver high-quality standards and effectively reach students (Meo, 2008).

Overall, the interdisciplinary and universally appealing lesson options are endless. This template invites you to collaborate with your colleagues to better connect to the students and the curriculum.

Interdisciplinary Unit Assignments on _____
English
Science
Mathematics
World Languages
Music
Art
Social Studies
Character Education

THE ROLE OF TECHNOLOGY FOR ADOLESCENTS IN INCLUSIVE CLASSROOMS

This fast-paced world quickly marches on, no longer with steps, but often with the click of a mouse, a remote, or the words, *"You've got mail"* Technology assists students of all abilities to process, demonstrate, retain, and share information and communication. The promise technology holds for students with disabilities is enormous and still growing beyond anyone's wildest imagination from even a decade ago.

A Web site entitled Teaching Moments (www.goalsettingforstudents.com) lists facts about teens, dubbed as the *instant everything generation.* Technology is explained as a release from boredom, which offers quick research with ideas immediately validated. The instantaneous communication of the Internet, social networking via the Web, and text messaging on cell phones offer ways to quickly explore the world without ever physically leaving your own. The site poignantly states that we are challenged to mentor adolescents without lectures. These teens are learning from us, yet asking us to see things from their vantage point, too.

Computer applications such as databases, concept-mapping, spreadsheets, and video conferencing are just some of today's technological tools. Multimedia simulations and computer-supported intentional learning environments (CSILE) further help students construct learning. Digital literacy now prepares all learners with access to a more global world. With digital storytelling and access to quick research, blogs, and reviews, newer venues of communication are now being explored.

> Digital-age literacy refers not only to the basic literacy of reading and writing, but also includes an understanding of scientific principles, economics, and global issues, as well as an ability to use technology to analyze information. Inventive thinking incorporates the cognitive skills necessary to grapple with the volume of information available with current technology, including higher-order abstract thought, flexibility, curiosity, and creativity. (Sheffield, 2007, p .2)

Advancements include interactive white boards that have replaced many chalkboards, sophisticated wheelchairs that allow students to see their peers at eye level, sound field systems that amplify voices, software with word prediction programs, talking Web sites, adaptable keyboards, a voice-activated mouse, cochlear implants, and incredible augmentative communication programs, just to name a few!

Even though technology offers incredible opportunities, it also needs to be accessible to students in effective ways. For example, when assigned research papers, online databases supply students with almost too much information to sift through. Students with learning disabilities may be distracted by pop-up ads or unable to distinguish which information site is a reliable source to cite. Students with fine motor issues, visual impairments, or physical and attention differences also require additional guidance to properly and efficiently navigate online.

While technology changes how students research and communicate information, instruction is still needed on proper ways to interact with online sites, as well as computer software and word processing programs, from Excel to Microsoft Word. Many students with physical disabilities and attention issues and those with or without disability classifications would benefit from instructional lessons on how to use computer language tools such as an online thesaurus and spell check. Teaching students how to properly cite references to avoid plagiarism is also something that requires direct skill instruction. I often assist students in computer labs to complete assigned research projects, be it for the History Day project or a biographical essay on a politician. As I circulate around the room, I invariably discover students with and without disabilities not making productive use of their time. Some of them will spend 15 to 20 minutes just deciding which font style, font size, or color of the letters that they will select. Adolescents love adding animations to their PowerPoint presentations, and will do so way before they have solidified the content of their slides, which in turn affects the quality of their product, since they have misallocated their computer lab time. In my own *pedagogical way*, I firmly offer better time management plans to *all* of these students.

One article on the *Wired* magazine Web site is an article by Terdiman (2005) titled "What Websites Do to Turn On Teens." The article matches several characteristics of adolescents to their computer usage behaviors. It reminds Web designers to not make the text too tiny. Now, the reasoning behind this has nothing to do with visual impairments, but is due to the fact that many teens do not sit close to the computer monitors. Rather, they often lean back, relaxing in their computer chairs, at a greater distance from the screen. In addition, adolescents like sites that acknowledge their sense of style and ones that have a degree of interactivity. Most important is to teach safe online communication skills, by advising teens to be leery of just how much personal information they disclose.

When used appropriately, technology allows students in inclusive classrooms to improve the process of accessing information and the quality of the product delivered. The following Web sites offer additional curricular information and technological opportunities to enhance and expand adolescent knowledge and to address everyone's strengths, interests, and abilities.

Adolescent Sites Worth Citing (Please note that adult supervision and monitoring on all Web sites is essential.)
www.thinkquest.org Invites teachers and students to choose, investigate, and collaborate on topics
www.nationalgeographic.com/xpeditions Interactive adventures
www.wise.berkeley.edu Web-based inquiry science environment
www.thinkers.co.nz/telementoring Reduces adolescent egocentrism by creating a collaborating network with other students and peers around the world
http://disabilityresources.org/KIDS.html www.disabilitystudiesforteachers.org/index.php www.disabilityresources.org/DIS-AWARE.html Sites for and about students with disabilities
www.factmonster.com Online almanac, dictionary, encyclopedia, and homework help www.sparknotes.com Offers study guides on different subjects
http://kidinfo.com Homework, student, teacher/parent reference
http://kids.nationalgeographic.com/kids Quizzes, videos, games, stories, and activities about people and places
http://bjpinchbeck.com Homework Helper
Community: createblog.com, MySpace.com, TeenChat.com Entertainment: RollingStone.com, CartoonNetwork.com
Sports: MLB.com, race-deZert.com
Shopping: www.clothesnet.com/teen.htm
http://lyrics.com Browse different musical artists
http://icom.museum/vlmp, www.museumstuff.com Virtually explore museums online
Games: www.funbrain.com, www.gamefaqs.com, www.dmoz.org/Kids_and_Teens/Games

Connecting Curriculum and Literature Materials

Review these sites and explore how these curriculum materials increase adolescent literacy.

Academic Therapy Publications	http://www.highnoonbooks.com
Curriculum Associates	http://www.curriculumassociates.com/products
Kids In Between	http://www.kidsinbetween.com
Great Source	www.greatsource.com
Steck Vaughn	http://steckvaughn.harcourtachieve.com/en-US/steckvaughn.htm
Remedial workbooks and high interest classics	http://www.mariinc.com/workremed3.html
Corrective Reading:	http://www.mcgraw-hill.co.uk/sra/correctivereading.htm
Scholastic System 44	http://www.marketwire.com/press-release/Scholastic-Inc-NASDAQ-SCHL-940083.html
Scholastic graded readers	http://www.scholastic.com/elt/graded.htm
Wilson Readers	http://www.wilsonlanguage.com

ADOLESCENT WEBQUEST FOR INCLUSIVE TEACHERS

This WebQuest invites you to explore online sites to gain more background knowledge on cognitive theories, discover additional instructional strategies, and expand your lesson deliveries to match the needs of adolescents in inclusive classrooms.

WebQuest Assignments	
Helping adolescents soak up the information	
Describe the three fundamental principles underlying the use of mnemonics that will help students with learning differences.	www.mindtools.com/memory.html
Understanding the social cognitive theory	
Explain the steps Bandura identified as part of the modeling process.	http://webspace.ship.edu/cgboer/bandura.html
Valuing constructivist learning and problem solving	
How does constructivism differ from more traditional ideas about teaching? How would this type of approach assist students with learning, physical, communication, and sensory issues to gain more understandings of abstract thought?	www.thirteen.org/edonline/concept2class/constructivism/index.html
Implementing effective instructional approaches for adolescents in inclusive classrooms	
Review these cites to identify meaningful lessons or applicable instructional approaches that relate to your curriculum area. Tell how you would apply or modify any of the ideas or lessons presented in these sites or periodicals to assist students in your inclusive classrooms. Also review this site to learn more about specific disabilities: www.nichcy.org	www.lessonplanspage.com http://teachers.net/lessons http://mathforum.org/teachers www.sitesforteachers.com www.nationalgeographic.com/geographyaction/habitats/educators.html http://teacher.scholastic.com/products/classmags/middleschool.htm http://teacher.scholastic.com/products/classmags/highschool.htm www.tolerance.org

8

Examining Exit Strategies That Prepare Adolescents to Enter the World

OVERVIEW **T**his chapter examines exit strategies that assist adolescents in inclusive classrooms to enter the world with the necessary skills, so they are ready to be part of their communities and global worlds as productive young adults.

Now that more adolescents with disabilities are included in general education classrooms, additional demands are placed upon school systems to not only include, but also educate and prepare these adolescents for productive adult lives. Oliver Wendell Holmes said it best when describing looking ahead:

> The great thing in this world is not so much where we stand, as what direction we are moving.

This last chapter looks at where many adolescents are heading when they exit high school. Door #1 is the one I hope is available to them, rather than Door #2, with no preparedness or direction for the postsecondary world.

Ex_{it} marks the spot!

excitement
exploration
expression
experimentation
experience
EXPERTISE

Door #1

?

Door #2

SPRINKLES AND CHERRIES: MORE THAN THE BASICS

Imagine entering an ice cream parlor with an array of flavors available as well as an extensive assortment of toppings, from hot fudge to crushed nuts, caramel, bananas, and more! Yummy, if you like ice cream, especially if there are sprinkles and cherries to top it off—la piece de resistance! Quite a culinary treat. Now here are some facts about ice cream that may dissuade you from ordering it, things like meaningless caloric content, high sugar, more fat, and little value, to name a few. Then what explains those long lines at ice cream stands? What is the appeal of this "feel good" ice cream that puts a smile on the faces of many? What's up with the sprinkles and cherries? Is ice cream synonymous with gluttony or waste? Do dieticians, nutritionists, health food advocates, vegans, and educational professionals value ice cream? Do adolescents like ice cream?

Now let's compare curriculum to ice cream. Does *curriculum* have the same flavorful appeal, or is it also viewed as containing meaningless nutritional content? The point here is that school experiences need to offer adolescents learning activities *topped with* multiple intelligences, sprinkles of constructivism, and other analogous extras that increase students' motivations. Schools that serve palatable courses that make adolescents smile, consequently have adolescents eagerly coming back for more servings. It's generally about connecting to adolescent lives with a flavorful relevant learning menu and some extras like sprinkles and cherries. The analogous toppings include involving learners in active classrooms, giving them a wide menu of ways to process the content, while honoring their hopes, strengths, and abilities. Suppose someone did not like sundaes. Couldn't a cone or a shake be an option? Students in inclusive classrooms need many options as well to stay engaged, inspired, and enthusiastic about learning without any *meltdowns,* but like with ice cream, more smiles!

This next quote sums up a real issue that educators need to address to improve all classrooms and include meaningful content, not just superfluous toppings:

> High schools have a propensity to cover lots of content *before* allowing students to use that content in authentic situations. (Wiggins & McTighe, 2008, p. 38.)

As the above authors point out, curriculum delivery must engage adolescents and enter their worlds. More research reports further:

> Such factors as departmental structure, subject-matter focus, lack of professional development opportunities, lack of common planning time, credit and graduation requirements, and course scheduling place limitations on the extent to which students with disabilities can access and benefit from a standards-based curriculum. (Deshler & Schumaker, 2006, p. 10)

With the many complexities involved, rather than focusing on limitations, let's consider the standards, but add the *extras*. Serving ice cream or curriculum certainly requires more than the basics; sometimes, the standards need cherries and sprinkles, too! A *balanced educational diet* is wise for all!

MEASURE THE LEARNING, NOT THE DISABILITIES! FORMATIVE, SUMMATIVE, AND *KIND* TESTS AND EVALUATIONS

Are tests valid assessments of student gains if they are not designed with students in mind? Prior chapters have emphasized the meanings of initials such as UbD, UDL, PBL, IEP, AYP, EBP, RtI, and NALB. In case you have forgotten, the translations are shown in the next table.

Initial Translations	
UbD	understanding by design
UDL	universally designed learning
PBL	problem-based learning
IEP	individualized education program
AYP	annual yearly progress
EBP	evidence-based practices
RtI	response to interventions
NCLB	No Child Left Behind
NALB (self-created)	No Adolescent Left Behind!

Assessments and evaluations are intended to check for understanding and to help teachers ascertain the levels and needs of students for diagnosis, instruction, or redirection. The sections in this book on assessments mention that kinder, appropriate ones let the students know at the onset the lesson's objectives and expected outcomes. Think about this analogy: *Why would you buy a train ticket if no one told you where you were going?* Students need to be on board, by knowing the learning stops scheduled and where the train is headed to achieve deeper understandings that have the best practices such as high-quality instruction, multiple intelligences, and meaningful curriculum as integral and ongoing inclusive components. Individuals with Disabilities Education Act amendments of 2004 require that all students with disabilities, even those with the most significant ones, participate in state- and districtwide assessments. This can be achieved by preparing students with the necessary background knowledge and then scaffolding as appropriate to help their baseline knowledge improve. Research reports the following conundrums:

Although data show that some students with disabilities are reaching the state-determined level of proficiency, many students with disabilities are still far from performing at this level. (Thurlow & Wiley, 2004)

Although there has been improvement in the reporting of assessment participation and performance data for students with disabilities, there is still much more that can be done. Since 1997, the National Center on Educational Outcomes has been collecting data on the inclusion of students with disabilities in statewide assessment systems. Unfortunately, there is still limited consensus among educators regarding appropriate achievement expectations for students with disabilities, particularly those with cognitive disabilities. (McGrew & Evans, 2003)

The report from McGrew and Evans (2003) confirms many of the factors outlined in prior chapters as reasons why students with cognitive disabilities have not achieved as many gains. These include the following teacher behaviors associated with the communication of low achievement expectancies (Cotton, 2001; Gottfredson, Marciciak, Birdseye, & Gottfredson, 1995).

Reasons for fewer gains include less student opportunities to learn or demonstrate knowledge of material. That means less wait time, with inappropriate feedback, criticism, reinforcement, and attention. Reinforcement needs to be realistic and responsive to adolescent needs. Even personal touches such as increasing eye contact and offering smiles spur students on and reward their efforts with realistic praise. Feedback also needs to be informative, not just offering the answer, but accompanying it with an explanation. In addition, students of all levels need stimulating, effective instruction with questions that encourage them to tackle higher-level curriculum questions. At all costs, educators need to avoid a Pygmalion or self-fulfilling prophecy that ignores the full potentials of students due to preconceived negative notions about their abilities.

Generally speaking, assessments are not the same across the board:

Students with disabilities participate in proficiency assessments in three primary ways: (1) participation in the general assessment without accommodations, (2) participation in the general assessment with accommodations, and (3) participation in an alternate assessment. (McGrew & Evans, 2003)

Self-assessment tools also help adolescent learners in inclusive classrooms to measure their learning strides and realize their strengths. These self-regulating tools are valuable for students of all abilities. They help organize personal profiles, by targeting students' stronger subjects, as well as those that need more sharpening. When students in middle schools develop this type of self-regulatory skill, they can become the masters of their learning and not be overwhelmed once they enter high school. With an easier transition, once the curriculum spirals with more course load demands, they already have clearer views of their capabilities. It is hoped that students will not be discouraged by a failure on a test but will realize that one particular test does not define their abilities and that they themselves are capable of that self-assessment! A sample table follows for adolescents to record their progress.

Keeping Track of My Progress on Quizzes, Reports, and Tests											
Subjects	Date	Date	Date	Date	Date	Date	Date	Date	Date	Date	Date

Comments:

Goals:

Subjects	Date	Date	Date	Date	Date	Date	Date	Date	Date	Date	Date

Comments:

Goals:

Formative assessments that offer more frequent feedback, when combined with summative ones, allow adolescents to average out their achievements over time. Tests that are kinder do not always have to measure or point out disabilities or weaker areas, but can be used as a baseline to establish a level of competency. Then students see their progress and are not discouraged by an assessment that translates to an unacceptable point value. Inclusive teachers who factor in effort and progress as indicators for grades, rather than solely relying on achievements, are acknowledging that adolescents in inclusive classrooms are not all the same. So why would assessments highlight their differences?

Class participation, homework assignments, notebook checks, and reflective journals are also learning indicators. If a student with learning difficulties tried his or her best and received a grade of 68 on an assessment, would it be a crime to give that student a grade of 70 if the homework, class participation, and work ethics are excellent? Other assessment indicators in this case would justify the grade adjustment. Each situation is a unique one that coteachers need to collaborate on to set up acceptable grading standards that apply to all students. Those *two points* have more than a two-point value; it's simply a kinder way to assess!

Most important, though, is that assessments and evaluations offer everyone accountability. Students need to know their capabilities and in what direction they need to stretch their adolescent minds and bodies. Families also need accurate and realistic views of their children, based upon school data: observational, behavioral, and written. Educators in inclusive environments then use the data to tweak their lessons to better match individual student needs.

HIGH AND REALISTIC EXPECTATIONS FOR ADOLESCENTS AS PRODUCTIVE ADULTS

Postsecondary decisions are tough ones for all adolescents with and without disabilities and their families. Turning points and forks in the road, as pointed out by Robert Frost in his poem "The Road Not Taken," often create dilemmas that do not always have quick remedies. *How does one define a productive adult? Can an adult who never attended college be a successful contributor to society?* Review the following research facts to reflect on these questions.

In 2006, the U.S. Department of Labor reported that postsecondary education or training is required for 90 percent of decent paying jobs. Without additional training, adolescents are not afforded the same opportunities for future successes as those students who go on to receive more educational acumen and job-related skills. Bridgeland, DiIulio, and Morrison point out statistics about adolescents from an extensive survey conducted in 2006. Many adolescents who left high school without graduating departed due to inadequate educational responses to circumstances in their lives. Even though most had minimum grade averages of C and initial career aspirations, they still dropped out of school due to personal or economic reasons; for example, 32 percent needed to make money for their family, and 26 percent had a baby to support. Some of these adolescents when questioned reported that if schools had offered additional support with more demands, they would have tried harder. The authors go on to mention factors such as the need for relevant curriculum, more individualization, and higher teacher expectations as part of remedying this dropout problem. Other factors of concern include not being able to catch up on schoolwork, too much freedom, and not enough rules.

Not all adolescents need to go to college to be successful, but if they do choose to attend a postsecondary training, then that additional experience should be a transferable and marketable one. In Swanson's analysis, *Learning and Earning* (2007), he points out different zones that the Bureau of Labor Statistics has to classify jobs, ranging from little to extensive preparation needed with regard to education, training, and experience. Job examples range from a taxi driver to a sheet-metal worker, retail sales clerk, teacher, librarian, engineer, and so on, with different levels of employment given different ratings. Higher education and career training consequently will yield opportunities for increased income. Upper-level jobs are sometimes closed to high school students who do not expand their skills beyond the academics and skills learned during their school years.

Maximizing postsecondary options with appropriate preparation translates to helping all inclusive students, including those with intellectual disabilities. The National Health and Medical Research Council project in Australia had promising results when it conducted a pilot study with students keeping an ASK (advocacy skills kit) Health Diary. The diary was used to collect and store personal health information and as a tool for students aged 13 to 18 to independently communicate information to health care providers and others when necessary (Carrington & Lennox, 2008) to develop increased self-advocacy skills. This promotion of independent living skills and more self-management was accomplished by implementing a health-based school curriculum, with strong personal connections. Staff helped students to concretely practice a way to communicate their needs across health areas in a bound Velcro notebook that included a personal section, advocacy tips, doctor information, and more.

Students with disabilities often need additional guidance when it comes to postsecondary decisions and available work options. The U.S. Business Leadership Network (www.usbln.org) is an online site that promotes the business imperative of including people with disabilities in the workforce. The ultimate point here is that postsecondary connections need to be offered to all populations, across the inclusive spectrum.

Inclusive teachers who have high, yet realistic expectations for their students help them to develop increased self-esteem. This translates to reaching for the sky without setting limits on opportunities. However, it is important to realize that some students need ladders as they reach different layers of the atmosphere to help them access postsecondary employment. If students only stop at the *troposphere*, they experience changing weather with incomes slightly above poverty level. Some adolescents with disabilities will soar with many jets into the *stratosphere* with work-related skills. Other adolescents move into the *mesosphere* with the meteors since they have more knowledge, training, and experience, while others aim higher into the *thermosphere* to meet up with space shuttles. When well prepared with high but applicable expectations, some adolescents may even explore their upper limits in the *exosphere*, if they have more extensive education, skills, and knowledge. Preparation for life after high school includes college-oriented courses, experiences with internships, work-related skills, job coaches, counseling, and life skills instruction and modeling (e.g., showing up at your job on time, community interactions, family training, and more).

Career and Technical Student Organizations (CTSOs) are funded through federal legislation by the U.S. Department of Education, with a purpose to connect classrooms with the outside workforce. Organizations such as these encourage adolescents to attempt challenges in fields such as technology, engineering, math, and business. Adolescents are able to be immersed in various environments that teach them job-related skills, such as getting along with peers and how to network. This is also an opportunity for some students to explore their inner career thoughts and at the same time bond with other adolescents who have similar interests. The following Web site offer services for adolescents that connect school to life:

SkillsUSA—www.skillsusa.org

Future Business Leaders of America (FBLA)—www.fbla-pbl.org

Family, Career, and Community Leaders of America (FCCLA)—www.fcclainc.org

Technology Student Association (TSA)—www.tsaweb.org

Institute on Disability, APEX II (Achievement in Dropout Prevention and Excellence)—www.iod.unh.edu/apex.html

The following organizations offer additional career support to adolescents in the form of internships, career academies, or targeted curriculum:

Ford Partnership for Advanced Studies—www.fordpas.org

National Academy Foundation—www.naf.org

ConnectEd—www.connectEdCalifornia.org

Society today is at such a wonderful apex; we are valuing all of our students as potential contributors, capable of achieving greatness, within interactive inclusive settings. Adolescents enter the postsecondary world as college students, participants in the workforce, members of the armed forces, or in the practice of a trade. Schools can prepare adolescents for their future lives as contributing and competent individuals. The world will sometimes be a differentiating one, but hopefully never again a segregating one.

In August 2008, the Higher Education Opportunity Act (HEOA) established a national center to help students, including those with intellectual disabilities, have more educational opportunities beyond high school. This involves improved services, accommodations, and ongoing support for both students and families with transitional services, academics, socialization, and independent living skills in higher education across the United States. Reports and analysis of successes of students in higher education will then yield better outcomes for generations of students who will follow. This Web site has information for students, families, and professionals to extend many more opportunities in higher education to students with intellectual disabilities: http://thinkcollege.net/(Calefati, 2009).

COMMUNITY INTEGRATIONS

In DiLeo's book *Raymond's Room* (2007), the author states, "A meaningful job and home in the community should be an option for everyone, regardless of label or perceived deficits" (p. 195). This includes bringing industry and communities into the classroom and taking students into the community within natural settings. A full range of community integrations is the desired goal for all students, with and without disabilities, so that they may live and function in inclusive postsecondary communities with coworkers, families, spouses, and their own children. This is more feasible when needs and concerns of adolescents are known and addressed ahead of time with appropriate preparations.

One study (Edwards, Patrick, & Topolski, 2003) that surveyed adolescents in Grades 7 through 12 asked them to identify physical, emotional, learning, or other disabilities through a TAP (Teen Assessment Project; Small, 1995) questionnaire. The survey asked adolescents about their disability levels, personal concerns, and community perceptions to gain individual input. Although the study was conducted in a rural community in the western United States, the following discussion thought seems applicable across the United States and in many other countries as well.

> Efforts to empower and include adolescents with disabilities in school, family, and community activities and working on ways to develop more peer support for adolescents with disabilities seem to be practical avenues of action that could make a positive difference in the lives of adolescents with disabilities. (Edwards et al., 2003)

The study investigated emotional and physical strain, misunderstandings, stereotypes, and how more awareness about the needs of students with disabilities yields less discomfort and more responsiveness in inclusive environments. It specifically suggests that the reduction of social and environmental barriers combined with the promotion of inclusion of adolescents with disabilities in school, family, and communities will improve their quality of life.

When classrooms connect to communities, real-life applications are possible. Since the learning is adhered to environmental contexts, adolescents are concretely shown reasons why they need to learn certain disciplines. Educators who invite business managers, office workers, sales associates, dentists, accountants, firefighters, journalists, parents, siblings, prior students, and more to share their personal job-related and school backgrounds with students are saying that the reason to learn concepts is not exclusively about receiving grades, but is related to achieving a fulfilling everyday life. Students in inclusive classrooms who hear these concrete personal testaments can better understand just why it all matters. For many students with learning disabilities—autism, Asperger syndrome, ADHD, behavioral issues, physical difficulties, and more—school has never been easy, since frustrations accompanied by societal roadblocks often interfere with these students displaying their competencies. Seeing and hearing adults in various fields who may have personally faced challenges can offer students increased reasons to further apply their strengths to circumvent academic, cognitive, perceptual, physical, or social difficulties and consequently achieve greater successes. Community-classroom collaborations that include scenarios with guest speakers, field site visits, e-mail contacts, and video-conferencing show that school connects to life. Community mentors who develop trusting relationships with adolescents are then able to serve as role models, confidants, and school motivators. Community collaboration translates into crucial conceptual applications—what education is all about!

The following *inclusion poem* highlights many factors concerning inclusion in the schools and how it can connect to community integrations.

Some don't know	We definitely need some more
The way inclusion for adolescents will go	Better classroom ideas
One thing is for sure	And less teacher fears
	More planned strategies

Focusing on abilities	So forget the label
Yes, more inclusion	Remember all are able
And less confusion	In different ways to succeed
More families amicably involved	To count, laugh, smile, and read
All conflicts mutually resolved	Let's give all a turn
Less opposition	To understand and learn
More transition	So don't be rude
To the community	Figure out a way to include
That's the reality	

Source: Adapted from Karten, T. (2008). *Embracing disabilities in the classroom: Strategies to maximize students' assets.* Thousand Oaks, CA: Corwin Press.

GLOBAL CONNECTIONS

I began this book by saying that sometimes adolescents think they live in a unique and separate world from the adults who preceded them. Years ago, this was especially true of students with disabilities who entered adolescence in a state of identity confusion, only to discover at this pivotal age that they would be placed in separate exclusive classes. Many received watered-down curriculum, which ill prepared them to productively live in their community, let alone in a global society. If schools offer adolescents a rich curriculum filled with relevant life experiences, then not only have school systems made personal connections, they also have more importantly made global ones for adolescents to apply across postsecondary experiences and diverse settings.

With inclusion in the general education classroom looked upon as the first option of service, adolescents are now afforded a chance for equal and full participation in a global society. Global connections involve sharpening academics, social attributes, technological acumen, communication levels, and feelings of self-efficacy to tackle whatever the world presents. Since inclusion has increased its prevalence in middle schools and high schools, adolescents with and without disabilities are integral parts of the school system, interacting with their peers. After high school, many of these teens are college-bound or become part of the workforce, possessing more skills and confidence to become productive members of a global society. No longer are they standing outside the circle looking in at others' accomplishments. The students with disabilities are also afforded more opportunities to achieve many diversified accomplishments.

Samantha Abeel, author of *My Thirteenth Winter* (2003), poignantly states,

I no longer comfort myself with ideas of my own difference and uniqueness. If anything, I struggle with the realization that I am normal, that I am, for the most part, just like everyone else. (p. 203)

Consult these sites for more global connections to help students of all abilities to connect to the world beyond their own backyard: www.pbs.org/wgbh/global connections; http://www.ccsf.edu/Resources/Tolerance/res.html; http://www.csun.edu/~hcedu013/plans.html

PROFESSIONAL DEVELOPMENT AND ENHANCEMENT

The National Board for Professional Standards (www.nbpts.org) has set forth the following five core propositions for accomplished teaching. They propose that teachers aspire to

1. commit to both their students and subjects, believing that all students can learn.

2. understand their subjects and offer students real-life connections.

3. monitor student learning.

4. learn and grow from professional and classroom experiences.

5. collaborate and network with professional organizations and colleagues.

Without professional development, teachers may as well surrender to stagnation. Whenever I conduct workshops, I recommend that teachers belong to professional organizations to continue their growth in their chosen fields. Whether your interests lie in art, music, science, English, history, exceptionalities, language, psychology, physical education, mathematics, or another field, there is always something more to learn that can then be transferred to your classrooms. Professional organizations offer opportunities to read journals, network with colleagues, affirm your strategies, attend workshops, share and learn ideas, and sometimes just release *pedagogical energy* to kind ears who know exactly what you are talking about. Productive partnerships are no longer an option, but a necessity. Most of all, the professional development is not just intended for personal enhancement, but must be oriented toward improving students' abilities, helping families, and supporting colleagues. The table on page 211 lists professional organizations for various fields.

An important part of professional development is reflection, which yields growth. Without that component, inclusive insights about adolescents will never be realized, achieved, and maximized. Try to reflect upon the following statements and see how much you remember, and definitely go back to the chapters to find the answers. You can construct similar curricular reflections for the adolescents in your inclusive environments as a way to revisit their learning. The reflective survey below is strictly a self-graded one. Answer the following questions as true (T) or false (F), and if the statement is false, change it to a true one.

___1. Adolescent learners go through a stage labeled by Erikson as *identity versus role confusion.*

___2. Teaching adolescents in inclusive classrooms requires monitoring of their achievements while trying to establish relevant curriculum connections.

___3. Universal design for learning is a proactive way to address adolescent needs.

___4. Sometimes, adolescents are more concerned with possibilities than actualities.

___5. Adolescent learners in inclusive environments require appropriate scaffolding.

___6. Academic failures can impact social and behavioral issues.

Professional Organizations	
Art	National Art Education Association—www.naea-reston.org
	The National Institute of Art & Disabilities (NIAD)—www.niadart.org
Curriculum	National Staff Development Council—www.nsdc.org
	Association for Supervision and Curriculum Development—www.ascd.org
English	National Council of Teachers of English—www.ncte.org
Exceptionalities	National Association of Special Education Teacher—www.naset.org/799.0.html
	Council for Exceptional Children—www.cec.sped.org
Music	National Association for Music Education—www.menc.org
Physical Education	National Association for Sport and Physical Education—www.aahperd.org/NASPE
Psychology	American Academy of Child and Adolescent Psychiatry—www.aacap.org
Reading	International Reading Association—www.reading.org
	International Dyslexia Association—www.interdys.org
Science	National Science Teachers Association—www.nsta.org
Social Studies	National Council for the Social Studies—www.ncss.org
Mathematics	National Council of Teachers of Mathematics—www.nctm.org

___7. Intelligence level is not absolute but can have multiple ways of being expressed.

___8. Cooperative learning and collaborative teaching de-emphasize competition and help learners of all abilities.

___9. The ultimate goal of inclusive experiences is for students to lead successful postsecondary lives.

__10. Educators can guide adolescents in inclusive classrooms to become self-regulated learners.

(By the way, all the statements are true!)

Since reflections help us all achieve growth, review and complete the survey on the next page.

PASSING THE TORCH

Learning is never a selfish concept, but is one that needs to be shared, with everyone included in the process. That's the whole premise behind educational systems.

Reflective Survey About Adolescents in Inclusive Environments

		High	Medium	Low	None
1.	Rate your knowledge about teaching adolescent learners.	High	Medium	Low	None
2.	Rate your confidence level in teaching adolescent learners.	High	Medium	Low	None
3.	Rate your motivation level to teach adolescent learners	High	Medium	Low	None

		Strongly agree	Somewhat agree	Somewhat disagree	Strongly disagree
4.	Scaffolding helps adolescents to learn.	1	2	3	4
5.	My main job focus as an educator is to deliver the content.	1	2	3	4
6.	Adolescent learners have unique needs.	1	2	3	4
7.	Collaboration with colleagues will enhance my teaching.	1	2	3	4
8.	Teaching adolescents requires the same approach as teaching younger learners.	1	2	3	4
9.	Family collaboration is nice, but not essential.	1	2	3	4
10.	I am well informed about the various psychosocial, behavioral, moral, and cognitive issues that adolescents face.	1	2	3	4
11.	Professional affiliations are important.	1	2	3	4
12.	Reflective practices are more essential for teachers newer to the field than veteran teachers.	1	2	3	4

List five instructional strategies that you plan to use as an educator of adolescents.
1.
2.
3.
4.
5.

(Optional) Additional comments about teaching adolescents in inclusive classrooms:

Families of adolescents with disabilities need to pass the torch to their children, siblings, grandchildren, cousins, nephews, nieces, friends, colleagues, coworkers, and more. Educators need to collaborate with those very same families and students so as to professionally ease this transitional phase to pass and light the torches. Empowerment is a strong tool in the hands of adolescents who, through inclusive experiences, are offered opportunities to shine. Empowerment involves trust and confidence in abilities, with the knowledge that with the right *educational doses of oxygen,* many illuminating achievements follow.

Inclusive adolescent classrooms are complex, and so are torches. The following lists a few different types of torches, their associated functions, and *enlightening* inclusion connections.

Torch	Function/Materials	Inclusion Connections
Cutting torch	Severs and burns away the metal in two or more pieces	This torch represents a time when students were not given access to inclusive classrooms, separated from socialization with their peers and challenging academics, cut away from society.
Unlit torch	Used for breathing life into a fire	This torch represents adolescent potentials to shine when properly fueled in inclusive settings
Welding torch	Unites or binds together two separate metal pieces	This torch represents adolescents connected with their peers to create empowering and strong social, learning, and life experiences.
Cooking torch	Used as a utensil for creative recipes like crème brûlée, other desserts, and more	This torch is adjustable and yields a palatable creation when used at the proper flame, just like the adaptations with curricular adjustments that adolescents in inclusive classrooms require.
Blow torch	used in construction to solder metal together	This torch produces hot flames fueled by oxygen, like students' minds that are fueled by study skills and self-help strategies that give adolescents the knowledge and preparatory tools to ignite the world.
Juggling torch	Performers may have fire torches that they juggle as props.	Inclusive teachers often have an impressive array of instructional tools, strategies, lessons, and schedules that they juggle to prevent any adolescent from being burnt.
Olympic torch	Initially commemorated theft of fire from Zeus by Prometheus, it also signifies the start of the Olympic games.	Inclusion needs to also travel across bodies of water and climb mountains by foot, bicycles, boats, and more, communicating its connective message to all living beings across the world. Like fire from Zeus, inclusion is an evolutionary process as well.
Statue of Liberty torch	Symbol of enlightenment, functions as a lighthouse, too!	Inclusion, too, is a symbol of the friendship and freedom to be part of a school setting and global society that is illuminated with worthwhile contributions.

The ancient Romans used some torches that were made of sulfur and lime that would not be extinguished when tossed into water. Inclusive torches for all adolescents in inclusive classrooms will hopefully be eternal ones that survive and thrive in many civilizations to come, by illuminating the world with their ongoing brilliance.

Bibliography and Resources

Abeel, S. (2003). *My thirteenth winter:* A memoir. New York: Scholastic.

Adolescents who live in poverty are more likely to be overweight. (2007, May 24–31). *JAMA: The Journal of the American Medical Association.* Retrieved August 16, 2008, from http://www.news-medical.net/?id=18112

Agran, M. (2006, May/June). Self-determination: Achieving a say-do correspondence. *TASH Connections, 32*(5/6). Retrieved September 26, 2008, from http://www.tash.org/express/06mayjun/agran.htm

Allen, J. (2007). *Inside words: Tools for teaching academic vocabulary, Grades 4–12.* Portland, ME: Stenhouse.

American Speech-Language-Hearing Association. 10801 Rockville Pike Rockville, MD 20852, (301) 897-5700 or (800) 638-8255. Accessible online at http://www.asha.org

Anderman, E., & Maehr, M. L. (1994). Motivation and schooling in the middle grades. *Review of Educational Research, 64,* 287–309.

Anderson, A., Kutash, K., & Duchnowski, A. J. (2001). A comparison of the academic progress of students with E/BD and students with LD. *Journal of Emotional and Behavioral Disorders, 9,* 106–115.

Anderson-Inman, L., Ditson, A., & Ditson, M. T. (1998). Computer-based concept mapping: Promoting meaningful learning in science for students with disabilities. *Information, Technology and Disabilities, 5.*

Baker, J. (2006). *The social skills picture book for high school and beyond.* Arlington, TX: Future Horizons.

Bandura, A. (1986). The explanatory and predictive scope of self-efficacy theory. *Journal of Clinical and Social Psychology, 4,* 359–373.

Bandura, A. (1994). Self-efficacy. In V. S. Ramachaudran (Ed.), *Encyclopedia of human behavior* (Vol. 4, pp. 71–81). New York: Academic Press.

Bauwens, J., & Hourcade, J. (2003) *Cooperative teaching: Rebuilding the schoolhouse for all students* (2nd ed.). Austin, TX: Pro-Ed.

Beale, A. (2005).Preparing students with learning disabilities for postsecondary education. *Techniques: Connecting Education and Careers, 80,* 24.

Bean, T., & Moni, K. (2003). Developing students' critical literacy: Exploring identity construction in young adult fiction. *Journal of Adolescent and Adult Literacy, 46,* 838–848.

Beddow, P. A., Kettler, R. J., & Elliott, S. N. (2008). *Test Accessibility and Modification Inventory (TAMI).* Nashville, TN: Vanderbilt University, Peabody College. Available online at http://peabody.vanderbilt.edu/tami.xml

Bender, W. (2002). *Differentiating instruction for students with learning disabilities.* Thousand Oaks, CA: Corwin Press.

Benner, G., Allor, J., & Mooney, P. (2008). An investigation of the academic processing speed of students with emotional and behavioral disorders served in public school settings. *Education and Treatment of Children, 31*(3), 307–332.

Berninger, V. W., & Richards, T. L. (2002). *Brain literacy for educators and psychologists.* Boston: Academic Press.

Biancarosa, G., & Snow, C. (2004). *Reading next: A vision for action and research in middle and high school literacy—A report to Carnegie Corporation of New York.* Washington, DC: Alliance for Excellent Education.

Bigelow, B. (1999). *World War II: Primary sources.* Detroit, MI: U.X.L.

Bloom, B., & Krathwohl, D. (1956). *Taxonomy of educational objectives: The classification of educational goals, by a committee of college and university examiners. Handbook I: Cognitive domain.* New York: Longmans, Green.

Boscolo, P., & Mason, L. (2001). Writing to learn, writing to transfer. In P. Tynjala, L. Mason, & K. Lonka (Eds.), *Writing as learning tool: Integrating theory and practice* (pp. 83–104). Dordrecht, Netherlands: Kluwer.

Boyle, J. R., & Yeager, N. (1997). Blueprints for learning: Using cognitive frameworks for understanding. *Teaching Exceptional Children, 29*(4), 26–31.

Bridgeland, J., Dilulio, J., & Morison, K. (2006, March). *The silent epidemic: Perspectives of high school dropouts.* Report by Civic Enterprise in association with Peter D. Hart Research Associates. Seattle, WA: Bill & Melinda Gates Foundation.

Bruner, J. (1986). *Actual minds, possible worlds.* Cambridge, MA: Harvard University Press.

Calefati, J. (2009). College is possible for students with intellectual disabilities. New support programs and federal funds can help students with intellectual disabilities. *U.S. News & World Report.* Retrieved February 13, 2009, from http://www.usnews.com/articles/education/2009/02/13/college-is-possible-for-students-with-intellectual-disabilities.html

Carrington, S., & Lennox, N. (2008). Advancing the curriculum for young people who have an intellectual disability. Advocacy in health: A pilot study. *Australasian Journal of Special Education, 32*(2), 177–186.

Casbarro, J. (2005). *Test anxiety and what you can do about it: A practical guide for teachers, parents, and kids.* Port Chester, NY: National Professional Resources.

Cash, R. (2003). When depression brings teens down. *Education Digest, 69*(3), 35–42.

CAST, Universal Design for Learning. http://www.cast.org/research/udl/index.html

Coleman, M., & Vaughn, S. (2000). Reading interventions for students with emotional/behavioral disorders. *Behavioral Disorders, 25*(2), 93–104.

Cooperative Learning Center (University of Minnesota). http://www.clcrc.com. Codirected by Roger T. Johnson and David W. Johnson.

Cotton, K. (2001, January). *Expectations and student outcomes.* Retrieved August 6, 2008, from http://www.nwrel.org/scpd/sirs/4/cu7.html

Council for Exceptional Children. (2003). *What every special educator must know: Ethics, standards, and guidelines for special educators.* Arlington, VA: Author.

Coutinho, M., & Oswald, D. (2004, October). Disproportionate representation of culturally and linguistically diverse students in special education: measuring the problem [Practitioner Brief Series]. Denver, CO: National Center for Culturally Responsive Educational Systems. Retrieved July 16, 2008, from http://www.nccrest.org/Briefs/students in SPED_Brief.pdf

Crawford, G. (2008). *Differentiation for the adolescent learner: Accommodating brain development, language, literacy, and special needs.* Thousand Oaks, CA: Corwin Press.

Curry, C., Cohen, L. G., & Lightbody, N. (2006, March). Universal design in science learning. *Science Teacher, 73*(3), 32–37.

Deno, S. L., Fuchs, L. S., Marston, D., & Shinn, M. (2001). Using curriculum-based measurement to establish growth standards for students with learning disabilities. *School Psychology Review, 30,* 507–524.

Deshler, D., & Schumaker, J. (2006). *Teaching adolescents with disabilities: Accessing the general education curriculum.* Thousand Oaks, CA: Corwin Press.

Deshler, D. D., Schumaker, J. B., Lenz, B. K., Bulgren, J. A., Hock, M. F., Knight, J., et al. (2001). Ensuring content-area learning by secondary students with learning disabilities. *Learning Disabilities Research and Practice, 16*(2), 96–108.

DeSimone, J., & Parmar, R. (2006). Middle school mathematics teachers' beliefs about inclusion of students with learning disabilities. *Learning Disabilities Research & Practice, 21*(2), 98.

Dickinson, D. (Ed.). (1991). *Creating the future: Perspectives on educational change.* New Horizons for Learning. Retrieved July 25, 2008, from http://www.newhorizons.org/future/Creating_the_Future/crfut_sternberg.html

Dieker, L. (2006). *Demystifying secondary inclusion: Powerful school-wide and classroom strategies.* Port Chester, NY: National Professional Resources.

DiLeo, D. (2007). *Raymond's room: Ending the segregation of people with disabilities.* St. Augustine, FL: Training Resource Network.

Dirks, E., Spyer, G., Lieshout, E., & Sonneville, L. (2008). Prevalence of combined reading and arithmetic disabilities. *Journal of Learning Disabilities, 41,* 260–473.

Duffy, H. (n.d.). *Meeting the needs of significantly struggling learners in high school: A look at approaches to tiered intervention.* Washington, DC: National High School Center, American Institutes for Research. Retrieved June 5, 2008, from http://www.rti4success.org/images/stories/high_school.pdf

DuPaul, G. J., & Henningson, P. N. (1993). Peer tutoring effects on the classroom performance of children with attention deficit hyperactivity disorder. *School Psychology Review, 22*(1), 134–143.

Dynarski, M., Clarke, L., Cobb, B., Finn, J., Rumberger, R., & Smink, J. (2008). *Dropout prevention: A practice guide* (NCEE 2008–4025). Washington, DC: National Center for Education Evaluation and Regional Assistance, Institute of Education Services, U.S. Department of Education. Retrieved September 23, 2008, from http://ies.ed.gov/ncee/wwc

Ecker, P. (1997). *John Dewey: 1859–1952.* Retrieved July 25, 2008, from http://www.bgsu.edu/departments/acs/1890s/dewey/dewey.html

Edwards, T., Patrick, D., & Topolski, T. (2003). Quality of life of adolescents with perceived disabilities. *Journal of Pediatric Psychology, 28*(4), 233–241. Retrieved February 16, 2009 from http://jpepsy.oxfordjournals.org/cgi/content/full/28/4/233

Elbaum, B., Vaughn, S., Hughes, M. T., & Moody, S. W. (2000). How effective are one-on-one tutoring programs in reading for elementary students at-risk for reading failure? A meta-analysis of the intervention research. *Journal of Educational Psychology, 92*(4), 605–619.

English Journal. NCTE: National Council of Teachers of English. http://www.ncte.org/journals

Erikson, E. H. (1963). *Childhood and society* (2nd ed.). New York: Norton.

Evers, R. (2007). *Career and technical student organizations: Extending employment preparation beyond the classroom.* Retrieved July 25, 2008, from http://www.schwablearning.org/articles.aspx?r=1136

Ferguson, P. (2002). A place in the family: An historical interpretation of research on parental reactions to having a child with a disability. *Journal of Special Education, 36*(3), 124–131.

Fisher, D., & Frey, N. (2007). *Checking for understanding: Formative assessment techniques for your classroom.* Alexandria, VA: Association for Supervision and Curriculum Development.

Forehand, M. (2005). Bloom's taxonomy: Original and revised. In M. Orey (Ed.), *Emerging perspectives on learning, teaching, and technology.* Retrieved August 6, 2008, from http://projects.coe.uga.edu/epltt

Fry, A. F., & Hale, S. (1996). Processing speed, working memory, and fluid intelligence: Evidence for a developmental cascade. *Psychological Science, 7,* 237–241.

Gardner, H. (2006). *Multiple intelligences: New horizons.* New York: Basic Books.

Gilberts, G. H., Agran, M., Hughes, C., & Wehmeyer, M. (2001). The effects of peer-delivered self-monitoring strategies on the participation of students with severe disabilities in general education classrooms. *Journal of the Association for Persons With Severe Handicaps, 26,* 25–36.

Gill, V. (2007). *The ten students you'll meet in your classroom: Classroom management tips for middle and high school teachers.* Thousand Oaks, CA: Corwin Press.

Gilligan, C. (1982). *In a different voice: Psychological theory and women's development.* Cambridge, MA: Harvard University Press.

Gore, M. C. (2004). *Successful inclusion strategies for secondary and middle school students: Keys to helping struggling learners access the curriculum.* Thousand Oaks, CA: Corwin Press.

Gottfredson, D. C., Marciniak, E. M., Birdseye, A. T., & Gottfredson, G. D. (1995). Increasing teacher expectations for student achievement. *Journal of Educational Research, 88*(3), 155–163.

Greenwood, C. R., Carta, J. J., & Maheady, L. (1991). Peer tutoring programs in the regular education classroom. In G. Stoner, M. R. Shinn, & H. M. Walker (Eds.), *Interventions for achievement and behavior problems* (pp. 179–200). Silver Spring, MD: National Association of School Psychologists.

Greenwood, C. R., Terry, B., Utley, C. A., Montagna, D., & Walker, D. (1993). Achievement, placement, and services: Middle school benefits of classwide peer tutoring used at the elementary school. *School Psychology Review, 22,* 497–516.

Gregory, G., & Chapman, C. (2002). *Differentiated instructional strategies: One size doesn't fit all.* Thousand Oaks, CA: Corwin Press.

Grigg, W., Donahue, P., & Dion, G. (2007). *The Nation's Report Card: 12th-grade reading and mathematics 2005* (NCES 2007.468). U.S. Department of Education, National Center for Education Statistics. Washington, DC: U.S. Government Printing Office. Available online at http://nces.ed.gov/nationsreportcard/pdf/main2005/2007468.pdf

Guthrie, J. T., & Humenick, N. M. (2004). Motivating students to read: Evidence for classroom practices that increase reading motivation and achievement. In P. McCardle & V. Chhabra (Eds.), *The voice of evidence in reading research* (pp. 329–54). Baltimore: Paul H. Brookes.

Hammeken, P. (2007). *The teacher's guide to inclusive education: 750 strategies for success.* Thousand Oaks, CA: Corwin Press.

Hankin, B. L., Abramson, L. Y., Moffitt, T. E., Silva, P. A., McGee, R., & Angell, K. E. (1998). Development of depression from preadolescence to young adulthood: Emerging gender differences in a 10-year longitudinal study. *Journal of Abnormal Psychology, 107,* 128–140.

Hare, T. A., Tottenham, N., Galvan, A., Voss, H. U., Glover, G. H., & Casey, B. J. (2008, May 15). Biological substrates of emotional reactivity and regulation in adolescence during an emotional go-nogo task. *Biological Psychiatry, 63,* 927–934.

Harry, B. (2002). Trends and issues in serving culturally diverse families of children with disabilities. *Journal of Special Education, 36*(3), 31–38, 47.

Harter, S. (1999). *The construction of the self: A developmental perspective.* New York: Guilford Press.

Hearts & Minds. (n.d.). *Children in poverty: America's ongoing war.* Retrieved August 16, 2008, from http://www.heartsandminds.org/articles/childpov.htm

Hirsch, C. R. (Ed.). (2007). *Perspectives on design and development of school mathematics curricula.* Reston, VA: National Council of Teachers of Mathematics.

Horowitz, J. L., & Garber, J. (2006). The prevention of depressive symptoms in children and adolescents: A meta-analytic review. *Journal of Consulting and Clinical Psychology, 74*(3), 401–415.

Horton, M., Kohl, J., & Kohl, H. (1997). *The long haul: An autobiography.* New York: Teachers College Press.

Hunter, R. (2004). *Madeline Hunter's mastery teaching: Increasing instructional effectiveness in elementary and secondary schools.* Thousand Oaks, CA: Corwin Press.

Institute for Research and Reform in Education. (n.d.). *First Things First* [Results achieved by schools using this school reform initiative]. Retrieved September 26, 2008, from http://www.irre.org/ftf/results.asp

International Child and Youth Care Network. (2001, September 19). Social pressures lead to adolescent rage. *Today.* Available at http://www.cyc-net.org/today2001/today010919.html

Jenkins, R. (2005). Interdisciplinary instruction in the inclusion classroom. *Teaching Exceptional Children, 27,* 5.

Johnson, D. R., Thurlow, M., Cosio, A., & Bremer, C. (2005, February). Diploma options for students with disabilities. *Information brief: Addressing trends and developments in secondary education and transition, 4*(1). Retrieved November 25, 2008, from http://www.ncset.org/publications/viewdesc.asp?id=1928

Johnson, D. W., & Johnson, R. T. (1999). *Learning together and alone: Cooperative, competitive, and individualistic learning* (5th ed.). Boston: Allyn & Bacon.

Johnson, D. W., & Johnson, R. T. (2003). *Joining together: Group theory and group skills* (8th ed.). Englewood Cliffs, NJ: Prentice Hall.

Johnson, R., Johnson, D., & Holubec, E. (1994). *Cooperative learning in the classroom.* Alexandria, VA: Association for Supervision and Curriculum Development.

Kagan, S. (1994). *Cooperative learning*. San Clemente, CA: Kagan Publishing.

Kamil, M. L., Borman, G. D., Dole, J., Kral, C. C., Salinger, T., & Torgesen, J. (2008). *Improving adolescent literacy: Effective classroom and intervention practices: A practice guide* (NCEE #2008-4027). Washington, DC: National Center for Education Evaluation and Regional Assistance, Institute of Education Sciences, U.S. Department of Education. Retrieved September 25, 2008, from http://ies.ed.gov/ncee/wwc

Karten, T. (2005). *Inclusion strategies that work! Research-based methods for the classroom.* Thousand Oaks, CA: Corwin Press.

Karten, T. (2007a). *Inclusion activities that work! Grades 6–8.* Thousand Oaks, CA: Corwin Press.

Karten, T. (2007b). *More inclusion strategies that work! Aligning student strengths with standards.* Thousand Oaks, CA: Corwin Press.

Karten, T. (2008a). *Embracing disabilities in the classroom: Strategies to maximize students' assets.* Thousand Oaks, CA: Corwin Press.

Karten, T. (2008b). *Facilitator's guide to more inclusion strategies that work!* Thousand Oaks, CA: Corwin Press.

Karten, T. (2008c). *Inclusion succeeds with effective strategies: Grades 6–12* [Laminated guide]. Port Chester, NY: National Professional Resources.

Keefe, E. B., Moore, V., & Duff, E. (2004). The four "knows" of collaborative teaching. *Teaching Exceptional Children, 3*(5), 36–42.

Kern, R., Libkuman, T., Otani, H., & Holmes, K. (2005, December). Emotional stimuli, divided attention, and memory. *Emotion, 5*(4), 408–417.

King-Sears, M. E. (2008). Using teacher and researcher data to evaluate the effects of self-management in an inclusive classroom. *Preventing School Failure, 52*(4), 25–36.

Kingsley, E. P. (1987). *Welcome to Holland.* Available at http://www.our-kids.org/Archives/Holland.html

Klein, S., & Schive, K. (Eds.). (2001).*You will dream new dreams: Inspiring personal stories by parents of children with disabilities.* New York: Kensington.

Klinger, J. K., & Vaughn, S. (2002). The changing roles and responsibilities of an LD specialist. *Learning Disability Quarterly, 25*(1), 19–32.

Kohlberg, L., & Turiel, E. (1971). Moral development and moral education. In G. Lesser (Ed.), *Psychology and educational practice.* Glenview, IL: Scott Foresman.

Kronick, R., & Hargis, C. (1998). *Dropouts: Who drops out and why and the recommended action.* Springfield, IL: Charles C Thomas.

Kryza, K., Stephens, S., & Duncan, A. (2007). *Inspiring middle and secondary learners: Honoring differences and creating community through differentiating instructional practices.* Thousand Oaks, CA: Corwin Press.

Lenters, K. (2006). Resistance, struggle, and the adolescent reader. *Journal of Adolescent & Adult Literacy, 50*(2), 136–146.

Lesley, M. (2008). Access and resistance to dominant forms of discourse: Critical literacy and "At risk" high school students, *Literacy Research and Instruction, 47*(3), 174–194.

Levine, M., & Barringer, M. (2008). Brain-based research helps to identify and treat slow learners. *Education Digest, 73*(9), 9–13.

Lindberg, J., Kelley, D., Walker-Wied, J., & Beckwith, K. (2007). *Common-sense classroom management for special education teachers, grades 6–12.* Thousand Oaks, CA: Corwin Press.

Linn, M., Lewis, C., Tsuchida, I., & Songer, N. (2002). Beyond fourth-grade science: Why do U.S. and Japanese students diverge? *Educational Researcher, 29*(3), 4–14.

Llewellyn, D. (2005). *Teaching high school science through inquiry.* Thousand Oaks, CA: Corwin Press.

Maag, J. W., & Reid, R. (2006). Depression among students with learning disabilities: Assessing the risk. *Journal of Learning Disabilities, 39*, 3–10.

Maehr, M., & Midgley, C. (1996). *Transforming school cultures.* Boulder, CO: Westview.

Magiera, K., Smith, G., Zigmond, N., & Gebauer, K. (2005). Benefits of co-teaching in secondary mathematics classes. *Teaching Exceptional Children, 37*(3), 20–24.

Marcia, J. E. (1966). Development and validation of ego identity statuses. *Journal of Personality and Social Psychology, 3*, 551–558.

Marsh, H. W. (1989). Age and gender effects in multiple dimensions of self-concept: Early adolescence to early adulthood. *Journal of Educational Psychology, 81,* 417–430.

Mastropieri, M. A., & Scruggs, T. E. (2006). *The inclusive classroom: Strategies for effective instruction* (3rd ed.).Upper Saddle River, NJ: Prentice Hall.

Mastropieri, M. A., Scruggs, T. E., Graetz, J., Norland, J., Gardizi, W., & McDuffie, K. (2005). Case studies in co-teaching in the content areas: Successes, failures, and challenges. *Intervention in School and Clinic, 40,* 260–270.

Mastropieri, M. A., Scruggs, T. E., Graetz, J., Norland, J., Gardizi, W., & McDuffie, K. (2007). Co-teaching in inclusive classrooms: A metasynthesis of qualitative research. *Teaching Exceptional Children, 73*(4), 392–416.

McGraw, J. (2000). *Life strategies for teens.* New York: Fireside.

McGrew, K. S., & Evans, J. (2003). *Expectations for students with cognitive disabilities: Is the cup half empty or half full? Can the cup flow over?* (Synthesis Report 55). Minneapolis: University of Minnesota, National Center on Educational Outcomes. Retrieved February 16, 2009, from http://education.umn.edu/NCEO/OnlinePubs/Synthesis55.html

McKellar, D. (2007). *How to survive middle-school math without losing your mind or breaking a nail.* New York: Hudson Street Press.

McLesky, J., & Waldron, N. (2002). Inclusion and school change: Teacher perceptions regarding curricular and instructional adaptations. *Teacher Education and Special Education, 25,* 53.

McNary, S., Glasgow, N., & Hicks, C. (2005). *What successful teachers do in inclusive classrooms.* Thousand Oaks, CA: Corwin Press.

Meeus, W. (1993, winter). Occupational identity development, school performance, and social support in adolescence: Findings of a Dutch study. *Adolescence.* Retrieved July 28, 2008, from http://findarticles.com/p/articles/mi_m2248/is_n112_v28/ai_14777755

Melber, L. (2004). Inquiry for everyone: Authentic science experiences for students with special needs. *Teaching Exceptional Children Plus, 1*(2). Retrieved December 12, 2008, from http://escholarship.bc.edu/education/tecplus/vol1/iss2

Melber, L., & Brown, K. (2008). Not like a regular science class: Informal science education for students with disabilities. *Clearing House, 82*(1), 35–39.

Meo, G. (2008). Curriculum planning for all learners: Applying universal design for learning (UDL) to a high school reading comprehension program. *Preventing School Failure, 52*(2), 21–30.

Moje, E. B. (2000). "To be part of the story": The literacy practices of gangsta adolescents. *Teachers College Record, 102*(3), 651–690.

Moje, E. B. (2002). But where are the youth? Integrating youth culture into literacy theory. *Educational Theory, 52,* 97–120.

Moje, E. B. (2007). Developing socially just subject-matter instruction: A review of the literature on disciplinary literacy teaching. *Review of Research in Education, 31,* 1–44.

Moje, E. B., Ciechanowski, K. M., Kramer, K. E., Ellis, L., Carrillo, R., & Collazo, T. (2004). Working toward third space in content area literacy: An examination of everyday funds of knowledge and Discourse. *Reading Research Quarterly, 39,* 1.

Montague, M., Enders, C., Dietz, S., Dixon, J., & Cavendish, W. (2008). A longitudinal study of depressive symptomology and self-concept in adolescents. *Journal of Special Education, 42*(2), 67–78.

Moran, S., Kornhaber, M., & Gardner, H. (2006). Orchestrating multiple intelligences. *Educational Leadership, 64,* 23–27.

National Association of State Directors of Special Education (NASDSE). (2006, May). *Myths about response to intervention (RtI) implementation.* Retrieved September 23, 2008, from http://www .nasdse.org/Portals/0/Documents/Download%20Publications/Myths%20about%20RtI.pdf

National Council of Teachers of English. (2006, April). *NCTE principles of adolescent literacy reform.* Available online at http://www.ncte.org/library/NCTEFiles/Resources/PolicyResearch/AdolLitPrinciples.pdf

National Council of Teachers of English. (2007). *Adolescent literacy: Policy research brief.* Ann Arbor: University of Michigan, James R. Squire Office of Policy Research.

National Health Interview Survey (NHIS). (1998–2002). The Parents with Disabilities and Their Teens Project. Accessed at http://www.lookingglass.org/publications/nhisf.php

National Middle School Association. http://www.nmsa.org

Nelson, J. R., Benner, G. J., & Cheney, D. (2005). An investigation of the language skills of students with emotional disturbance served in public school settings. *Journal of Special Education, 39*(2), 97–105.

New Jersey Department of Education. (2004, October). *New Jersey Core curriculum content standards.* Retrieved August 16, 2008, from http://www.nj.gov/education/cccs/cccs.pdf

National Science Teacher's Association. http://www.nsta.org/publications/journals.aspx

Nunley, K. (2006). *Differentiating the high school classroom: Solution strategies for 18 common obstacles.* Thousand Oaks, CA: Corwin Press.

Ogden, C. L., Carroll, M., Curtin, L., et al. (2006). Prevalence of overweight and obesity in the United States, 1999-2004. *JAMA, 295,* 1549–1555.

Oswald, D. P., & Coutinho, M. J. (2005). *Disproportionate representation of minority students in special education: Measuring the problem.* The National Center for Culturally Responsive Systems of the National Institute for School Improvement at the University of Denver. Practitioner Brief Series. Denver, CO.

Pescatore, C. (2007). Current events as empowering literacy: For English and social studies teachers. *Journal of Adolescent & Adult Literacy, 51*(4), 326–339.

Piaget, J. (1965). *The moral judgment of the child.* New York: The Free Press.

Pierangelo, R., & Giuliani, G. (2007). *EDM: The educator's diagnostic manual of disabilities and disorders.* San Francisco: Jossey-Bass.

Pierce, K. L., & Schreibman, L. (1994). Teaching daily living skills to children with autism in unsupervised settings through pictorial self-management. *Journal of Applied Behavior Analysis, 27,* 471–481.

Pipher, M. (2005) *Reviving Ophelia: Saving the selves of adolescent girls.* New York: Riverhead Trade.

Power, F. C., Higgins, A., & Kohlberg, L. (1989). *Lawrence Kohlberg's approach to moral education.* New York: Columbia University Press.

Prince George's County Public Schools. (n.d.). *A guide to cooperative learning.* Available at http://www.pgcps.pg.k12.md.us/~elc/learning1.html

Pullin, D. (2005). When one size does not fit all—The special challenges of accountability testing for students with disabilities. *Annual Yearbook of the National Society for the Student of Education, 104*(2), 199–222.

Rao, U., Hammen, C., & Daley, S. E. (1999). Continuity of depression during the transition to adulthood: A 5-year longitudinal study of young women. *Journal of the American Academy of Child and Adolescent Psychiatry, 38*(7), 908–915.

Rauscher, F. H., Shaw, G. L, & Ky, K. N. (1993, October 14). Music and spatial task performance. *Nature, 365*(6447), 611.

Recording for the Blind & Dyslexic. 20 Roszel Road, Princeton, NJ 08540. (609) 452-0606.

Ross, T. (2008, February 13). "Five hours of culture" planned for schools. *Independent.* Retrieved August 6, 2008, from http://www.independent.co.uk/news/education/education-news/five-hours-of-culture-planned-for-schools-781697.html

Ryan, A. (2001). The classroom social environment and changes in adolescents' motivation and engagement during middle school. *American Educational Research Journal, 38,* 437–460.

Santa, C. (2006). A vision for adolescent literacy: Ours or theirs? *Journal of Adolescent and Adult Literacy, 49*(6), 466–476.

Scheuermann, A., & Van Garderen, D. (2008). Analyzing students' use of graphic representations: Determining misconceptions and error patterns for instruction. *Mathematics Teaching in the Middle School, 13*(8), 471–477.

Schloss, P. J., Smith, M. A., & Schloss, C. A. (2001*). Instructional methods for secondary students with learning and behavior problems.* Boston: Allyn & Bacon.

Shah, A. (n.d.). Causes of poverty. *Global Issues.* Retrieved August 16, 2006, from http://www.globalissues.org/issue/2/causes-of-poverty

Sheffield, C. (2007, summer). Technology and the gifted adolescent: Higher order thinking, 21st century literacy, and the Digital Native. *Meridian: A Middle School Computer Technologies Journal, 10*(2). Retrieved August 15, 2008, from http://www.ncsu.edu/meridian/sum2007

Slavin, R. E. (1995). *Cooperative learning.* Boston: Allyn & Bacon.

Small, S. A. (1995). Enhancing contexts of adolescent development: The role of community-based action research. In L. J. Crockett & A. C. Crouter (Eds.), *Pathways through adolescence: Individual development in relation to social context.* Mahwah, NJ: Lawrence Erlbaum.

Snowman, J., McCown, R., & Biehler, R. (2008). *Psychology applied to teaching* (12th ed.). Boston: Houghton Mifflin.

Sousa, D. (2005). *How the brain learns to read.* Thousand Oaks, CA: Corwin Press.

Southern Regional Education Board. (n.d.). *Making Middle Grades Work: An enhanced design to get all students to standards.* Available at http://www.sreb.org/programs/middlegrades/publications/06V15_MMGW_Brochure.pdf

Special Parents Information Network (SPIN). http://spinsc.org/default.asp?page=webresources.htm

Spooner, F., Ahlgrim-Delzell, L., Kohprasert, K., Baker, J., & Courtade, G. (2008). Content analysis of science performance indicators in alternate assessment. *Remedial and Special Education, 29,* 343–351.

Steele, M. M. (2002). Strategies for helping students who have learning disabilities in mathematics. *Mathematics Teaching in the Middle School, 8,* 140–143.

Sternberg, R. (1996). *Successful intelligence: How practical and creative intelligence determine success in life.* New York: Simon & Schuster.

Sternberg, R. (1997). *Thinking styles.* Cambridge, UK: Cambridge University Press.

Sternberg, R. (2006). Recognizing neglected strengths. *Educational Leadership, 64,* 30–35.

Sterzer, P., Stadler, C., Krebs, A., Kleinschmidt, A., & Poustka, F. (2005, January 1). Abnormal neural responses to emotional visual stimuli in adolescents with conduct disorder. *Biological Psychiatry, 57*(1), 7–15.

Strangeman, N., Hitchcock, C., Hall, T., Meo, G., & Coyne, P. (2006). *Response-to-instruction and universal design for learning: How might they intersect in the general education classroom?* Washington, DC: The Access Center.

Swanson, C. (2004). *Who graduates? Who doesn't? A statistical portrait of public high school graduation, class of 2001.* Washington, DC: The Urban Institute.

Swanson, C. (2007, June 12). Learning and earning. *Education Week [Special issue]: Ready for What? Preparing Students for College Careers, and Life After High School, 26*(40), 15–20.

Swanson, C. (November 3, 2008). *Report: Special education in America.* Bethesda, MD: Editorial Projects in Education Research Center. Retrieved November 10, 2008, from http://www.edweek.org/rc/articles/2008/10/27/special_education_in_america.html

Sylwester, R. (2005). *How to explain a brain.* Thousand Oaks, CA: Corwin Press.

Sylwester, R. (2007). *The adolescent brain: Reaching for autonomy.* Thousand Oaks, CA: Corwin Press.

Teaching Tolerance Magazine, A Project of the Southern Poverty Law Center. http://www.tolerance.org/teach/resources/index.jsp

Terdiman, D. (2005, February 8). What websites do to turn on teens. *Wired.* Retrieved May 30, 2008, from http://www.wired.com/culture/lifestyle/news/2005/02/66514

Thoma, C. A., Nathanson, R., Baker, S. R., & Tamura, R. (2002). Self-determination: What do special educators know and where do they learn it? *Remedial and Special Education, 23,* 242–247.

Thousand, J., Villa, R., & Nevin, A. (2007). *Differentiating instruction: Collaborative planning and teaching for universally designed learning.* Thousand Oaks, CA: Corwin Press.

Thurlow, M. L., & Wiley, H. I. (2004). *Almost there in public reporting of assessment results for students with disabilities* (Technical Report 39). Minneapolis: University of Minnesota, National Center on Educational Outcomes. Retrieved September 10, 2008, from http://education.umn.edu/NCEO/OnlinePubs/Technical39.htm

Tomlinson, C., Kaplan, S., Renzulli, J., Purcell, J., Leppien, J., & Burns, D. (2002). *The parallel curriculum: A design to develop high potential and challenge high-ability learners.* Thousand Oaks, CA: Corwin Press.

Tomlinson, C., & McTighe, J. (2006). *Integrating differentiated instruction and understanding by design: Connecting content and kids.* Alexandria, Virginia: Association for Supervision and Curriculum Development.

UNICEF. (2006). *The state of the world's children.* Retrieved September 12, 2008, from http://www.unicef.org/sowc

U.S. Department of Labor. (2006). *America's dynamic workforce.* Washington, DC: Author. Available at http://www.dol.gov/asp/media/reports/workforce2006/ ADW2006_Full_Text.pdf

Villa, R., & Thousand, J. (2003). Making inclusive education work. *Educational Leadership, 61,* 19.

Vygotsky, L. S. (1978). *Mind in society: The development of higher psychological processes.* Cambridge, MA: Harvard University Press.

Wagner, K. *What is a fixed-ratio schedule?* Retrieved February 16, 2009, from http://psychology .about.com/od/findex/g/def_fixedratio.htm

Wehmeyer, M. (2006). Self-determination and individuals with severe disabilities: Re-examining meanings and misinterpretations. *Research and Practice for Persons with Severe Disabilities, 30,* 113–120.

Wehmeyer, M. L., Agran, M., & Hughes, C. (1998). *Teaching self-determination to youth with disabilities: Basic skills for successful transition.* Baltimore: Paul H. Brookes.

Wiggins, G., & McTighe, J. (2008). Put understanding first. *Educational Leadership, 65*(19), 36–41.

Willis, J. (2007). *Brain-friendly strategies for the inclusion classroom.* Alexandria, VA: Association for Supervision and Curriculum Development.

Wolf, A. (2002). *Get out of my life, but first could you drive me and Cheryl to the mall: A parent's guide to the new teenager.* New York: Farrar, Straus and Giroux.

Woodcock, R. W., McGrew, K. S., & Mather, N. (2001). *Woodcock-Johnson III Tests of Achievement.* Itasca, IL: Riverside.

Zirkel, P., & Gischlar, K. (2008). Due process hearings under the IDEA: A longitudinal frequency analysis. *Journal of Special Education Leadership, 21*(1), 22–31.

Index

Abeel, Samantha, 82, 209
Above average skill student
    accommodations for, 22, 86
    classroom strategy for, 4
Above average students, 44–45
Academic goals, setting, 17, 20, 58–61
Accessibility and Modification Inventory
    (TAMI), 139
Accessories, learning, 82
Accommodations, 22, 86, 128–134, 155
    conduct disorders, 86
    curriculum connections, 160–164
    documentation chart, 133–134
    graphic organizers, 9, 18, 52, 108, 131, 181–189
    On line resources, 86
    scenarios and weaning plans for, 131–133, 155
    study guides, 9, 108, 181–183
    testing, 139
    vs. modifications, 131
Accountability, 128, 130–134
Achievement for Latinos Through Academic
    Success (ALAS), 13
Acrostic, lesson/environment, 38–39
Adaptation, 65
    vs. organization, 55
Adequate yearly progress (AYP), 3, 109
Administrators, 11–16
    inclusion implementation, 17
    proactive strategies, 14–15
Adolescent Autonomy Checklist, 88
Adolescent emotional elevator, 68–69
Adolescent moods, 67
Adolescent movie options, 39–42
Adolescent statements, 44–47, 175–176
Advanced cognitive abilities, student with,
    statements about school experience, 44–46
Advance planners, 6
Age-level characteristics, of adolescents, 50–51
Anchor activities and ongoing stations
    (sample), 175–181
    anchor activities/materials (sample), 178
    classroom scenario, 175–177

planner for (sample), 179
station/center directions, 177, 179–181
Web sites for, 180–181
Art and the Alphabet: A Tactile Experience, 169
Art Beyond Sight: Yellow Pages, 169
Art connections, 168–170, 178
ASK (advocacy skills kit)
    Health Diary, 206
Asperger syndrome, student with
    ability/strategy overview,
        6–7, 184–186
    accommodations for, 22, 86
    reading comprehension, 155
    statements about school experience, 44
Assessments, 118–120, 135–144, 202–205
    assessment quiz, 140–141
    assessment quiz answer key, 141
    assessment quiz answers, explanation of,
        141–144
    baseline behavior, 101
    curriculum-based, 75
    formative, 202–205
    ongoing, 141–142
    options, 160–161
    rubrics for, 136–137
    rubric template, 138
    summative, 14, 143, 202–205
    Web sites for, 144
Attention deficit hyperactivity disorder
    (ADHD), student with, 5, 85, 86, 96
Attention issues, student with, on school
    experience, 44
Australia, 145, 206
Autism, student with
    ability/strategy overview, 184–186
    accommodations for, 22, 86
    classroom strategies for, 6
    music therapy for, 168

Baseline assessment, 101
Bauwens, J., 24
Beddow, P., 139

Behavior Assessment System for Children–
Teacher Rating Scales
(BASC-TRS), 101
Behavior intervention plan (BIP), 98
Behavior reinforcement, 99–101
accommodations and, 22
baseline assessments, 101
consequences, 99
at fixed intervals, 97
functional behavioral analysis, 100
intervention plan, 97
modification, 102
positive behavior support, 99–100
primary prevention, 100
reinforcement *vs.* punishment, 100
research on, 100
secondary prevention, 100
tertiary prevention, 100
at variable intervals, 97
Benefits of a problem-solving approach, 152
Biancarosa, G., 11–12
Biology, inclusion connections, 20, 189
Bloom, B., 151
Blooming verbs, 152
Bloom's Taxonomy, 151–152
Boardmaker software, 71
Bodily-kinesthetic learning,
52, 60, 70, 71–73, 118
Books about teens and differences, 41–43
Boyle, J. R., 183
Brain-based research, 61–64, 158
Bridgeland, J., 205
Bruner, J., 102, 121

Campaigning for adolescents, 89–90
slogans for, 90
Camp counselor, inclusive, 144
Capping learning, in intelligent ways, 76–77
Career Academics dropout prevention
program, 13
Career and Technical Student Organizations
(CTSOs), 206–207
Career support Web sites, 207
Casbarro, J., 135–136
Center for Applied Specialized Technology
(CAST), 116
Cerebral classroom cortex, 63
Character education, 55
Check and Connect dropout prevention
program, 13
Chemistry inclusion connections, 19, 33, 189
CHOICES, 24
Classroom cerebellum, 63
Classroom cerebrum, 63
Classroom discussion, benefits of, 142
Classroom hypothalamus, 63
Classroom medulla, 63
Classroom spinal cord, 63

Classwide peer tutoring, 146
Coach, inclusive, 144
Cognitive and psychological theories, 50–77
adolescent brain and, 61–64
BIG ideas to better reach adolescents, 53
bodily-kinesthetic learning, 70, 71–73
capping learning in intelligent
ways, 75–77
classroom scenarios related to, 57–61
cognitive theory of Piaget, 55, 56
emotional stimuli, 66–69
experts on, 51–57
gender theory, 55, 57
identity status model, 54–55
moral reasoning, 55
multiple intelligences, 52, 75
prior knowledge, 64–66
progressive education, 51–52
stage theory of development, 54
translating research into practice, 62
triarchic theory, 75
zone of proximal development, 54, 59, 143
Cognitive factors, defining, 8–9
Cohesive climate, 128
Collaboration. *See* Coteaching and collaboration
Communication disorders, 22, 86
Community, connecting with, 17, 207–209
Competence building, 149–150
Computer-supported intentional learning
environments (CSILE), 197
Concept map, differences, 189
Conduct disorders, 69, 86
See also Behavior reinforcement
Confusions *vs.* consistencies, 81–82
Connecting school to life, Web sites, 207
Constructivist strategies, 121, 122
Constructivist teachers, 122
Cooperative learning, 25, 124–128, 155, 176
checklist/rating scale for, 126127
Jigsaw, 126
non-examples/examples of, 125–126
Numbered Heads Together, 126
Roundtable, 126
Send a Problem, 126
Think-Pair-Share, 96, 126
Coteaching and collaboration
advantages of, 24
curriculum application, literacy lesson, 31
curriculum application, mathematics, 31–32
curriculum application, social studies, 32–33
family–school collaboration, 33–34
implementation issues, 25–26, 30
Inclusive Solutions & Ideas, 27–29
interdisciplinary lessons, 33
positive actions for, 30
shared responsibilities, 25
Course planner (sample), 19
Coutinho, M. J., 115

Critical thinking, skills 151
CTSOs (Career and Technical Student
    Organizations), 206–207
Cultural diversity, of students, 85
Curriculum
    connecting skills with, 104–105
    examples of, 20
    Web sites for supports/lessons/strategies,
        154, 180–181
Curriculum-based assessment (CBA), 75, 106
Curriculum-based measurement, 158
Curriculum graphic organizers (CGOs), 181–189
    ancient Egypt study guide (sample), 182–183
    benefits of, 181
    conceptual organization, 188–189
    organizational chart, 189 (sample)
    sequencing chart, 183, 187 (sample)
    storyboard, 188 (sample)
    study guides, 181–183
    See also Graphic organizers
Curriculum overload, 181
Curriculum representations, 170–175

Data documentation, 133–134
Daydreamers and doodlers, connecting to, 90–97
    by honoring differences, 91, 96
    by increasing metacognition, 91
    through student self-rating, 96–97, 98–99
    through study skills, 91–96
Deafness and hearing impaired, students with
    accommodations for, 22, 86
    classroom strategies for, 4
Democratic inclusive classroom, 52, 101–103
Department store, adolescent, 81–82
    cognitive shops, 81
    emotional accessories, 81
    physical items, 81
    social/moral sweets, 81
Depression, online resources for, 5, 86, 101
Deshler, D., 52
Developmental disorder, online resources for, 86
Dewey, J., 51–52, 63, 102
Differentiating instruction, 121–124
    planning stage examples, 124
Digital literacy, 197
Digital portfolio, 143
DiIulio, J., 205
DiLeo, D., 207
Direct instruction, 14
Disability awareness parent/guardian rubric, 84
Disability awareness peer rubric, 83 (always
    underline the abilities)
Disability awareness Web sites, 86
Disability awareness WebQuest, 195
Discrimination instructional process, 97

Discussion, 69
Division on Career Development and
    Transition, 106
Down syndrome, 5, 174
Dropout Prevention: A Practice Guide (IES), 12–13
Dropout prevention programs, 12–13
Duncan, A., 52–53
Dyscalculia, 82, 86, 155, 209
Dysgraphia, 86, 116
Dyslexia, 86, 155

Eating disorders,, 79
E.C.M.O.W. (every child makes out well), 116
Educational implications, 58–61
Elliott, S., 139
Emerging visuals, 71
Emotional disorders, classroom strategies for, 5
Emotional elevator, 68–69
Emotional stimuli, 66–69
Endo-learner, 120
English, inclusion connections, 31, 33, 77, 115,
    160, 161, 188
Environment
    classroom environment, defining, 8
    reflective survey, 212
    See also Inclusive settings
Environmental sciences, inclusion
    connections, 162
Erikson, E., 54
ETB, 113
Evans, J., 203
Executive dysfunction, online resources for, 86
Existentialist intelligences, 52
Exit cards, 142
Exit strategies, 200–214
    community connections, 207–209
    formative/summative evaluations, 202–205
    global connections, 209
    high and realistic expectations, 205–207
    meaningful balanced content, 201–202
    passing the torch, 211, 213–214
    professional development and enhancement,
        210–211
Exo-learner, 120
Expectations, 205
Extended school year (ESY) program, 106
Extra-credit assignments, 143–144
Extroverted student, 96
Eyewitness Books, 71

Family
    collaboration with school, 33–34
    disability awareness rubric, 84
    as mentor, 146–147
    support for students, 87–88

Feedback, 142
Ferguson, P., 88
First Things First dropout prevention
    program, 13
Forehand, M., 151
Formative assessment, 14, 143
Four C's, 136
Functional behavioral analysis, 100

Gardner, H., 52, 57, 60, 63, 75
Gender issues, 85–86, 110
Gender theory, 55, 57
Generalization instructional process, 97
Geometry, inclusive connections, 20
Gilligan, C., 55–56, 60
Gischlar, K., 106
Global connections, 77, 164, 180, 209
GMMA (Give Me My Answers), 115
Good-bye childhood syndrome, 78–79
Gore, M., 53
Graphic organizers, 9, 18, 52, 108, 131
    See also Curriculum graphic organizers
Guardians. See Family
Guru, inclusive, 144

Hearing impaired, students with. See Deaf and
    hearing impairments, students with
High School Redirection, 13
Hourcade, J., 24
Hunter, M., 71

Identity status model, 54–55
Inclusive classroom
    advantages for all students, 36–37
    checklist for, 9–10, 11
    ratings on practices, 9–11
Inclusive settings, 38–47
    adolescent statements about experience, 44–47
    films depicting adolescents, 39–41
    lesson/environment acrostic, 38–39
    literature depicting adolescents, 41–42
not-so-great/great lessons (samples),
    40Inclusive Solutions & Ideas (ISI), 27–29
Inclusive strategy list, 149–150
Inclusive survey, 212
Independent living skills, 88, 205–208
Individualized education program (IEP), 3
    adolescent attendance at meetings, 105
    goal implementation, 106
    implementation issues, 108
    least restrictive environment, 80, 103, 105
    transition statement, 106–107
Individuals with Disabilities Education Act
    (IDEA), 106, 108
Information processing, 64–66

Initial translations, 202
In service, 14
Inspiration Software, 51
Instruction
    differentiating, 121–124
    direct, 14
    discrimination process, 97
    generalization process, 97
Intellectual disabilities
    accommodations for, 22, 86
    classroom strategies for, 5–6
    post secondary opportunities, 207
Intelligence quotient (IQ), 75
Intelligences. See Multiple intelligences
Interdisciplinary lessons and thematic units,
    33, 164, 180, 189–196
    unit assignments, 192–193 (sample),
        195 (sample), 196 (sample)
Interdisciplinary teacher teams, 14
Interpersonal intelligences, 60, 73
Interpersonal/intrapersonal intelligences,
    52, 59, 60, 73
Introverted student, 96

Japan, 90
Jigsaw, 126, 188

Kagan, 126
Kettler, R., 139
Kinesthetic connections, 70–75
Kingsley, E., 87
Klein, S., 87
Kohlberg, L., 55, 57, 61, 62, 63
Krulik, N., 82
Kryza, K., 52–53

Labeling students, 68, 85
Language skills, 64
Learning accessories, 82
Learning differences, students with, 4, 22, 32,
    53, 86, 91, 96, 108, 112–115, 120, 141,
Learning and Earning (Swanson), 205–206
Least restrictive environment (LRE),
    80, 103, 105
Lesson plan template (sample), 156
Lin, M., 61, 63
Literacy and numeration skills, 11–14, 31, 154–160
    grade level standards and objectives (sample),
        160–164
    student ability coding sheet (sample), 159
Literature about student differences, 41–43
Logical-mathematical intelligences, 52, 60, 118

Making Middle Grades Work (MMGW), 16
Manipulatives, 25, 116, 149, 168, 172–175

Marcia, J., 54–55
Math recipe project rubric, 136
Mathematics, inclusion connections, 31–32, 57, 76, 89, 137, 139, 155, 163, 172, 178, 187, 192,
McAfee, J., 82
McGraw, J., 52
McGrew, K. S., 203
McKellar, D., 89
McTighe, J., 117, 120
MENC (National Association for Music Education), 167
Mental self-government, 103
Mentors, 144–147
    families as, 146–147
    mentoring chart, 146
    peer mentors, 145–146
    skills for, 145–146
    teacher to newer teacher, 147
    types of, 144–145
Metacognition, 91
Mobility impairments, classroom strategies for, 7
Mobility International USA, 47
Modeling, 9, 54, 130
Modifications vs. accommodations, 131
Moral reasoning, 55Morrison, K., 205
Motivation, 118–119
Movies about teens and differences, 39–42
Mozart effect, 167
Multicultural education, 180
Multidimensional Self Concept Scale (MSCS), 101
Multiple curriculum representations, 170–172
    chart (sample), 171
Multiple intelligences, 9, 33, 43, 63, 118–119
    bodily-kinesthetic, 52, 60, 73, 118
    existentialist, 52
    Gardner theory on, 52, 75
    interpersonal/intrapersonal, 52, 59, 60, 73
    logical-mathematical, 52, 60, 118
    musical-rhythmic, 52, 118, 167
    naturalist, 52
    verbal-linguistic, 52, 60, 118
    visual-spatial, 52, 118
Musical-rhythmic intelligences, 52, 118, 167
Myers-Briggs Type Indicator (MBTI), 91

National Assessment of Educational Progress (NEAP), 154
National Association for Music Education (MENC), 167
National Board for Professional Standards, 210
National Center for Accessible Media Web site, 117
National Health Interview Survey (NHIS), 87
National Instructional Materials Accessibility Standard (NIMAS), 117
Naturalist intelligences, 52
Negative differentiation, circumventing, 122–123

New Zealand, 145
No Child Left Behind (NCLB), 3, 109
Numbered Heads Together, 126
Nutrition and Health, 79

Obsessive compulsive disorder, online resources for, 86
Office of Special Education Program (OSEP), 99
Ongoing assessments, 141–142
Oppositional defiant disorder (ODD), 86, 135
Orff, C., 167
Oswald, M. J., 115
Other health impairments (OHI), 80
Other school activities, defining, 9

Paraeducators, 25–26
Parents. See Family
PBS Web site, 209
Peer mentors, 25, 145–146
Peer rubric, 83
Peer support, 82–83
    disability awareness rubric, 83
Peer tutoring, 17, 146
People-first language, 85
People searches, 73
Perceptual issues, 132–133
Philosophy, of school district, 10–11
Physical education, inclusion connections, 178, 211
Physical impairment, online resources for, 86
Piaget's cognitive theory, 55, 56, 59, 62
Pics4Learning, 71
Pilot, inclusive, 144
Pipher, M., 79
Planning, 16–20
Poetry, music, and art, 158, 165–170
    art therapy, 168–170
    art Web sites, 169–170
    benefits of, 158, 165
    music therapy, 166–168
    music Web sites, 167–168
    poetry Web sites, 166
Portfolio, digital, 143
Positive behavior support (PBS), 100
Positive interdependence, 128
Postsecondary decisions, 109, 202–207
Premack principle, 43
Prior knowledge, 52, 64–66, 82
Proactive strategies, 14–15, 53, 149–150, 156
Problem-based learning (PBL), 151–154
    benefits of problem-solving approach, 152
    Blooming verbs for, 152
    Lessons, 104–105
    outline and sample topics for, 152–154
    Web sites for, 154
Professional development, 14, 15–16, 210–211
Professional organizations, list of, 211
Progressive education, 51–52
Project Wisdom, 55

Quantum Opportunities Program, 13

Reflection
 necessity of, 144
 survey about adolescent, 212
 for teacher, 22–23, 43–44, 210–211
Reflective lessons, 23, 40
Response to intervention (RtI), 3, 8, 109, 112–115
RtI sandwich, 114
 tiers in, 113–114
Rote learning, 100, 191
Roundtable, 126
Rubric
 assessment, 136–137
 disability awareness parent/guardian, 84
 disability awareness peer, 83
 presentation for book skit, 137–138

Sample lesson plan template, 156
Scaffolding, 9, 52, 54
 baseline knowledge, 203
 benefits of, 143, 183
 cognitive skills, 60
 intervention, 114
 moral, 55
 psychological, 56
Scheduling issues, 16
Science, inclusion connections, 19, 20, 33, 76,
  133, 181, 186, 189, 192
Schive, K., 87
Schloss, C. A., 183
Schloss, P. J., 183
Schumaker, J., 52
Self-efficacy, 67
Self-esteem, student, 67–68, 206
Self-monitoring, 102
Self-rating, student, 96–97, 98–99
Self-regulated learner, 102–103
Send a Problem, 126
Sensory and kinesthetic ideas, 70–75
Sensory disabilities, student with, 71
Sequencing chart, 183, 187 (sample)
Skinner, B. F., 97
Slater Software, 71
SMART board, 130
Smith, M. A., 183
Snow, C., 11–12
Snowball effect, 115
Social goals, setting, 17
Social journal (sample), 66, 67
Social studies, inclusion connections, 20, 76, 178
Societal pressures, on adolescents, 79–80
S.O.S., 192
Sousa, D., 64
Spanish, inclusion connections, 20, 76, 132–133
Specific learning disabilities (SLD), 4, 22, 32, 53,
  80, 86, 91–96, 108, 113, 120
Spontaneous cooperative teacher, 128

Stage theory of development, 54
Standardized tests, 75, 143
Standards, as confusing to students, 142
Static visuals, 71
Station and center planner, 179
Statistics, on students with disabilities, 80–81
Stephens, S., 52–53
Sternberg, R., 52, 57, 60, 75, 176–77, 03
Stock analyst, inclusive, 144
Storyboard, 188 (sample)
Strategic lessons, 162-164
Strategic tutoring, 14
Striving Readers Act, 154
Student ability coding sheet (sample), 159
Student crises, defining, 9
Student data documentation, 134
Student differences, classroom strategies for, 4–8
Student dynamics, defining, 8
Student Pledge, 35–36
Student responsibility, 34–36
Student search, 73–74
Students without disabilities, 36–37
Study guides [accommodations], 9, 108, 181–183
Study skills, 25, 91–96, 180
Summative assessment, 14, 143
Swanson, C., 205–206
Sylwester, R., 51–52, 62, 63–64

Talent Development High School Model, 13
Teachers
 constructivist, 122
 interdisciplinary teams, 14
 mentoring of, 147
 organization issues, 18
 planning by, 16, 18
 preparation by, 18–21
 professional development, 14, 15–16, 210–211
 reflection by, 22–23, 43–44, 210–211
 relationship with parents, 87–88
 scheduling issues, 16, 17
 statements about good, 46–47
 statements about school experience by, 46
 tracing lessons, 68
 See also Coteaching and collaboration
Teaching Moments, 196–197
Team members, 28, 108–109
Technology, 196–198
 adolescent WebQuest for teacher, 198–199
 computer-supported environments, 197
 implementation strategies, 15
 multimedia tool, 110
 WebQuest assignments, 199
Telling About Yourself (T.A.Y.) (template), 107
Terdiman, D., 197–198
Test anxiety, 135–136
Tests
 formats issues, 137, 139, 140, 143
 standardized, 75, 143

teacher comments on, 142
universal design, 103
See also Assessments
Theoretical frameworks, 58–61
Think-Pair-Share, 96, 119, 126
Tomlinson, C., 117
Top-down control, 69
Tourette's syndrome, online resources for, 86
Tour guide, inclusive, 144
Trainer, inclusive, 144
Transistion statement (IEP), 106–107
Traumatic brain disorder Web sites, 86
Traumatic brain injury (TBI), classroom
     strategies for, 7–8
Trial-and-error method, of handling emotional
     stimuli, 66
Triarchic theory, 75
Tutors, 17, 144, 146
Twelve Together dropout prevention
     program, 13
Twice exceptional, online resources for, 86

UDL (universally designed lesson), 115–119,
     194–195
  major principles of, 103, 115–116
  preplanning template, 118–119
  preplanning template (sample), 119
  Web sites for, 117
UbD (understanding by design), 117, 120, 143
Universal test design, 103

Usborne Books, 71
U.S. Business Leadership Network, 206

Verbal-linguistic intelligences, 52, 60, 118
Visual elements, adding to curriculum, 71
Visual impairments/blindness
     accommodations for, 22, 86
  art therapy for, 169
  classroom strategies for, 8
Visual-spatial intelligences, 52, 118
VSA arts, 70
Vygotsky, L. S., 54, 57, 62,143

WebQuest, 110, 195, 198–199
Web sites, adolescent sites worth citing, 198–199
"What Websites Do to Turn on Teens," 197–198
Wiggins, G., 120
Wolf, A., 81–82
Wong, H., 34
World history, inclusion connections,
     20, 32, 77, 170–171
Wright's Law, 106
Writing workshop, 17

Yeager, N., 183
Youth Empowerment Seminars (YES!), 145

Zirkel, P., 106
Zone of proximal development (ZPD),
     54, 59, 143

CORWIN

A SAGE Company